Challenging Corporate Social Responsibility

T0300090

The concept of Corporate Social Responsibility (CSR) has become increasingly widespread, as businesses seek to incorporate socially responsible behaviors while still being accountable to shareholders. Indeed some research has suggested that CSR in itself can form the basis of good PR by promoting consumers' purchase decisions.

Arguing that this approach is a dangerous oversimplification, this book takes a deeper look at the concept of CSR in a particularly challenging context – casino gaming. Originally the province of seedy, backdoor establishments in isolated cities, casino gaming has become a multibillion-dollar global industry. Drawing on in-depth research in Las Vegas, this unique study examines how and why corporations in the casino industry interpret and engage in CSR through community support, environmental issues, labor rights, and corporate governance.

Through in-depth analysis of CSR in this industry, this book adds a new dimension to the debate on the role of CSR and public relations in business. Given the burgeoning relationship between CSR and corporate PR, the book seeks to illuminate CSR's complexities, contradictions, and moral obligations. It will be of interest to all scholars of public relations, corporate communications, and corporate reputation.

Jessalynn R. Strauss is Assistant Professor of Strategic Communication at Elon University, USA. She has several years of experience in public relations and marketing communication and her research interests include public relations, corporate social responsibility, nonprofit organizations, and the history and culture of Las Vegas

Routledge New Directions in Public Relations and Communication Research
Edited by Kevin Moloney

Routledge New Directions in Public Relations and Communication Research is a new forum for the publication of books of original research in PR and related types of communication. Its remit is to publish critical and challenging responses to continuities and fractures in contemporary PR thinking and practice, and its essential yet contested role in market-orientated, capitalist, liberal democracies around the world. The series reflects the multiple and inter-disciplinary forms PR takes in a post-Grunigian world: the expanding roles which it performs, and the increasing number of countries in which it is practised.

The series will examine current trends and explore new thinking on the key questions which impact upon PR and communications including:

- Is the evolution of persuasive communications in Central and Eastern Europe, China, Latin America, Japan, the Middle East, and South East Asia developing new forms or following Western models?
- What has been the impact of postmodern sociologies, cultural studies, and methodologies which are often critical of the traditional, conservative role of PR in capitalist political economies, and in patriarchy, gender, and ethnic roles?
- What is the impact of digital social media on politics, individual privacy, and PR practice? Is new technology changing the nature of content communicated, or simply reaching bigger audiences faster? Is digital PR a cause or a consequence of political and cultural change?

Books in this series will be of interest to academics and researchers involved in these expanding fields of study, as well as students undertaking advanced studies in this area.

Public Relations and Nation Building
Influencing Israel
Margalit Toledano and David McKie

Gender and Public Relations
Critical perspectives on voice, image and identity
Edited by Christine Daymon and Kristin Demetrious

Pathways to Public Relations
Histories of practice and profession
Edited by Burton Saint John III, Margot Opdycke Lamme and Jacquie L'Etang

Positioning Theory and Strategic Communications
A new approach to public relations research and practice
Melanie James

Public Relations and the History of Ideas
Simon Moore

Public Relations Ethics and Professionalism
The shadow of excellence
Johanna Fawkes

Power, Diversity and Public Relations
Lee Edwards

The Public Relations of Everything
The ancient, modern and postmodern dramatic history of an idea
Robert E. Brown

Political Reputation Management
The strategy myth
Christian Schnee

Corporate Social Responsibility, Sustainability and Public Relations
Negotiating multiple complex challenges
Donnalyn Pompper

Challenging Corporate Social Responsibility
Lessons for public relations from the casino industry
Jessalynn R. Strauss

This fantastic book provides a thoughtful, accessible, and thorough treatment of Corporate Social Responsibility as a public relations strategy that offers both opportunities and challenges. Using the casino industry as a case study, Jessalynn Strauss gives us an intriguing glimpse into the past, current, and future state of the relationship between business and society.

Steve May, *Associate Professor,*
The University of North Carolina at Chapel Hill, USA

This book is a thoughtful and comprehensive examination of Corporate Social Responsibility, an area of study with enormous implications for the practice of modern public relations. In this eminently readable study, Dr. Strauss seamlessly weaves theoretical insights with a fascinating discussion of the growing world-wide gaming industry.

Kathleen Stansberry, *Associate Professor,*
Cleveland State University, USA

This well-written, well-researched book begins with an irresistible hook: Bugsy Siegel and other gangsters may be the founders of casino CSR. As Strauss traces CSR through casinos in Las Vegas, Australia, Macau, and Canada, we gain detailed insights into broad, cutting-edge concerns, including the paradoxical social downsides of CSR.

Charles Marsh, *Professor, University of Kansas, USA*

Jessalynn Strauss' case studies demonstrate how adeptly vice industries have adapted to ethical demands and societal trends to establish community and good-will within their environments. This is a worthwhile book that will challenge and upend assumptions as well as shine a light on the history and legacy of an industry many have ignored.

Natalie T. J. Tindall, *Associate Professor,*
Georgia State University, USA

Challenging Corporate Social Responsibility

Lessons for public relations from the casino industry

Jessalynn R. Strauss

LONDON AND NEW YORK

First published 2015
by Routledge

2 Park Square, Milton Park, Abingdon, Oxfordshire OX14 4RN
52 Vanderbilt Avenue, New York, NY 10017

Routledge is an imprint of the Taylor & Francis Group, an informa business

First issued in paperback 2019

British Library Cataloguing in Publication Data
A catalogue record for this book is available from the British Library

Library of Congress Cataloging in Publication Data
Strauss, Jessalynn R.
Challenging corporate social responsibility : lessons for public relations
from the casino industry / Jessalynn R. Strauss.
pages cm. – (Routledge new directions in public relations and
communication research)
Includes bibliographical references and index.
1. Casinos–Social aspects. 2. Social responsibility of business. 3. Casinos–Social
aspects–Nevada–Las Vegas. 4. Casinos–Social aspects–Case studies.
I. Title.
HV6711.S77 2015
658.4'08–dc23
2014036183

ISBN: 978-0-415-70637-7 (hbk)
ISBN: 978-0-367-86854-3 (pbk)

Typeset in Times New Roman
by Swales & Willis Ltd, Exeter, Devon, UK

Contents

Acknowledgements   viii

1 Introduction   1

2 CSR: walking the walk, talking the talk   9

3 The casino industry grows up   49

4 Understanding the global casino industry   70

5 Casino city in the desert: history and context of Las Vegas,
   Nevada   85

6 CSR in Las Vegas   101

7 Trouble points: implications of strategic CSR   115

8 Conclusions and future directions   123

Appendix   133
References   134
Index   156

Acknowledgements

They say it takes a village to raise a child, and I've found the same is certainly true of writing a book. I wish to briefly express my gratitude to those who have helped make this endeavor possible (and in some cases, tolerable or even enjoyable).

All professional acknowledgments must begin with my adviser, mentor, and friend, Dr. Pat Curtin, for your years of guidance, support, and valuable life lessons. Thanks also to Dr. Janet Wasko, for overseeing my very first academic foray into CSR in the casino industry, and to Drs. Tom Bivins, Tiffany Gallicano, and Renee Irvin for their service on the committee for my doctoral dissertation, which formed the basis for this book, and for the part they played in helping me grow as a scholar.

I extend my gratitude to my graduate school colleagues at the University of Oregon who helped me get this project off the ground; to my colleagues at Xavier University, for encouraging me to keep it going; and to my colleagues at Elon University, for their support as I brought it to fruition. My thanks especially to Dean Janice Walker at Xavier University for enabling me to present this research at conferences and ultimately secure a contract for this book's publication, and to Dean Paul Parsons at Elon University, for providing summer funding that allowed me time to finish this book without teaching obligations.

Additionally, I wish to acknowledge Dr. David Schwartz, at the UNLV Center for Gaming Research, for his support and advice as I entered the brave new world of gambling research, and Dr. Kevin Moloney, whose advice during the process of proposing and completing this book has been much appreciated. A final thanks to my fall 2014 semester Strategic Writing students for their assistance with the final proofreading of this book in a remarkable group effort.

On a personal note, I'd like to say that this book wouldn't have been possible without the help of a great number of family and friends; there have been so many of you who have contributed in your way. I lost both of my parents while I was writing this book and I dedicate my efforts to their memory – much like many of my professional accomplishments, this book wouldn't have been possible without them. Thank you to my father, Martin Strauss, for always supporting me as I traveled down the road to my dream of being a college professor – I couldn't have done it without you. To my mother, Rosalia Strauss, my thanks for the tremendous example you set for me, and for telling me that you were proud of me for getting my PhD. Whenever I wonder if I'm really good enough to be doing this, I remember those words and suddenly I'm not concerned anymore.

Thank you to my brother, Joel, for being my rock during this past year; to my friend and editor extraordinaire, Grace; to my soul sister, Hillary, who always had a pep talk when I needed one; and to my co-conspirator in world travels, Michael, for his friendship and support. Thanks especially to my dear Allan, for the count-less words of encouragement you've given, gourmet meals you've cooked, and selfless decisions you've made to help me achieve over the years.

This book was written in coffee shops from Dublin, Ireland to Saxapahaw, NC to Healdsburg, CA. I would be remiss not to thank the baristas at Brother Hubbard for their delicious flat whites and glorious coffee art, the Catch-22 coffee shop for its inspiring views of the Haw River, and the multitude of Starbucks worldwide that have provided me with espresso, a laptop plug, and free Wi-Fi.

1 Introduction

Casino gaming is big business. According to the American Gaming Association, the industry's professional and lobbying arm in the United States, the top 20 casino markets in the US alone combined to bring in over $17.5 billion in the year 2012. In some of those top-20 markets, gaming is the dominant industry, the "only show in town," much like 1950s-era Detroit or 1920s-era Pittsburgh. In Las Vegas, 1 in 10 residents work in the casino gaming or related tourism industry.

Internationally, the casino industry continues to grow. In the tiny Chinese city of Macau, profits from casino gaming far eclipse those of Las Vegas despite the fact that this Special Administrative Region (SAR) measures less than 30 square kilometers in size. Casino gambling has emerged in metropolitan cities and small municipalities alike in countries across the globe. In fact, only a handful of countries have thus far resisted the urge to legalize gambling, largely because governments see the potential to reap tremendous tax windfalls from casino profits.

Although the desire to gamble can be traced to the early days of mankind, the existence of casino gaming as a legally sanctioned enterprise is actually quite new. In fact, some countries have legalized gambling only in the last 50 years, and the spread of casinos in the United States (outside of Nevada, where gambling has been legal since 1931) has occurred primarily in the last 25 years. The expansion of casino gaming as an industry has brought considerable revenue to both corporations and governments as this new industry continues to evolve and establish its identity and place in cities around the world.

Consider that the name itself holds some interesting clues to the evolution of this particular industry. Originally referred to as "gambling" operations, casinos found themselves hard-pressed to find investors who would bankroll an endeavor with such a morally dubious character. Industry executives latched onto the word "gaming" to present a somewhat more corporatized and sanitized investment opportunity. As gambling has expanded into the online realm, the phrase "casino gaming" came to represent those land-based casino gaming locations that have expanded into communities around the world.

This book steps into the rapid expansion of the casino gaming industry to consider the role that corporate social responsibility (CSR) can and should play in a world where legalized gambling exists alongside traditional industries such as manufacturing and information technology. Wood (1991, p. 695) describes CSR as the idea that "business and society are interwoven rather than distinct entities," suggesting that society expects corporations to enact behaviors deemed socially appropriate and necessary. This book parses what that statement might mean in the casino industry: How have casinos become a part of our society, and what expectations does society have of corporations whose business is gambling?

Additionally, this book considers that the CSR function operates as both a matter of business operations (i.e. CSR as a business strategy that positively impacts the bottom line) and as an element of successful public relations (CSR helps build and maintain relationships with important publics), highlighting the differences between these approaches and examining where they might overlap. In doing so, it raises important questions about how corporations can enact CSR programs in ways that are both ethical and effective.

It also considers whether certain industries, by their nature, might be more or less capable of corporate social responsibility as we know it: can a casino, racetrack, or lottery, which profits from others' losses, ever be truly responsible? Does society have additional requirements of these corporations, and must they work harder to meet societal expectations of responsibility? How does the equation change when casinos and lotteries are run by (or generate profits for) local or national governments, and do the significant taxes paid by casinos on their profits affect the balance of responsibility in the industry?

This book starts in the city of Las Vegas, Nevada. If there was ever a city built by gambling, it was Las Vegas: Except for a brief stint as a railroad stop in the early 1900s, Las Vegas has never had an identity that was not tied to its dominant industry, casino gaming. However, the story of the casino industry, and the discussion of what role corporate social responsibility might play in that industry, expands far beyond that city's borders.

Legalized gambling now exists worldwide, generating taxes and revenues that feed the coffers of governments at an astronomical rate. In fact, as Buchanan and Johnson (2007) suggest, it is very possible that just as there are concerns that patrons might become unhealthily attached to the thrills of gambling, the governments that have voted to legalize casinos may be similarly addicted to the revenues that they generate. The complicated connection between the casino gaming industry and the government, which varies broadly based on jurisdiction, adds another wrinkle to the study of social responsibility in this industry.

This book seeks to examine the nature of corporate social responsibility in the casino gaming industry by returning to Wood's (1991) foundational definition: the recognition of societal expectations for corporate behavior and the corporation's actions to meet or exceed those expectations. In doing so, it seeks to highlight some of the complexities and considerations of CSR in the gaming industry that may raise larger questions for those corporations seeking to enact a CSR program. It also considers how the government's involvement in casino operations might affect the way that social responsibility is enacted by these casinos.

***

In 1961, a business owner in Las Vegas, NV donated a plot of land to a local Catholic parish so that a church could be constructed to hold services for the congregation. Completed in 1963, the Guardian Angel Cathedral has stood for over 50 years while buildings were constructed, demolished and replaced by other buildings all around it. The church sits on the Las Vegas Boulevard in the proximity of the Riviera hotel-casino, which is notable in the city for its longevity: The Riviera was originally built in 1955, and at the ripe old age of 59, it stands as the sixth-oldest Las Vegas casino still in operation.

This donation was unusual for a number of reasons. For starters, the man who donated the land wasn't a member of the congregation, and he wasn't even Catholic, he was Jewish. Among his many philanthropic endeavors, for many years he served as a prominent fundraiser for the organization United Jewish Appeal; he also helped fund the construction of the temple for the only Jewish congregation in Las Vegas.

This man was also no ordinary business owner. He was Moe Dalitz, part owner of the Desert Inn casino. In his life prior to moving to Las Vegas – before he became a noted philanthropist and community member – Dalitz was a member of the Cleveland crime syndicate, a notoriously brutal operation that held a prominent place among East Coast Mob families.

Dalitz was not necessarily an exception in the early years of Las Vegas's casino industry. Gambling operations in the US had, for many years, been run illegally and generated great financial profit for criminal operations. Nevada, the first state to legalize gambling in 1931, provided a haven for men like Dalitz to turn their illegal endeavors into legitimate business establishments. The transition from gangster to community pillar, it seems, was not very difficult – not in Las Vegas.

And so it would seem that the earliest vestiges of corporate social responsibility in the casino gaming industry emanated from the most unlikely of sources: The mobsters and organized crime bosses who built and ran Las Vegas's early casinos, primarily as a front for skimming profits and laundering money from illegal operations. These men had been feared in their earlier lives, but once they arrived in Las Vegas, some were ultimately respected as pillars of the community. Even reputed mobsters like Benjamin Siegel, who was given the name "Bugsy" because his cavalier attitude toward murder made him seem crazy, gave back to the community by hosting a benefit for a local writer battling cancer.

Although Las Vegas's early days were characterized by the prevalence of organized crime, changes in casino ownership in the 1960s and 1970s altered the city's landscape dramatically in a number of ways. When reclusive billionaire Howard Hughes came to Las Vegas in 1966, his purchase of several casino properties through his wholly owned Summa Corporation paved the way for the Nevada Gaming Commission to authorize corporations with multiple shareholders to own and operate casinos in the late 1960s.

Once the state's gaming commission made it legal for corporations to own casinos, the individual owner-operators of Las Vegas's early casinos were essentially forced out by these corporate owners' access to capital for improvements and expansion (Schwartz, 2003). Today, the casinos in Las Vegas are primarily owned and operated by one of five corporations, each of which owns multiple casinos in the Las Vegas market. MGM Resorts International (11 casinos), Caesars Entertainment (eight casinos), and Las Vegas Sands (two casinos) operate multiple casino properties on the well-known Las Vegas Strip; Boyd Gaming (seven casinos) and Station Casinos (18 casinos) operate in the city's downtown area and in the suburban areas away from the Strip.

Although these corporations do engage significantly in community causes, it is still not uncommon to hear Las Vegas residents declare that the city was "better" when casinos were owned by the Mob (Coolican, 2012). This statement, which is anecdotally quite common among the city's long-time residents, should give us pause: The people of Las Vegas indicate that they prefer men like Moe Dalitz and Bugsy Siegel to the corporations that run today's casinos, even though these corporations sponsor carefully planned and executed foundations and other corporate social responsibility programs.

In Las Vegas, at least, social responsibility seems no match for the prevailing belief that the only thing worse than a mobster is a corporation.

***

There is no more polarizing figure in the history of Macau's gaming industry – and none more important – than Stanley Ho. In 1962, Ho's company STDM (Sociedade de Turismos y Diversões de Macau) won the monopoly license to operate casinos in Macau. In the second half of the 20th century, Ho built not only a personal empire of casinos but also infrastructure improvements, such as ferries to the Chinese mainland, that supported those casinos' success and also contributed generally to the city's growth.

In 2001, the Chinese government – which took over governance of Macau from Portugal in 1999 – decided to open up Macau's casino industry and granted two additional casino licenses. In order to modernize and advance the industry, the government chose to grant licenses to outside interests that had opened casinos in places such as Las Vegas (Wynn Resorts). These operators then extended sublicenses to other casino corporations, and the number of corporations involved in Macau's casino industry grew to six.

Ho was understandably upset to lose his monopoly over the lucrative Macau casino industry. Although he still had a significant share of the gaming revenue, he was forced to compete with well-capitalized investors from outside of Macau, a distinct disadvantage from his previous position. Internal struggles within Ho's casino corporation, now known as SJM (Sociedade de Jogos de Macau), further complicated his efforts to remain dominant in Macau's casino industry.

Ho lashed out publicly against what he thought were unfair practices by his competitors. Organized gambling trips, or "junkets," from mainland China and elsewhere in Asia had kept the VIP rooms of Ho's casinos profitable during the monopoly years, but these groups were increasingly patronizing casinos owned by Wynn or Las Vegas Sands, which had entered the market as subcontractors to the license awarded to Galaxy Entertainment Group. Ho claimed that the large casinos and VIP rooms built by the American corporations made it impossible for his own rooms to compete.

In his efforts to gain a firm footing for his casino enterprises, Ho also relied on the advantage that Wynn, Sands, and Galaxy could not compete with: history. After all, Ho had been responsible for a great deal of Macau's non-gaming development during the STDM monopoly years, and his was the only Macanese corporation given a license by the Chinese government in 2001. Ho began promoting his own casinos' record of hiring Macau residents for top-level management jobs – many other corporations had been bringing in foreign workers for these positions – and openly challenging other casino corporations for not doing enough to help the community and the natural environment of Macau. He even accused other corporations of making casino jobs so attractive that young Macanese were dropping out of school to work for these casino corporations.

Ho's ability to profit from casino gambling had convinced the Chinese government that Macau held a significant potential for profitable gambling enterprises, prompting the government to open Macau's historical monopoly and attempt to Westernize its casino industry. The story of Macau's casino industry is still being written, but it remains to be seen whether the former Portuguese colony will thrive or ultimately become a victim of its own success – much like its leading figure, Stanley Ho.

***

When people think of Las Vegas and Macau – and, in general, about the multibillion-dollar casino industry that has become prominent throughout the world – they are unlikely to think next about philanthropy and community involvement. When they think of the significant water and energy resources used by 5000+ room hotels in Macau or the neon used to light Las Vegas's Strip, they are unlikely to think about environmental sustainability. When they think of the tens of thousands of employees that are needed to run a successful hotel-casino operation, many of whom are in low-level service jobs, they are unlikely to think about responsible labor practices.

But the truth is that these responsible practices do exist in the modern casino industry. In fact, the transition of casino gaming to a corporate industry with the usual trappings of stockholders and government regulatory document filings helped fuel the development of corporate social responsibility in the casino industry, and the expectation of such behavior by large corporations has no doubt contributed to the prominent place that CSR holds on the websites of many major casino gaming corporations.

The face of legalized gambling varies considerably across the world, and with the introduction of new technologies, it continues to evolve every day. "Gambling" as a term can cover a wide variety of enterprises including but not limited to lotteries, sports betting, and more traditional forms of casino games as are found in gambling hubs like Las Vegas or Macau. In addition, technology now makes it possible for people to gamble anywhere, at any time, through online gambling sites. Because these forms of gambling are so different in the way they are perceived by society, and in the type of expectations that might be placed on them for socially responsible behavior, this book looks primarily at the industry that operates gambling in physical casinos, hence it will primarily use the term "casino industry." The decision to focus on bricks-and-mortar casinos, to the exclusion of lotteries and online gambling, allows the discussion to be more specifically located in the context of a particular community.

Ultimately, the discussion of corporate social responsibility in the casino industry calls into question some of the fundamental assumptions that have buttressed the wide-scale proliferation of CSR in that industry. Are there certain industries that, by their nature, are incapable of exhibiting social responsibility? If the casino industry is capable of being socially responsible, what might that look like? Does the reality of CSR in this industry reflect the idealized standards that society might hold for it, and is it motivated by purpose or profit? Does it matter?

***

The city of Las Vegas was built around gambling. Without a steady stream of workers from the Hoover Dam – who were forbidden to gamble (among other things) in their government-sponsored work camp at Boulder City – Las Vegas might have dried up after the town's railroad station ceased operations in the mid-1920s and people no longer had a reason to visit the isolated desert outpost. City leaders attempted to promote Las Vegas as a tourism and leisure destination, but their efforts did not meet with much success until casino hotels and resorts started popping up along Highway 97, now known as the infamous Las Vegas Strip. As such, the community and the gaming industry in Las Vegas have always been intertwined.

But gaming has now come to communities where it has no historical connection. You can visit legal casinos in locations from Cincinnati, Ohio to Sydney, Australia; from Vancouver, Canada to Nassau, Bahamas; and from Lima, Peru to Johannesburg, South Africa. Publicly held casino corporations look to expand into untapped markets in regions of the world that are just now legalizing gambling. Government-run casinos in Canada and Australia, among others, bring tremendous revenues to balance those countries' expenditures.

The rapid expansion of legalized gambling should come as no surprise. In a time where governments are constantly seeking new sources of revenue, the successful casino industry has had no problems winning over new converts. As moral opposition to gambling has largely fallen away, corporations have stepped forward with attractive proposals to increase jobs in communities that have fallen on hard times and provide revenues to governments that desperately need them.

But, much like any kind of economic development, the expansion of casinos comes at a price. What that price might be, exactly, is often hard to determine objectively, and thus hard to compare to the potential benefits in the sort of costs-vs-benefits framework that so often drives public policy decisions. The decision to legalize gambling often comes in less-than-ideal economic conditions, and so the promises of economic development made by governments and corporations alike are attractive to those who are in charge of making such decisions.

In many places around the world, however, the discussion of whether gambling should be legalized is largely moot: Casinos have come to play a large role in producing revenues for governments where they exist, whether these are direct revenues or taxes collected on corporate profits, and to take away these substantial funds is largely unthinkable. It seems likely at this point that legalized gambling is here to stay, and if it is, it seems important to begin meaningful discussions about the role that CSR plays in this growing casino industry. This book attempts, in part, to further that conversation.

But as corporations increasingly use their socially responsible efforts to promote and advance their relationships with significant stakeholders – the traditional province of public relations professionals – it is important to look closely at this practice to ensure that it is being done ethically, and to look at any ways it might be negatively affecting any of the stakeholders it purports to be helping. An industry-specific look at CSR in the casino industry reveals a number of concerning disconnects between ostensibly pro-social CSR efforts and the recent trend toward a strategic enactment of CSR – the so-called "business case" for CSR that evolved in response to opposition from Milton Friedman, among others. A deeper look, however, reveals that this attempt to generate a "win–win" situation for both business interests and society may in fact do as much harm as it does good.

***

This book provides the background in both CSR and the casino industry necessary to understand the particular complexities that evolve from enacting a program of corporate social responsibility in a casino industry or by a government that operates casinos to generate public revenues. After providing this background, it looks at a specific case study of Las Vegas, Nevada, a site chosen for its enduring relationship with the casino industry and also for the intrinsic interest it generates as a community with a dominant industry (casinos and tourism). Finally, the book identifies and discusses inconsistencies shown by the Las Vegas case study and discusses what this might mean for the future enactment of CSR in the casino industry as well as for the role of CSR in successful and ethical public relations practice.

Chapter 2 provides an extensive review of literature on the topic of corporate social responsibility. It considers a number of different approaches to CSR, including the use of CSR for strategic purposes as a way to drive corporate profit.

Chapters 3 and 4 provide background on the casino industry sufficient for readers to understand the complexities of CSR in this industry even if they are not familiar with the industry at all. After Chapter 3 discusses some general aspects of the casino industry and the role that casinos have come to play in our society, Chapter 4 gives three short case studies of the development in casino gaming in Canada, Australia, and Macau. These three locations were chosen for their variety and ability to demonstrate differences among gaming locations, but they share common elements as well.

Chapter 5 provides background on the book's primary case study of Las Vegas, Nevada. Knowing the context and history of Las Vegas, the reader can further understand how this community is affected by the casino industry in a number of physical, environmental, and social ways. Chapter 6 specifically looks at three illustrative elements of CSR in the Las Vegas casino industry – labor relations, environmental impact, and community engagement – that highlight specific elements of this topic for further discussion.

Chapter 7 explores further these inconsistencies identified in the Las Vegas case study and discusses at length why a "business case" for CSR might be so problematic in the casino industry for a number of reasons. Because this research looks only at one industry and is primarily qualitative in nature, it makes no claims to generalizability; however, Chapter 8 brings up some points for future discussion and suggests ways in which the conversation can and should be moved forward on this important issue.

2 CSR

Walking the walk, talking the talk

In over 30 years of concerted research on CSR, or corporate social responsibility, about the only thing that academics agree on is that no one can really agree upon the definition of CSR or the role that it should play in today's world. A number of deep-seated social, political, and economic beliefs affect a person's perception of corporate social responsibility – what it is, whether it's good or bad, how it should be done, whether it should be done – and this complexity makes it difficult to have a coherent conversation about the construct in the academic literature (Dahlsrud, 2008).

This chapter eschews any attempts to create a new definition for CSR, or to synthesize existing definitions – examples of these efforts abound in the existing literature on corporate social responsibility. Instead, the chapter pulls together existing academic literature on corporate social responsibility from a number of interdisciplinary fields in order to consider how CSR is perceived differently from a number of perspectives such as business managers, corporate owners, public relations practitioners, and business ethicists. After describing the history of CSR and its many definitions, it examines the ways in which CSR is very much socially and culturally constructed by the expectations of stakeholders in a particular situation.

The chapter then examines the "business case" for CSR, an approach that has become popular as a theoretical middle-ground approach to CSR and panacea to those who feel that CSR is not in the corporation's best financial interests. However, there are nonbusiness reasons for participation in CSR, and this chapter also examines those, which are primarily ethical/normative in nature. It also looks at the effects of CSR on society, including the possible negative side effects of a strategic CSR approach that emphasizes the financial benefits of CSR. In the course of implementing a CSR strategy, a corporation often interacts with nonprofits/NGOs, and so this chapter also lays the groundwork for understanding these organizations.

Public relations practitioners figure prominently in the CSR debate because of their important role in communicating the corporation's prosocial deeds to a wider audience. In the business case for CSR, as will be demonstrated here, there is little to no motivation for a corporation to engage in CSR if its actions are not widely known. However, the communication of CSR to various stakeholder audiences is complex and must be considered carefully. This chapter looks especially at the way that CSR messages are communicated to stakeholders such as employees, the local community, and the news media.

The actual contours of the definition of CSR have been debated (often heatedly) for several decades, and the debate continues in the academic literature. Because the concept is rooted in social and cultural expectations and standards, the definition of a "socially responsible" corporation has evolved over time, and an understanding of the history of CSR is an important first step in fully understanding the concept itself.

History of corporate social responsibility

The concept of corporate social responsibility has its roots in post-industrial Britain (Smith, 2003) and late 19th-century America (Hall, 1987), when businessmen such as John Rockefeller and Andrew Carnegie put a significant amount of money and effort into improving living conditions for their employees and contributed financially to their communities. The motivation for these efforts was twofold: to address public distrust of the large fortunes these businessmen had amassed and to create a sort of "welfare capitalism" aimed primarily at improving the workforce and consequently increasing efficiency and business production. Many of these early business tycoons were highly paternalistic, imposing a particular moral agenda on workers (Smith, 2003). Early examples of CSR primarily took the form of charitable donations, often to the company's local community or some cause with which it was affiliated (Clark, 2000).

Public concern over the role of business in society rose in the early 20th century as corporations began to amass large amounts of capital resources. Some became concerned that these businesses, which had gained such power via resource control, were not being held to any specific responsibilities (Wood, 1991). The idea of such a power imbalance became even more troubling in the 1950s as anti-corporate, anti-capitalism movements fueled concerns that practices of large corporations were overwhelming and tainting all business in America (Heath & Ni, 2008).

Calls for a philosophy of corporate social responsibility grew louder in the United States and UK in the 1960s as activist movements targeted corporate practices they considered socially or environmentally detrimental (Smith, 2003). Activist movements were typified by the efforts of Ralph Nader, whose 1965 book *Unsafe At Any Speed* attacked the auto industry for dangerous production practices in the manufacturing of automobiles. The prominence of these activists and the growing antibusiness sentiment of the era fundamentally changed the way that corporations communicated with their stakeholders (Clark, 2000). As corporations increasingly used communication tactics to improve their reputations, their participation in socially responsible activities – a category that was beginning to expand beyond mere philanthropy into environmental stewardship, full disclosure of financial information to investors, and attention to diversity – was a crucial element of the effort to rehabilitate tarnished images.

Academic research on the topic of CSR has fragmented into several approaches: justifying or negating the ethical basis for corporate social responsibility (e.g. Donaldson, 1982; Jones, 1999; Smith, 2003); attempting to measure CSR's impact on a company's financial profit (e.g. Bhattacharya & Sen, 2004; Simpson & Kohers, 2002); defining and operationalizing related concepts such as corporate social performance (CSP) and corporate citizenship (e.g. Clarkson, 1995; Knox & Maslan, 2004; Lewis, 2001); and finally, assessing the state of CSR research (e.g. Carroll, 1999; Cheney, Roper, & May, 2007; Griffin & Mahon, 1997; Wood, 1991). Academics continue to struggle with the process of measuring aspects of corporate social responsibility (Heath & Ni, 2008), and a great deal of the early research, which suggested that CSR practices would positively affect purchase intentions, was not reflected in real-world observation (Sen, Bhattacharya, & Korschun, 2006).

Scholars agree that the discussion about CSR has amplified considerably concurrent with the process of globalization (Dahlsrud, 2008; Frynas, 2005; Jamali & Mirshak, 2007; Martin, 2002; Smith, 2003; Starck & Kruckeberg, 2004). The expansion of multinational corporations into new markets has led to concern about corporations' impact on local communities, especially in developing countries (Garriga & Melé, 2004). From a business perspective, effective CSR has been pitched as a tool that can facilitate corporate expansion by "priming" a new community to look favorably on the company (Gardberg & Fombrun, 2006; Porter & Kramer, 2002).

Because definitions and terminology abound in the discussion of corporate social responsibility, it is nearly impossible to list them all here. Instead, the next two sections highlight different working definitions of CSR and some of the aspects of the concept that are often discussed and examined separately.

Varying definitions and terminology in the CSR discussion

On a macro level, CSR is perhaps best generally defined as corporations' attempt to operationalize the belief "that business and society are interwoven rather than distinct entities; therefore, society has certain expectations for appropriate business behavior and outcomes" (Wood, 1991, p. 695). This general definition of the motivations for CSR, rather than the explicit actions taken by individual corporations, seems especially appropriate to the research being undertaken here, which is concerned with the interaction between business and society in an industry that has some negative externalities on the society in which the business operates. Wood's definition also suggests the importance of societal expectations for the level and type of CSR a corporation will engage in; this construct will be discussed in detail in a later section.

Wood's choice of the word "interwoven" is echoed in other definitions of CSR that use terminology such as "interdependence" (Heath & Ni, 2008, p. 17), "integrated" (Pedersen, 2006, p. 157) and "inexorably involved" (McKie, qtd. in Vogel, 2005, p. 32). She goes on to further refine elements of CSR at an institutional level (as institutions in society, businesses are granted a "license to operate" which may be revoked if they are socially irresponsible) and an organizational level, attributing a responsibility to businesses for any impacts they have on society (Wood, 1991).

Heath and Ni (2008, p. 3) see CSR as an inevitable outcome of the ongoing relationship between business and society, stating that, "by whatever name, interests of organizations cannot long be at odds with mutual interest and common good." The business–society relationship is at the heart of many conceptualizations of CSR (Maignan, Ferrell, & Ferrell, 2005), but increasingly this relationship is less popular as a justification for CSR than one based on the potential for financial profit (Wheeler, Colbert, & Freeman, 2003). It seems reasonable on a gut level that most people would expect corporations to engage in some basic level of social responsibility: If a business could repair, reduce, or atone for its environmental impact, or make a donation that could benefit its local community, why wouldn't it? When the conversation about CSR becomes more nuanced, however, the role of ethics in business becomes a significant sticky wicket.

The very term itself can be controversial. The use of "corporate" may be too limiting (Cheney, Roper, & May, 2007; Schoenberger-Orgad & McKie, 2005), as this behavior is common in small to medium-sized businesses as well as larger corporations; if the need for CSR is predicated on a business's obligation to society, there is no reason that this should apply solely to large corporations and not to smaller businesses. Some researchers have tried to replace the word "social" with "societal," hoping to clarify that this construct refers to the business's relationship with society writ large, and not just with other stakeholders (Hoeffler & Keller, 2002; van Marrewijk, 2003). The word "responsibility" invokes an ethical/duty-based approach with a Kantian sense of obligation, but the increasing turn toward a business case for CSR leaves one to wonder what place there is, if any, for normative views in the discussion of CSR.

The word "responsibility" creates a conflict in the definitions of CSR, where a notable bifurcation exists between a corporation's purported duty to meet its obligations (including legal/regulatory standards) or correct harms it may have caused and the idea that corporations should go above and beyond those obligations into what Carroll (1991) calls *discretionary* CSR, also known as corporate philanthropy. Philanthropy, be it strategic or altruistic, plays an important role in the discussion of CSR and will be addressed in a later section.

Some definitions of CSR suggest that if the corporation has the resources and knowledge to address a problem in society, it should do so voluntarily due to its relative power and ability to improve social conditions (Moir, 2001; Newell, 2008) – whether or not the corporation was responsible for the social problem in the first place. In an article called "Misery loves companies," Margolis and Walsh (2003, p. 270) summarize one of the primary contradictions in CSR thusly:

> The repeated calls for corporate action to ameliorate social ills reflect an underlying tension. On the one hand, misery loves companies. The sheer magnitude of problems, from malnutrition and HIV to illiteracy and homelessness, inspires a turn toward all available sources of aid, most

notably corporations. Especially when those problems are juxtaposed to the wealth-creation capabilities of firms – or to the ills that firms may have helped to create – firms become an understandable target of appeals. On the other hand, a sturdy and persistent theoretical argument in economics suggests that such corporate involvement is misguided.

McWilliams and Siegel (2001, p. 117) even go so far as to clearly define CSR as "actions that appear to further some social good, beyond the interests of the firm and that which is required by law" (see also Doane, 2005). However, others imply that CSR actions are most legitimate when they are ameliorating the corporation's own actions/impacts on society (Pava & Krausz, 1997), implying that companies without an impact on society are somehow excused from an obligation to engage in CSR.

Many of those who advocate prioritizing and valuing CSR base their opinion on an ethical foundation (Jones, 1999). Definitions of CSR often reference normative concepts (Clarkson, 1995), including corporate values (Knox & Maslan, 2004). Some of those who support CSR justify it on a "social contract" basis: When it comes into being, the corporation enters into an implicit social contract with all stakeholders, not just its stockholders (Evan & Freeman, 1988). CSR can also be justified based on a "license to operate" viewpoint, which suggests that businesses "owe" a certain amount to society for being allowed to exist and benefit from society's norms and economic structure (Smith, 2003). In the absence of a business justification for CSR, some scholars suggest that the corporation's moral obligation to its stakeholders should serve as an adequate motivation for CSR (Smith, 2003).

Many definitions locate CSR in the relationship between a corporation and its stakeholders (Sweeney & Coughlan, 2008); this includes but is not limited to a company's owners and/or financial shareholders (Clarkson, 1995; Snider, Hill, & Martin, 2003). Locating CSR within the organization–public relationship occurs on both a theoretical (Donaldson & Preston, 1995) and an operational (Basu & Palazzo, 2008) level: CSR is both how corporations think about stakeholder relationships and how they act toward/communicate with those stakeholders. The vast body of stakeholder management literature in business can be brought to bear on CSR in this context, and CSR communication with stakeholders – either before, to understand what the stakeholders expect, or after, to report on the corporation's action – falls squarely into the role of the public relations practitioner. This significant overlap may account for the vast popularity and quantity of CSR research that has been published primarily in the last 30 years.

CSR is often described in terms of the benefits that it provides for the corporation, a concept that will be discussed in greater depth as part of the examination of the business case for CSR. With respect to definitions of CSR, however, it seems telling to note the elements of definitions for CSR that allude to these benefits, such as "the management of risk, as the avoidance of damage to the company's reputation" (Skapinker, 2004, NP); "increasingly important to competitive success" (Porter, Kramer, & Zadek, 2006, p. 90); and "legitimizing a corporation's activities and increasing corporate acceptance" (Palazzo & Richter, 2005, p. 390), speak to a wide range of benefits the corporation hopes to reap from socially responsible behavior.

A nuanced consideration of the nature and definition of CSR must consider corporate motivations for engaging in socially responsible behavior; however, this is a complicated endeavor. Because corporate strategic decisions about CSR are made by individuals at the management level, a corporation's involvement (or lack of it) in CSR actions often reflects the morality of the individuals who make these decisions (Carroll, 1991). Although it is often done for the sake of convenience, it may not be correct to talk about the "conscience" or "morals" of a corporation – these anthropomorphizations can inaccurately represent the reality of decisions made by corporations to engage in CSR activities (McMillan, 2007).

However, the suggestion by Bivins (2009) that a corporation's responsibilities to its stakeholders can be classified as either moral or functional obligations can be useful here in broadly identifying corporate motivations for engaging in socially responsible behavior. Following Bivins' classification, a corporation may engage in CSR in order to fulfill functional obligations – things it must do to ensure its continued survival. In this sense, a corporation is typically more obligated to those stakeholders on whom its existence depends or those with whom it is interdependent (see also Rawlins, 2006).

In addition to this functional obligation to engage in CSR, corporations also have moral obligations to stakeholders that usually align along an axis of power; as a rule of thumb, corporations are morally obligated to those stakeholder groups over which they hold power (Bivins, 2009). In deciding how it will enact a policy of corporate social responsibility, a corporation may have to decide which stakeholders it is obligated to and how it will fulfill both moral and functional obligations. Engaging in socially responsible actions, and communicating those actions to the appropriate stakeholder groups, might be one way in which a corporation can fulfill obligations of both types.

Because CSR is situational, relative to industry and stakeholder group, an overall "umbrella" definition of CSR may be impossible and unproductive (Blowfield & Frynas, 2005; Campbell, 2007; Dahlsrud, 2008; Griffin & Mahon, 1997; van Marrewijk, 2003). In fact, it might be more productive to think of CSR as an evolving concept, more of a discussion, by which the relationship between organization and stakeholder can be sustained and the role of the corporation in society can be continually re-evaluated (Guthey & Morsing, 2014; Miles, Munilla, & Darroch, 2006).

While a corporation's obligations and the actions it takes to address these duties can vary across industries, most research recognizes certain aspects of corporate social responsibility including labor relations, environmental sustainability, and community support or philanthropy. The sources that discuss these categories of socially responsible action vary from academic research to professional ranking services to socially responsible investing services.

Social investment firm Kinder, Lydenburg and Domini (KLD) created an index of social responsibility for investors who were interested in using their funds to support responsible corporations. These ratings, which were made available by subscription, subsequently have become popularly used in academic research about corporate social responsibility (e.g. Blanco, Guillamón-Saorín, & Guiral, 2013; Cai, Jo, & Pan, 2012; Simpson & Kohers, 2002). Sharfman (1996) established the validity of the KLD dimensions and their suitability for further academic research. As the rankings have evolved, at some time the KLD database has ranked companies on dimensions of social responsibility including community support, diversity, employee support, environment, non-US operations, corporate governance, and product.

In their discussion of exclusion factors in screening for corporate social investment (CSI) funds, de Colle and York (2009) explore the complexity of deeming particular stocks "irresponsible" due solely to a failure in one of these dimensions of CSR. For instance, they highlight wine- and beer-making firms that employ environmentally sensitive practices above and beyond the norm but still make a product, alcohol, which could be considered irresponsible because of its potential for abuse. (A section in chapter 3 will discuss the complex nature of the "vice" industries, among them alcohol and gambling, with respect to corporate social responsibility.) Rather than excluding companies based on a purported failure in responsibility on one of the KLD dimensions (labor relations, environmental sustainability, etc.), the authors suggest that still other aspects of CSR would be more appropriate measuring sticks, such as the corporation's relationships with its stakeholders – especially its local communities – and the managerial decisions to enact socially responsible behavior where appropriate.

Researchers have attempted to collapse these different elements into one single measure of CSR for the sake of expediency, but the complicated, situational nature of corporate social responsibility makes this problematic. Instead, the elements of corporate social responsibility are best analyzed individually (Godfrey, Merrill, & Hansen, 2009). This suggests that a nuanced evaluation of corporations' social responsibility is incredibly time-consuming, which has led to the rise of CSR rankings by dedicated private services. These rankings have served to improve the visibility and transparency of corporations' CSR efforts (Pirsch, Gupta, & Grau, 2007); however, these rating systems have been primarily useful to academics and investors and have not facilitated any real change among corporations (Scalet & Kelly, 2010).

CSR as a social and cultural construct

Further complicating the discussion of corporate social responsibility is the fact that CSR is a construct that is fundamentally rooted in societal expectations of corporate stakeholders; therefore, it is influenced by cultural aspects of a society with regard to economic principles and political relationships between business, people, and governments. This section examines the ways that CSR is socially constructed through the expectation of various stakeholder publics and the way that cultural and political beliefs influence these expectations.

Stakeholder expectations and the social construction of CSR

Discussing societal expectations of responsible corporate behavior poses a number of operational challenges. As mentioned previously, the word "responsible" is contested, with varying opinions on whether this obligation is moral or functional in nature, whether the corporation should meet or exceed expectations of responsibility, and exactly to whom the corporation is obligated. Additionally, the idea of a corporation's responsibility to society does not allow for differences between corporations' obligations to varied stakeholders and the way that "responsible" behavior may be fundamentally different across groups (Murray & Montanari, 1986). Finally, this concept suggests that expectations are fixed, when in fact they vary over time based on changing sentiment and mores (Campbell, 2007; Heath & Ni, 2008; Morsing & Schultz, 2006; Rowley & Berman, 2000).

Societal perceptions of socially responsible behavior – and society's expectations for corporations to engage in such behavior – set the standard for CSR by a particular corporation in a particular industry, often in a particular time and place. Schultz, Castelló, and Morsing (2013) suggest that corporate social responsibility can also illuminate the mores of the time; the fact that there is no agreed-upon, permanent definition of CSR echoes the diversity of opinions in a modern society (Frederick, 1986).

However, the fact that CSR is built on social expectations can also serve to set the bar so low for corporations' socially responsible behavior that the corporation's efforts do not provide an adequate benefit to society. If members of a society have naturally low expectations for corporate involvement in prosocial behavior, or if a corporation has a history of irresponsible behavior, expectations for CSR behavior by that corporation might be low. Although stakeholder pressure serves as a primary driver of CSR behavior, stakeholders might not be likely to engage in this sort of activism if the corporation or industry is financially or culturally important, or if the society relies heavily on the corporation or industry for taxes and jobs (Rowley & Berman, 2000).

Society's perspectives of corporations and their socially responsible (or not) behavior are mediated by a number of influences, including the news (Tench, Bowd, & Jones, 2007). This adds another complication to the societal construction of CSR, and the ways that corporations engage with the news media regarding their CSR efforts provides a challenge that will be explored later in this chapter. However, the news media are not the only stakeholders that corporations engage with as a part of their CSR efforts. Using stakeholder theory in the discussion of CSR allows for an exploration of the nuances in expectations across different stakeholder publics. Expectations occur at multiple levels: the individual member of society, the firm itself, the industry, the nation, etc. (Jones, 1999). Institutional or industry norms about the role of social responsibility in corporate behavior often influence CSR actions considerably, but their effect is mediated by other factors from society writ large (Campbell, 2007).

Cultural influences on corporate social responsibility

Academic research has examined the idea of cultural differences in corporate social responsibility (e.g. Birth, Illia, Lurati, & Zamparini, 2008 on CSR in Sweden; Lewin, Sakano, Stephens, & Victor, 1995 on corporate citizenship in Japan; Midttun, Gautesen, & Gjølberg, 2006 on CSR in Western Europe), but it has only begun to piece together the map of cultural influences on how CSR is perceived and practiced in corporations around the world. Cultural difference can affect societal perspectives on what constitutes socially responsible action and to what degree this action is expected of corporations (Birth, Illia, Lurati, & Zamparini, 2008; Elving, 2013).

Contemporary perceptions of CSR in differing countries are affected, most obviously, by the history of CSR in that country. Therefore, the United States' perspective on CSR is based in the welfare capitalism of Andrew Carnegie and John Rockefeller, whose socially responsible projects (pools, libraries) were significant in size but not too sophisticated. Cultural values can also affect the way that CSR is perceived. A 2000 report by the World Business Council for Sustainable Development found, among others, that Taiwanese perceptions of CSR mirrored that country's cultural focus on future generations and the environment and that Ghanaians thought that CSR should empower people, respect local culture, and fill in for government shortcomings (Holme & Watts, 2000).

Because CSR is popularly used by corporations expanding into new markets, especially in developing countries, its association with globalization might cast it in a negative light for some cultures, as some critics see inherent problems with the rapid expansion of multinational corporations (Garriga & Melé, 2004). CSR as a function of the corporation's plans for international expansion can be problematic: Some cultures may be skeptical of institutions overall, especially when businesses and governments are known to be corrupt (Suchman, 1995). An overall skepticism toward corporations pervades many cultures and may influence perceptions of CSR (Wagner, Lutz, & Weitz, 2009).

The use of CSR in developing countries, and the cultural perceptions of this behavior, creates some particular landmines in the CSR discussion. These countries often evidence corruption in government and business and do not have high expectations for socially responsible behavior by corporations (Doane, 2005). Even cultures that do not prioritize CSR, however, were willing to acknowledge it as a positive investment for multinational corporations (Holme & Watts, 2000) – a testament to the pervasive and persuasive development of a business justification for CSR.

In some developing countries, incoming corporations *are* expected to contribute to local communities, possibly because of preconceptions about the corporation and its industry (Gardberg & Fombrun, 2006), and often because governments are incapable of/unwilling to do what is necessary in this regard (Frynas, 2005). This perpetuates an image of the corporation as the provider of services that are traditionally expected of governments, such as public works and schools – a conception of CSR that is troublingly outside the scope of most definitions and seems unsustainable in the long run; most corporations are ill-equipped to perform this kind of community building, and their efforts often fail (Frynas, 2005).

Increasing globalization and the presence of multinational organizations have significantly affected cultural perspectives on CSR. Han (2011) found that multinational casino firms in Macao had often brought in "Western" approaches to CSR, which were then mimicked by domestic corporations and eventually started to displace traditional ideas about business and society that had existed for years. Japanese firms that have expanded beyond that country's borders have found that expectations for CSR are considerably higher and have adjusted their practices accordingly, both outside of Japan and inside (Lewin, Sakano, Stephens, & Victor, 1995). Local media coverage of multinational corporations' CSR actions has helped popularize these companies' responsible actions in countries like South Korea, Brazil, Malaysia, Mexico, Argentina, Hungary, and Poland (Smith, 1994).

Different cultures' perspectives on political and economic systems will also influence the way that societies talk about CSR, as this construct is fundamentally tied to systems such as capitalism and democracy (Jones, 1999; Matten & Moon, 2008). Cultural characteristics can affect perceptions of the appropriate role of government in legislating corporations' CSR behavior. Although the US is hesitant to enact regulation that could be construed as detrimental to business (Langlois & Schlegelmilch, 1990), many other cultures have reacted favorably to the introduction of government standards for corporate social responsibility, notably in the European Union (González & Martinez, 2004). In Japan, a "symbiotic, non-adversarial relation between Japanese industry and the Japanese government" (Lewin, Sakano, Stephens, & Victor, 1995, p. 83) encourages the government to take a hands-off approach to regulating CSR as long as firms are meeting their economic obligations.

On a micro level, corporate or industry culture can also influence the way CSR behaviors are perceived and enacted (Heath & Ni, 2008; Jones, 1999). Organizational values and culture can also determine what level of CSR actions corporations will strive to achieve and how stakeholders will be prioritized when this becomes necessary (Maignan, Ferrell, & Ferrell, 2005). Because the casino industry generates negative social costs and these corporations are expected to address these externalities, the decision by these corporations to engage in CSR is not so much a "will we or won't we," but a "how much and how often" (Smith & Kumar, 2013).

The business case for CSR

The concept of CSR might have evolved into its current place in today's discourse about business and society sooner had its development not been significantly stifled by economist Milton Friedman in the 1960s and 1970s. Responding to calls from Bowen (1953) and Davis (1960) for business to have a positive impact on society, Friedman (1962, 1970) stepped in with a hardline interpretation of free-market capitalism that posited corporate social responsibility as an unethical breach of the corporation's responsibility to produce value for its stakeholders (Lantos, 2001; Margolis & Walsh, 2003). Ever since this intervention, CSR supporters have been trying to rationalize their ideas about the corporation's obligations to society with Friedman's bottom-line mentality. In the need to provide an economic justification to assuage Friedman's concerns, the business case for CSR was born (Schoenberger-Orgad & McKie, 2005); its mottoes and principles have been popularized in business schools, "where CSR is usually justified as enabling managers either to protect firms from external threats (e.g. risk management) or to benefit from external opportunities (e.g. new product development through partnerships with NGOs)" (Blowfield & Frynas, 2005, p. 512).

Given the popularity of CSR in the academic and trade literature, it is almost difficult to imagine that there are those who oppose integrating CSR actions into a business. The opposition to CSR usually denies or downplays the fiscal opportunities in CSR and focuses on an institutional approach (governments and nonprofits are responsible for responding to social problems, not businesses) or a property rights argument (the shareholder's right to make money from the company reflects the fact that investment represents stock ownership) (Jones, 1999). This perspective is grounded in Friedman's assertion that the shareholder's interests are the corporation's sole obligation, even at the expense of other stakeholders.

Friedman's objections to CSR, while seemingly straightforward, relied on a number of unsubstantiated assumptions; his suggestions that "social and economic objectives are separate and distinct, so that a corporation's social spending comes at the expense of its economic results" (Porter & Kramer, 2002, p. 58) and that corporations are no better equipped to address social problems than individuals are easily refuted. Friedman's zero-sum argument, that CSR actions took profits away from shareholders (to give to nonprofit causes), made sense when CSR was primarily corporate philanthropy (Stroup, Neubert, & Anderson Jr, 1987). However, more nuanced contemporary CSR actions rely less on cash donations and more on the use of resources to build and maintain relationships – something that the corporation is already doing, ostensibly, in the pursuit of its business objectives.

Opposition to the use of CSR often falls into the categories known as "misappropriation" and "misallocation": The use of funds which otherwise would go to corporate shareholders, without their permission, for CSR efforts, and the expenditure of these funds on actions that are unlikely to directly generate profit for or otherwise benefit the firm (Margolis & Walsh, 2003). The moral responsibility of the corporate managers becomes especially interesting and complex here: while some would argue that it is most ethical for managers to prioritize the financial advancement of shareholders, it is also true that these shareholders might have their own concerns about nonbusiness issues such as the environment, labor relations, etc. that should be respected by and represented in managers' decisions (Paine, 1996).

While the corporation may not be the right choice to fill the vacuum of social responsibility created by growing individuality (McMillan, 2007), there are clearly needs in our society to be addressed. By partnering with appropriate nonprofit organizations, corporations can bring specific knowledge and resources to address social problems more efficiently and effectively (Pearce & Doh, 2005). As corporations grow larger and wield more power, they increasingly hold the resources to tackle large-scale societal problems that are lacking in individuals or NGOs. Any argument along these lines, however, will likely be met with a Friedmanesque rejoinder that the corporation's shareholders, not the world and its problems, should be the corporation's primary concern.

In an attempt to refute the primacy of shareholders' financial interests that had stifled further expansion of CSR, scholars began to approach the concept from a new direction: They suggested that managers should adopt CSR principles and practices because doing so would allow the corporation to be more financially successful (Heath & Ni, 2008; Rowley & Berman, 2000). Over the ensuing years, scholars have developed the contours of this business case for CSR. Research has identified the kinds of benefits CSR can produce for a company, some of which are directly financial (e.g. purchase decisions, ability to charge higher prices for products) and some more indirect (e.g. reputation and eased government regulations).

This section of the chapter will examine the evolution of the business case for CSR and how it has been applied for use in management situations. It will look at the shareholder primacy argument introduced by Friedman and examine how this economic construct has been melded into contemporary discussions of CSR. A discussion about how CSR is affected by financial crisis will set the stage for an examination of the notion of altruism in business and how strategic CSR has emerged as a way to allay Friedman's concerns by producing value for the corporation and its shareholders. Finally, this section will begin to look broadly at the societal-level implications of corporations operating under a CSR strategy that is based on the financial bottom line.

Evolution of the business case for CSR

The idea that CSR actions should ultimately benefit a company's shareholders is not a new one: Until the restriction was removed by a Supreme Court decision in 1954, businesses had been limited to philanthropic donations that would directly further the corporation's interests (Varadarajan & Menon, 1988). Where early CSR was primarily informal and consisted of philanthropic donations to executives' favored projects (Cheney, Roper, & May 2007; Smith, 1994), the introduction of a business case for CSR has led to more formalized processes as the success or failure of CSR actions are now included in the business's overall financial health (Frynas, 2005).

The rumblings of early calls for CSR emerged in the 1950s and escalated in the 1960s when labor and product safety issues began to come to light (Lantos, 2001). CSR took a more formalized, managerial turn in the 1970s in response to social pressures on businesses to act in a prosocial manner (Frederick, 1994). Early CSR efforts were voluntary, and, later, certain industries saw a phase where these actions were mandated by government regulation (Stroup, Neubert, & Anderson Jr., 1987). For instance, in 1977 the Community Reinvestment Act established regulation that forced banks to lend in low-income communities based on obligation, not necessarily on expected return (Barr, 2005).

The turn toward a business justification allowed managers to cast their CSR decisions in a more objective light and removed the specter of moral thinking from these actions; this allowed them to support or defend actions based on business principles, not moral ones (Frederick, 1994). For example, in the light of economic downturns and forced layoffs, companies have been able to defend their

CSR actions as investments in the company's business success (Smith, 1994). The new, business-oriented CSR strives "to achieve a synergistic outcome by targeting corporate resources at societal problems or issues that resonate with the core values and mission of the firm" (Saiia, Carroll, & Buchholtz, 2003, p. 170). Put simply, the current thinking is that strategic CSR is good business, and that managers would be acting irresponsibly toward shareholders if they did *not* engage in this practice (Lantos, 2001).

In a final stage of this evolution, the very organizations that companies' CSR actions are intended to benefit have begun to adapt to this rhetorical framework for CSR as a business strategy. In the wake of CSR's popularity as a driver of profitability, NGOs and nonprofits have adjusted their strategies to appeal to corporations' bottom line when propositioning them for financial assistance (Doane, 2005; Vogel, 2005). Ironically, the strategic turn in CSR practice has limited these nonprofits' opportunity to benefit from corporate philanthropy, since rules for giving are now more narrowly circumscribed and often tailored to benefit the financial success of the firm (Vogel, 2005).

Of course, because conceptions of CSR are tied to society's expectation of the firm's obligations, this current perspective on CSR is subject to change (Campbell, 2007; Zadek, 2004). For now, however, CSR scholars have found a way to appease CSR's critics by framing the concept as a solid business investment. By highlighting CSR's ability to create value – whether financial or less tangible value that can be used in pursuit of eventual financial success – CSR development can coexist more peacefully with the interests of financial stakeholders (Wheeler, Colbert, & Freeman, 2003).

The double-edged sword of shareholder primacy

Prioritizing shareholders in the discussion about CSR is the only way to acquiesce to Milton Friedman's assertions and make the business case for CSR. If CSR can truly help a corporation provide greater benefits to its shareholders (or, in the case of a smaller company, provide profits to its owners), then Friedman's zero-sum argument is moot. In fact, if CSR can provide added value for the corporation – and, hence, for its shareholders – by providing more benefits than the costs required to achieve them, then it would be against Friedman's own standards for a corporation *not* to engage in CSR.

The prioritization of shareholders above other stakeholders suggests that CSR can be instrumental in a corporation's pursuit of financial success – the so-called business case. Martin (2002) points out, however, that the instrumental view of CSR is only one of two perspectives on corporate social responsibility – a nonbusiness, moral view of CSR suggests that the corporation does what is right regardless of whether it has a positive, neutral, or negative effect on value for shareholders. Obviously, though, this view of CSR is incompatible with Friedman's assertions and the business case for CSR.

However, a myopic view of shareholder primacy can have serious consequences, which are articulated well by Boatright (1996, p. 228):

The fiduciary duty to act in the interests of shareholders creates a presumption that firms are free to externalize costs whenever possible and may even have an obligation to do so when shareholders benefit. Thus, takeovers that inflict great losses on bondholders, employees, and communities are justified on the grounds that they maximize the wealth of shareholders. Pollution, customer injuries, and plant relocation are further externalities that corporations feel free to externalize as a matter of course.

When considering industries that might already be producing negative externalities, such as gambling, this blithe acceptance of potential externalities in the name of shareholder primacy is especially troubling.

As Boatright (1996, p. 236) continues, such a focus on creating shareholder value "gives management a free hand to impose negative externalities and other harms on society, and, indeed, *it may even create an obligation on managers to do so* at every opportunity" (emphasis added). While this single-minded pursuit of shareholder value might seem dramatically over-exaggerated, attempts to suggest that corporations prioritize stakeholders fairly may be misleading (Gioia, 1999). Ignoring moral obligations to other stakeholders can easily be justified by the pursuit of shareholder wealth and the manager's moral obligation to prioritize this stakeholder (Paine, 1996). However, as Cragg (2002) points out, the corporation's use of financial duty to shareholders superseding obligations to other stakeholders is a logical red herring, as the corporation simultaneously honors other obligations (to government by paying taxes and following laws, to local communities by following zoning rules and other agreements, etc.) because it would face consequences for not doing so.

CSR in an economic crisis

This issue of shareholder primacy becomes especially sharp when a corporation encounters financial crisis. In many industries, corporations are feeling economic pressures that threaten their very survival (Vogel, 2005). Under strained economic conditions, it becomes even more crucial – and even more difficult – to address the business case for CSR and demonstrate its ability to provide shareholders with additional value. Because CSR has traditionally been associated with philanthropy, a discretionary or "add-on" engagement, it can seem like an optional expense in times of financial crisis (Swanson, 1995; Vogel, 2005).

Campbell (2007) identifies weak financial performance or an unhealthy economy as two of several factors that might prevent a corporation from engaging in CSR. Spending on CSR might be more prevalent in companies that are enjoying financial success and have discretionary income for extra expenditures (Miles & Covin, 2000; Waddock & Graves, 1997). This creates what Waddock and Graves (1997, p. 307) refer to as a "virtuous circle" where the firm's resources enable its CSR actions, which in turn produce further financial success.

Many of the misconceptions that suggest corporations should cut back on CSR in a financial crisis presume that these actions are done purely out of altruism; if this were true, then these expenditures would necessarily be low in the pecking order for justifiable expenses. However, in justifying the business case for CSR, scholars have addressed the misconception of CSR as an altruistic act, and in fact have exposed the weaknesses of an altruistic approach. The next section defines and identifies the differences between altruistic and strategic CSR.

The downside of altruism and the rise of strategic CSR

At the far end of the CSR spectrum, corporate altruism includes giving that has no ulterior motive and no prospect of reward or return (Saiia, Carroll, & Buchholtz, 2003). The very opposite of the business case for CSR, corporate altruism sounds extremely idealistic and impractical, not to mention in direct opposition to Friedman's principles of shareholder primacy. Husted and de Jesus Salazar (2006, p. 80) examine the theoretical idea of the altruistic firm, which they define as a firm willing to "work until social profits[1] are zero, but not to accept negative social profits – such an action would not be altruistic, but foolish. Even Mother Theresa [sic] took time to eat and sleep."

Webb and Mohr (1998) examined consumer perception of altruism and found that, although consumers wished to believe that corporations engaged in CSR for purely altruistic reasons, those same consumers tended to be skeptical if the corporations communicated an altruistic motivation without acknowledging that the corporation was benefiting from CSR as well. Here, it seems that consumers were concerned with a perceived lack of transparency, not the idea that the corporation's motives were at least partially self-serving. This is only one of many reasons why communicating CSR to stakeholder publics is so complex; this topic will be explored in depth later in this chapter.

Because a corporation's strategic decisions about CSR are made by individuals at the management level, a corporation's involvement (or lack of involvement) in CSR actions often reflects the morality of the individuals who make these decisions (Basu & Palazzo, 2008; Carroll, 1991; Moir, 2001). That corporations become involved in CSR at the behest of notable executives can be problematic. Managers' decisions about a corporation's appropriate engagement in CSR may not adequately fit societal expectations or be properly aligned with the values of the firm. If these executives who supported CSR are no longer with the firm, the firm's commitment to CSR may leave as well (Basu & Palazzo, 2008). Managers may be influenced by corporate culture to make decisions about CSR that do not align with their personal morals and ethics (Murphy, Öberseder, & Laczniak, 2013). A bottom-line orientation towards CSR on the part of managers may signal to lower-level employees that financial success is the only objective of the firm, and employees in turn may act accordingly, as happened in the case of Enron (Sims & Brinkmann, 2003).

Ultimately, the purely altruistic firm is not as successful as one that uses CSR strategically for the simple reason that the latter is more financially sustainable due to its focus on making profits in a responsible way (Husted & de Jesus Salazar, 2006). This suggests that managers and executives who are motivated to engage in CSR should direct their corporations toward CSR for strategic reasons that will benefit the corporation's bottom line (Porter & Kramer, 2002), even if their primary motivations are moral.

While strategic CSR involves a number of facets, at its heart it is an orientation toward the business case for CSR (i.e. these actions should ultimately support the corporation's financial profitability). Discussions of strategic CSR often feature an explicit or implicit cost/benefit analysis of the investment in CSR actions and attention to the CSR action's "fit" with the company and its values, concepts that will be explored in the following section.

CSR as a cost–benefit proposition

In order to make the case for CSR, scholars have long discussed the benefits that a strategic CSR program can bring to a corporation. The costs of CSR are fairly straightforward and include human resources (employees' time) and in-kind and financial donations. The literature ascribes a number of benefits to be obtained from engaging in CSR, including *improved brand equality* (Blumenthal & Bergstrom, 2003; Garriga & Melé, 2004; Hoeffler & Keller, 2002; Murphy, Öberseder, & Laczniak, 2013), which often leads to *increased purchase decisions* (Bhattacharya & Sen, 2004; Lewis, 2001; Groza, Pronschinske, & Walker, 2011; Lichtenstein, Drumright, & Braig, 2004; Smith, 2003), *decreased price sensitivity* (Miles & Covin, 2000), *improved employee support* (Frynas, 2005; Lee, Song, Lee, Lee, & Bernhard, 2013; Maignan, Ferrell, & Hult, 1999; Smith, 2003; Smith & Kumar, 2013), *ease in attracting qualified employees* (Birth, Illia, Lurati, & Zamparini, 2008; Bloom, Hoeffler, Keller, & Meza, 2006; Greening & Turban, 2000; Lantos, 2001; Murray & Montanari, 1986; Vong & Wong, 2013), *smoother relationships with stakeholders* of all sorts (Du, Bhattacharya, & Sen, 2007, 2010; Heath & Ni, 2008; Holme & Watts, 2000; Morsing & Schultz, 2006), *positive "reputational capital"*, (Gardberg & Fombrun, 2006, p. 330), *reduced firm risk* (Jo & Na, 2012; Paine, 2000), *more support from consumers in crisis situations* (Bhattacharya & Sen, 2004), and *eased regulation and government relations* (Frynas, 2005; Smith, 1994; Vong & Wong, 2013). Companies that see no benefit from CSR are less likely to engage in these actions (Keim, 1978); however, these companies can find themselves subject to increased government regulation (Heath & Ryan, 1989) and litigation costs related to their actions (Lantos, 2001).

CSR actions are perhaps easier to justify, even to skeptics or opponents of the practice, when they are directly tied to product sales. Some research has shown that a corporation's engagement in CSR will make consumers decide to purchase its products (Lichtenstein, Drumwright, & Braig, 2004) and that corporations active in CSR can even charge a higher price for their products (Bloom, Hoeffler, Keller, & Meza, 2006; Miles & Covin, 2000). The increase in purchase decisions is often attributed to a consumer's desire to affiliate with the identity of socially responsible companies by purchasing their products (Aguilera, Rupp, Williams, & Ganapathi, 2007). Customers also wish to signal support for socially responsible behaviors by purchasing the products of corporations that choose to act in this way (Maignan, Ferrell, & Hult, 1999). However, Fry et al. (1982) note a theoretical "free rider" problem with the notion that consumers will support CSR actions: Because an individual consumer is unlikely to influence the actions of the firm, consumers can reasonably think that their decisions on whether to patronize socially responsible firms is unlikely to make a difference – they will benefit from the firm's contribution to the public good regardless of whether they patronize the firm.

Engaging in CSR can also help augment a corporation's brand identity. Du, Bhattacharya, and Sen (2007, p. 225) suggest that a corporate identity based on CSR is "not only more memorable but also more anthropomorphic, enabling consumers to identify with it more readily than with others based on more conventional positioning strategies" and making customers more likely to identify with the brand. Cause-related marketing – the use of partnerships with nonprofits or causes to promote product sales – are popular tools to build a corporation's CSR brand identity. Doing this well, however, can be difficult: In order for consumers to transfer positive feelings as a result of a CSR campaign, they have to be aware of the cause, feel that it is relevant/meaningful, and be willing to transfer feelings about the cause onto the company (Hoeffler & Keller, 2002).

Identification with a CSR-friendly brand is an important component of the competitive advantage generated by corporate social responsibility (Garriga & Melé, 2004; Heath & Ni, 2008; Miles & Covin, 2000; Porter & Kramer, 2002; Vogel, 2005). This is often an attractive proposition to corporations that have recently suffered a blow to their reputation or that operate in a societally controversial industry (Yoon, Gürhan-Canli, & Schwarz, 2006). However, Yoon, Gürhan-Canli, and Schwarz (2006) suggest that expecting customers to naively replace a preconception of corporate misdeeds with a socially responsible façade might be unreasonable.

Increased attention to CSR efforts can even help some businesses realize savings unassociated with the traditional benefits of CSR by reconsidering or re-inventing operational processes. This is especially true in environmental CSR, where attention to this area may help create processes that are both environmentally friendly and financially efficient (Azzone & Noci, 1998; Burke & Lodgson, 1996; Smith & Kumar, 2013). Because these advances often occur when companies are pressured to engage in CSR, the existence of that pressure is important in driving the mechanism of innovation (Blanco, Guillamón-Saorín, & Guiral, 2013).

In order to remain in line with conventional business thinking, many scholars recommend, as do McWilliams and Siegel (2001, p. 125), that "managers should treat decisions regarding CSR precisely as they treat all investment decisions." CSR is frequently framed in investment terms in the academic literature (see Du, Bhattacharya, & Sen, 2010; Groza, Pronschinske, & Walker, 2011; Hess, Rogovsky, & Dunfee, 2002; Holme & Watts, 2000; Husted & de Jesus Salazar, 2006; Zadek, 2004). Even traditional philanthropic contributions can be framed in this way, as can decisions to promote employee welfare and environmental protection (Porter & Kramer, 2002). However, without a strategic plan to employ CSR as an investment strategy, many business scholars would argue, these efforts can fall into Friedman's characterization of CSR as a misappropriation of shareholder profits (Porter, Kramer, & Zadek, 2006).

An understanding of CSR as an investment, or as a balance of costs and benefits, necessarily implies certain things about a corporation's CSR behavior. For instance, this sort of calculus suggests that a corporation should minimize CSR costs, which is difficult to do in certain industries, especially ones that outsource production (Haigh & Jones, 2006). Corporations might chose to engage in certain CSR actions over others because of lower costs (Blowfield & Frynas, 2005) and might be less willing to expend CSR costs if financial performance has been poor or the firm has limited access to capital (Dhaliwal, Li, Tsang, & Yang, 2011; Waddock & Graves, 1997).

However, in order to reap the benefits promised by CSR (and offset its costs), key stakeholders must be aware of the company's actions (Bhattacharya & Sen, 2004). A later section will discuss the complexities of communicating the company's CSR actions to a variety of publics, as ensuring consumer support based on a company's CSR actions is not merely a matter of communicating a simple message (Du, Bhattacharya, & Sen, 2007; see also Elving, 2013; Wagner, Lutz, & Weitz, 2009).

Strategic CSR and the notion of fit

One of the more complex constructs in the discussion of CSR is the idea of fit, or the alignment between a corporation's business and its CSR efforts. Should a corporation engage in CSR behaviors that closely match the nature of the corporation, or do such actions merely make the corporation seem self-serving? Because the fit of a corporation's CSR actions relies on the perceptions of differing stakeholder publics, this is a difficult concept to measure; in fact, the degree of fit might affect a corporation's CSR actions both positively and negatively. This section explores the complicated and still somewhat uncertain role that fit plays in mediating the overall success (or failure) of a company's CSR efforts.

Fit has become a popular topic in discussions of strategic CSR. In order to provide the maximum return on the company's CSR investment, scholars have suggested that corporations should engage in actions that most closely match the company's strengths (Hess, Rogovsky, & Dunfee, 2002; Pearce & Doh, 2005) and organizational values (Maignan, Ferrell, & Ferrell, 2005; Saiia, Carroll, & Buchholtz, 2003). The rationale for a high fit between the corporation and its CSR actions lies in cognitive processing: If stakeholders are required to think too much about the corporation's CSR actions, they might be more likely to question the corporation's motives (Du, Bhattacharya, & Sen, 2010). Varadarajan and Menon (1988) suggested that a corporation could use fit to strategic advantage by targeting its CSR efforts toward issues and causes that were important to the firm's key stakeholders (see also Hess, Rogovsky, & Dunfee, 2002).

However, fit has not always been a desirable characteristic in CSR efforts. In early philanthropy, corporations (through their foundations) chose to give primarily to unrelated causes in order to give the appearance that the foundations were independent from the corporation (Smith, 1994). Even in today's corporate philanthropy, a degree of removal from the business's interests can help overcome consumer skepticism of corporate motivation (Porter & Kramer, 2002). Because CSR is a social construct based on elements such as industry and culture, it follows that fit is a concept that is defined situationally with no "one size fits all" approach (Heath & Ni, 2008).

Research has suggested that the fit of CSR actions with the company's overall reputation could benefit the corporation by reducing consumer skepticism (Du, Bhattacharya, & Sen, 2007; Pava & Krausz, 1997) and encouraging purchase decisions (Bhattacharya & Sen, 2004), thus providing maximum benefit to society through CSR actions (Porter, Kramer, & Zadek, 2006) and ensuring that CSR retains a primary place in the corporate culture over time (Burke & Lodgson, 1996). However, fit between a corporation and its social causes could actually hurt a corporation if publics perceived that the firm was acting in its own self-interest but communicating a prosocial objective (Bloom, Hoeffler, Keller, & Meza, 2006; Forehand & Grier, 2003). This is especially true in corporations with bad reputations, where Elving (2013) found that high fit led to consumer skepticism.

Fit between a company and its CSR efforts can also help communicate a consistent story to stakeholder publics (Blumenthal & Bergstrom, 2003). Companies that routinely engage in CSR receive better responses from stakeholder publics to their efforts than do companies with occasional CSR efforts (Du, Bhattacharya, & Sen, 2007).

Logically, it would seem that corporations that create some sort of negative externality should choose to engage in CSR activities that address this negative aspect of their reputation (Lewis, 2001; Lichtenstein, Drumwright, & Braig, 2004; Margolis & Walsh, 2003). However, in controversial or vice industries, this would lead corporations to support causes such as problem gambling and alcoholism, which are unlikely to create benefit for the corporation because they remind the public about the negative externalities generated by the corporation's operations. In their examination of CSR in the tobacco industry, Palazzo and Richter (2005) found that these corporations' actions were perceived to be so socially irresponsible that they had no choice of generating positive benefits by engaging in CSR – they could only hope to avoid generating negative reputation. By the logic extended above in the business case for CSR, this would suggest that these corporations not engage in CSR at all, regardless of the negative externalities their product causes (see also Lindorff, Prior Jonson, & McGuire, 2012).

Measurement of strategic CSR initiatives

Evaluation and measurement of CSR efforts and their success is inherent in the business case for CSR (Hess, Rogovsky, & Dunfee, 2002; Smith, 2003). Unfortunately, it is difficult to quantify – and therefore measure – corporate social responsibility and to determine its effect on the bottom line (Heath & Ni, 2008). Still, this effort has comprised a major strain in the CSR literature

(Basu & Palazzo, 2008; Beliveau, Cottrill, & O'Neill, 1994; Griffin & Mahon, 1997; Jones, 1999; Rowley & Berman, 2000, Sweeney & Coughlan, 2008).

The measurement of CSR is complicated by the fact that these actions are industry- and context-specific (Graafland, Eijffinger, & Smid, 2004; Rowley & Berman, 2000; Vogel, 2005). Research that aims to evaluate the effectiveness of CSR efforts attempts to measure a variety of things, including perceptions and actions of stakeholders (internal and external), elements of the context that motivate CSR action, and the company's financial performance based on the actions (the business case for CSR) (Basu & Palazzo, 2008). CSR scholars also often measure aspects of corporate social responsibility according to the KLD index, as mentioned earlier (Vogel, 2005). Burke and Logsdon (1996) suggest that companies themselves can also measure strategic elements of their CSR efforts, including fit, proactivity, voluntariness, and visibility of CSR actions; this kind of comprehensive, wide-ranging approach to evaluating CSR efforts may encourage businesses to think about their impact beyond the bottom line.

CSR measurement frequently assesses stakeholder perspectives and behavior – after all, this is often the desired end result of most companies' engagement in CSR. However, the measurement of CSR efforts needs also to consider the amount of social impact that the actions are having (Margolis & Walsh, 2003; Murray & Montanari, 1986; Porter, Kramer, & Zadek, 2006). In considering how "Misery loves companies," Margolis and Walsh (2003, p. 282) suggest that it is important to learn more about whether corporations' CSR actions are actually making progress in addressing social ills, suggesting that the business case for CSR obscures the intention of doing good in society and prevents companies from truly assessing their impact:

> For example, if corporate responses to social misery are evaluated only in terms of their instrumental benefits for the firm and its shareholders, we never learn about their impact on society, most notably on the intended beneficiaries of these initiatives. Nor do we investigate the conditions under which it is permissible to act on stakeholder interests that are inconsistent with shareholder interests.

A focus on measuring a business' prosocial behavior and whether it can impact the firm's financial bottom line – a requirement for making the business case for CSR – is certainly valuable to the conversation about corporate social responsibility, but it is equally important to identify stakeholders' expectations for social responsibility (Moir, 2001). In fact, the business case for CSR considers only what actions might be beneficial to the firm, not what actions might positively impact the stakeholders who are the intended recipients of the corporation's largesse (L'Etang, 1994).

Societal implications of corporate social responsibility

Defining the proper relationship between business and society is at the heart of the debate over corporate social responsibility. This section looks at the impacts of CSR on society, including potential dangers of CSR. It also examines the way that businesses interact with nonprofits through CSR and considers how nonprofits and other activist groups play a vital role in pressuring corporations to act in socially responsible ways.

The business case for CSR follows an enlightened self-interest model – the idea that socially responsible behavior will advance business profits, as required by Friedman. But this perspective also requires that the corporation consider how it might benefit society and meet stakeholder expectations so that it can continue to operate and thrive (Moir, 2001). Fundamental to the dialogue over CSR is the idea that the corporation's impact on society is not merely economic (Dahlsrud, 2008). In the event that these noneconomic impacts may be negative in nature, "there is the expectation by many that businesses that cause harm to the community should be part of the cure" (Buchanan & Johnson, 2007, p. 2841).

There is no agreement on the scope of business's obligation to society; however, since governments are no longer capable of providing many social services they had previously (Frynas, 2005; Jamali & Mirshak, 2007; Smith, 2003), the corporation has emerged to fill a vacuum of social responsibility created by growing individuality. However, because business may be ill-suited to take on the role (Blowfield & Frynas, 2005; McMillan, 2007), CSR may have negative impacts on society in addition to its expected benefits.

By tying business performance to socially responsible behavior (and vice versa), the business case for CSR hopes to give corporations a financial reason for contributing to society (Frankental, 2001). But giving CSR a business imperative creates the risk that firms might engage in deceptive behavior such that they are *perceived* as socially responsible, even if their actions might not be (Cai, Jo, & Pan, 2012; Hamil, 1999; Smith, 1994). In fact, managers need only to make their companies *appear* socially responsible in order to receive the rewards of CSR behavior (Cragg, 2002), since consumers' perceptions of the company need not necessarily be rooted in reality to impact their behaviors based on those perceptions (Ellen, Webb, & Mohr, 2006). Managers might also be encouraged to do just enough to be socially responsible, and no more, making sure to publicize their "just-enough" efforts substantially (Murray & Montanari, 1986; Waddock & Graves, 1997). Although today's companies have extensive codes of ethics, one does not have to look far to see examples of corporations where unethical behaviors have been enabled in spite of these codes – for example, Enron (Sims & Brinkmann, 2003).

The perception that corporations are being socially responsible, even if they are not, can allow for them to benefit from less stringent government regulation and lower tax burdens, which might hide behavior (e.g. tax avoidance) that would be considered irresponsible (Doane, 2005). In order to promote expansion into new global markets, corporations may become involved in development behavior that is outside of their purview – doing more harm than good when these projects ultimately fail – or prioritize social projects based on their suitability to enhance the bottom line rather than need in the community (Frynas, 2005; Margolis & Walsh, 2003).

The business case for CSR also gives preference to CSR's potential to promote the corporation's financial success and not the ability of the corporation's efforts to have a positive social impact (L'Etang, 1994; Sims & Brinkmann, 2003).

> The corporation motivated by self-interest is unlikely to give full considera-
> tion to the needs and interests of a recipient. The company's perception of
> these needs is likely to be distorted by its primarily self-interested motivation.
> In such cases the relationship with the recipient is thus exploitative because
> what is important for the corporation is what the recipient can do for the
> corporation (in terms of contributing to their corporate social responsibil-
> ity profile/portfolio, promotional brochures and press releases) not what the
> company can do for the recipient as defined and evaluated by the recipient.
>
> (L'Etang, 1994, p. 118)

Corporations might also prioritize certain stakeholders and spend resources on those groups because the business case suggests a better return on investment, even if other stakeholders are being ignored or exploited, "making somewhat of a mockery of the ethical lineage of the CSR concept" (Haigh & Jones, 2006, p. 3). Ultimately, the idea that business success can be "purchased" via CSR is fatally flawed, as primary stakeholders may continue to participate in your business endeavors, even if you treat them unethically. This may lead to good financial performance even when ethical stakeholder management is not practiced (Cragg, 2002).

CSR as a business investment suggests that choices for socially responsible behavior should be made by a financial calculation – return on investment – rather than a dialogue with stakeholders about the appropriate engagement between the business and society (Wheeler, Fabig, & Boele, 2002). While CSR programs may be initially enacted for the purposes of ethical, two-way symmetrical communica-tion, subsequent efforts to communicate the results of these programs may be more one-way (publicity); in addition, the efforts may be discontinued if it is no longer necessary to maintain a relationship with the public in question (L'Etang, 1994).

Ultimately, however, a key danger of the business case for CSR is its impli-cation that financial profit should be the sole motivator for business behavior, implying that all other considerations (e.g. ethical obligations) should be ignored if they do not have a profit potential (Blowfield & Frynas, 2005).

> In a world that recognizes only economic rationality, it becomes not merely
> difficult but impossible to frame persuasive objections to any of the practices
> mentioned above – child labor, deceit, etc. Non-economic values to which we
> might appeal – such as dignity, fair play, good citizenship – are, standing on
> their own, impotent to persuade or motivate in the absence of an economic
> payoff.
>
> (Paine, 2000, p. 328)

A business case for CSR suggests that corporations overlook issues – like the right for labor to associate in unions and the need for a living wage – because addressing them may be detrimental to the corporation's bottom line (Blowfield & Frynas, 2005).

Haigh and Jones (2006, p. 3) suggest that CSR is a poor attempt to solve the negative externalities inherently generated by a capitalist economy, suggesting that "while some CSR initiatives might generate positive or mitigating effects on externalities, they cannot fundamentally alter the externalising engine that powers every business firm and is the primary source of capitalist pathologies" (see also Doane, 2005). The single-minded use of economic reasoning, a hallmark of the business case for CSR, lies at the center of the modern debate over the role of corporations (Richter, 2010). The valorization of economic reasoning subverts the need to consider ethical considerations and "rather than being a domain of rationality capable of challenging economics, ethics is conceived only as a tool of economics" (Paine, 2000, p. 327).

Nonprofits and their role in corporate social responsibility

Just as some would argue that businesses are not responsible for solving society's problems – nor are they obligated to – it is clear that nonprofits alone lack the resources to address the totality of society's needs. Working together, however, nonprofits and corporations might be able to use their resources toward a solution – and CSR advocates would suggest that they should do so (Pearce & Doh, 2005; Porter & Kramer, 2002).

Ultimately, a partnership between a corporation and a nonprofit should serve the strategic needs of both (Saiia, Carroll, & Buchholtz, 2003). This section talks briefly about the history of nonprofits (primarily in the US) and NGOs (nongovernmental organizations) before identifying some of the salient issues that affect the relationships between nonprofits and corporations under the mantle of corporate social responsibility.

Salamon (2002, pp. 3–4) defined the unique character of nonprofit organizations as a byproduct of two fundamentally US notions: individuality and community. Nonprofit organizations

> embody two seemingly contradictory impulses that form the heart of American character: a deep-seated commitment to freedom and individual initiative and an equally fundamental realization that people live in communities and consequently have responsibilities that extend beyond themselves. Uniquely among American institutions, those [organizations] in the nonprofit sector blend these competing impulses, creating a special class of entities dedicated to mobilizing *private initiative for the common good.*
>
> (Emphasis original)

The history of nonprofit organizations, and the evolution of their partnerships with entities in the private sector, has significantly affected the role that these organizations play in today's US society. Although these organizations most often serve in a service provider or advocacy role, they can fill a range of functions, including the expression of creative impulses, of individuality, or of ethnic identity (Salamon, 2002).

Today's nonprofit organizations face many challenges, including the challenge of maintaining public trust, competition from for-profit service providers, the constant need to procure and/or generate funding, and current pressures to improve measurement of outcomes and effectiveness (Salamon, 2002). These challenges contribute to today's nonprofits' need to establish the financial security that will ensure their survival. In order to accomplish this, many nonprofit organizations (specifically, those which provide social services or fulfill an educational, religious, or scientific purpose) are given a 501(c)(3) designation by the Internal Revenue Service, which means that donations to these organizations are tax-exempt for the donor (Boris & Steuerle, 2006). This provides a more tangible financial benefit to corporations that donate to these nonprofit organizations in addition to the benefits of CSR described previously, such as goodwill, a positive reputation, increased employee morale, and consumer loyalty.

Corporate giving to nonprofit organizations dates back to the beginning of the 20th century and can include cash, in-kind donations of goods or services, meeting space, free publicity, marketing assistance, loaned executives, sponsorships, or licensing fees. Roughly 75% of corporate giving today goes directly to nonprofit organizations, with the remainder going to foundations established by the corporation, which then give to causes as they see fit (Lenkowsky, 2002). At the turn of the most recent century, corporate involvement with nonprofit organizations was expected to grow stronger, as pressure increased for business to contribute to society through CSR efforts (Levy, 1999).

Because early CSR primarily took the form of financial donations and other kinds of corporate philanthropy (Cheney, Roper, & May, 2007; Hess, Rogovsky, & Dunfee, 2002), corporate social responsibility is often conflated with corporate philanthropy. Although philanthropy still exists as a subset of CSR actions, it exists to a far less prominent degree and is complemented with other actions that promote the company's social responsibility. Because early corporate philanthropy was not strategic or related to the company's business objectives, it was often considered tangential to the corporation's primary function. In some countries where CSR is not quite as developed as a strategic concept, corporate social responsibility is still limited to voluntary philanthropy (Jamali & Mirshak, 2007).

Carroll (1991) identified philanthropy as the voluntary actions of a corporation to act in ways that are beneficial to society, especially to the local community through the support of education, the performing arts, and general quality of life in the community. Philanthropic actions performed by Andrew Carnegie and his 19th-century contemporaries were ostensibly rooted in the public good (Pearce & Doh, 2005), but also served the purposes of these philanthropists by providing better employees. The business case for CSR echoes the self-serving welfare capitalism of Carnegie and his ilk.

Under a business case for CSR, however, corporate philanthropy does not fare so well. Aupperle, Carroll, and Hatfield (1985) found that business executives ranked obligations to engage in corporate philanthropy last out of Carroll's (1991) four dimensions of CSR (economic, legal, ethical, discretionary/voluntary). Porter and Kramer (2002, p.57) suggest that corporate philanthropy is a fool's errand because "giving more does not satisfy the critics – the more companies donate, the more is expected of them. And executives find it hard, if not impossible, to justify charitable expenditures in terms of bottom-line benefit." While the application of strategic business principles can certainly help corporations use philanthropy to its best ends (Porter & Kramer, 2002), the decision to engage widely in corporate philanthropy is not always supported by the business case for CSR.

It should come as no surprise, then, that the economic downturn of 2008 understandably affected the viability of corporate giving and forced many companies to re-evaluate their involvement in CSR. Many corporations have also made an effort to change their giving priorities in order to follow "strategies that align philanthropy with business goals" (American Association of Fund-Raising Counsel, 2009, p. 71). From a normative perspective, companies were expected to continue doing the good works that had earned them consumer support, among other benefits, during the economic boom times of the early 2000s (Quelch & Jocz, 2009). However, many corporations were forced to reallocate resources previously designated to corporate giving in order to keep their companies afloat, and many began favoring forms of CSR that had been prevalent in the past, such as support for employee volunteer efforts, over cash or in-kind donations (Welch & Welch, 2009). Ultimately, though, even the most financially strapped corporations – US credit giant Citigroup is an example – could not abandon CSR efforts entirely for fear of the negative exposure such a move would generate ("A stress test," 2009; Quelch & Jocz, 2009).

Nonprofits and NGOs primarily enter the CSR discussion as drivers of corporate involvement in social issues (Clarkson, 1995; Crawford & Gram, 1978; Frynas, 2005; Haigh & Jones, 2006). Pressure applied, often publicly, by these organizations often exposes corporate wrongdoing and factors into a corporation's decision to engage in socially responsible behavior (Campbell, 2007; Frankental, 2001). Corporations, in turn, can gain reputational advantage by rising to the challenge, "brandishing CSR as the friendly face of capitalism" (Doane, 2005, p. 23).

As partners to corporations, nonprofits help facilitate CSR efforts in hopes of gaining some benefit, either financial or reputational, from their association with the corporation (Aguilera, Rupp, Williams, & Ganapathi, 2007; Bhattacharya & Sen, 2004; Lichtenstein, Drumwright, & Braig, 2004). By affiliating with a company that has strong customer support and a favorable reputation, a nonprofit can appropriate those positive characteristics and often will get new donors; however, partnership with a company with a tarnished past carries some risk (Lichtenstein, Drumwright, & Braig, 2004). Conversely, a partnership with a nonprofit can indicate that a corporation's corporate social responsibility is at an adequate level (Crawford & Gram, 1978).

Nonprofits can also benefit from corporate partnership beyond mere financial contributions. The decision by a corporation to partner with or donate money to a nonprofit signals to other potential donors that the nonprofit is credible and worthy of future investment (Porter & Kramer, 2002). Beyond financial donations, corporations often bring skills, knowledge, and technology to social tasks that the nonprofit may be lacking due to resource shortages. Affiliation with a well-known corporation can help a nonprofit gain credibility and awareness.

With responsibility for social change increasingly taken up by corporations, activist publics have become a salient stakeholder for corporations. However, because they do not always affect the company's ability to make money (and thus do not have much leverage), these stakeholders have a secondary position (Den Hond & De Bakker, 2007; Lindgreen, Swaen, & Johnston, 2009; see also Crawford & Gram, 1978). However, activist publics that are able to secure media coverage of their concerns are much more likely to see results:

> in today's turbulent, media-intensive, globally connected social environment, corporations may be "forced" through "social blackmail," or the pressure applied by an activist minority of stakeholders, such as nongovernmental organiza-tions (NGOs), to engage in activities that are more stringent than either legally required or necessary to achieve the firm's strategic and financial objectives.
> (Munilla & Miles, 2005, p. 374; see also Midttun,
> Gautesen, & Gjølberg, 2006; Smith, 2003;
> Wagner, Lutz, & Weitz, 2009)

This suggestion that media coverage of activist groups' pressure can force a cor-poration to engage in CSR beyond what is recommended by the business case will come to bear later in the discussion of CSR in the casino industry. Additionally, such "forced" efforts to respond to activist pressure often come across as insincere and self-interested (Groza, Pronschinske, & Walker, 2011) and thus may not pro-vide the usual benefits of CSR.

Because corporate support of nonprofits is often tied to media coverage and the corporations' public image and reputation, some critics of CSR complain that cor-porations' efforts are merely token actions, as indicated by the fact that they rarely support controversial nonprofits (Hamil, 1999). As mentioned previously, choice of nonprofits to support is narrowly proscribed by the business case for CSR: Only nonprofits that can ultimately advance the corporation's bottom line should be supported. Even uncontroversial nonprofits may be passed over for corporate support if they do not fit with the corporation's desired brand image (Blumenthal & Bergstrom, 2003).

This preference for certain nonprofits over others, which is based on corpo-rate goals and not on desired social impact, calls into question the corporations' sense of procedural justice, which Kim (2007, p. 171) describes as "perceived fairness of the procedures used to make decisions." This includes having formal-ized rules for a process and applying them consistently. By following procedures in a consistent manner, organizations can reduce both the potential bias in the decision-making process and the appearance of such bias to those affected by the organization's decisions, such as nonprofits.

While acknowledging that pressure from nonprofits can be effective, Martin (2002, p. 74) suggests that, "even more effective than consumer agitation, perhaps, is peer encouragement. By publicizing their successes on the strategic frontier, business leaders can encourage further innovation by other companies" (see also Weaver, Trevino, & Cochran, 1999). Increasingly, the inclination to corporate philanthropy comes from within, as a management strategy designed to improve reputation and create product differentiation (Saiia, Carroll, & Buchholtz, 2003). In addition,

> firms may be compelled to react to the first-mover CSR strategies of their competitors where they believe that failing to do so would disadvantage them vis à vis market positioning . . . In these cases, even where the CSR strategy has not been proven a "winner" (in terms of net payback), other firms will imitate it because they perceive the costs of not doing so are prohibitive.
>
> (Haigh & Jones, 2006, p. 2)

However, an increased use of CSR might not necessarily earn the promised benefits, especially in certain industries where firms are not expected to be socially responsible or where the industry is saturated with socially responsible firms (Vogel, 2005).

The interaction between nonprofits and corporations is inherently problematic because it is a relationship marked by an extreme imbalance of power: Because it is to some degree dependent on the corporation for financial support, the nonprofit is unable to leverage a great deal of pressure on the corporation (Rowley & Moldoveanu, 2003). Instead, nonprofits rely on corporations to take an ethical approach to CSR, including the responsible use of business power (Garriga & Melé, 2004; Schultz, Castelló, & Morsing, 2013), and they presume that corporations will abide by a sense of procedural justice. However, without any kind of regulatory force to ensure either of these, nonprofits are often left in a powerless situation. In addition, the focus on the business case for CSR necessarily detracts from ethical considerations, as the two are often considered incompatible, or the business case given precedence when the two conflict (Paine, 2000).

The relative lack of power held by nonprofits affects their relationships with corporations in the CSR context in a number of ways. Nonprofits are not only less able to exert pressure on the corporation to act in socially responsible ways, but are also less likely to be prioritized as stakeholders when the corporation communicates about CSR (Pedersen, 2006). The following section unpacks the complicated concept of communicating CSR to a variety of stakeholders.

Communicating CSR

Communication is key to the success of corporate social responsibility (Moreno & Capriotti, 2009). A great body of academic research has revealed that communicating CSR actions to a corporation's stakeholders is far more complicated than merely delivering a message on a website or in an annual report (Rim & Song, 2013; Sweeney & Coughlan, 2008). However, without high awareness of a corporation's CSR actions among its stakeholders, the corporation might not reap the intended rewards of CSR – a key justification of the business case (Du, Bhattacharya, & Sen, 2010; Godfrey, Merrill, & Hansen, 2009; Heath & Ni, 2008; Jones, Bowd, & Tench, 2009; Murray & Montanari, 1986). This establishes a key role for public relations in the enactment of successful strategic CSR (Hess, Rogovsky, & Dunfee, 2002; Lantos, 2001), but also opens up the possibility that communicators may be inauthentic in their portrayal of CSR in order to achieve business objectives (Buchanan, Elliott, & Johnson, 2009).

Stakeholder theory and the communication of CSR

At the center of the debate over corporate social responsibility is the extent to which a corporation is obligated to benefit society. Because the idea of a corporation's responsibility to society is rather nebulous, many scholars have preferred a stakeholder-based approach, which identifies specific publics with which the corporation has some sort of connection (Clarkson, 1995; Maignan, Ferrell, & Ferrell, 2005). Although the definitions of stakeholder in the CSR literature are as varied as the definitions of CSR itself, many invoke Freeman's (1984, p. 46) definition of a stakeholder as "any group or individual who can affect or is affected by the achievement of the organization's objectives." Some studies have defined stakeholders more broadly, without the consequential element, as "persons or groups with legitimate interests in procedural and/or substantive aspects of corporate activity" (Donaldson & Preston, 1995, p. 67); for this definition, it is the stakeholders' interest in the company, not the company's interest in the stakeholders, which defines them as such.

Stakeholder theory, which prioritizes publics into categories of primary and secondary stakeholders according to their ability to affect the firm, suggests that CSR communication should address primary stakeholders first (Sweeney & Coughlan, 2008). Successful corporations thrive at balancing obligations to and communication with various stakeholders over the long term (Kimery & Rinehart, 1998). An ethical orientation suggests that CSR decisions should be made with fairness to all stakeholders and should not prioritize primary stakeholders (i.e. shareholders) to the detriment of others; however, this is not always enacted in practice (Paine, 1996). At the very least, CSR decisions should treat all stakeholders, even secondary ones, humanely if not fairly if the corporation is to engage in ethical communication (Waddock & Smith, 2000).

Depending on resources, corporations may be forced into communicating with some stakeholders and excluding others; they may also make the decision not to communicate with publics for other reasons, as will be discussed later (Smith, 2003). The identification of stakeholder publics and the necessity for the corporation to communicate with these publics can change over time depending on environmental factors – such as time-sensitivity of the issue and the importance of a claim to the stakeholder public that makes it (Mitchell, Agle, & Wood, 1997) – and can also vary across industries (Jones, 1999; Murray & Montanari, 1986).

Kimery and Rinehart (1998) suggest that corporations can identify four groups of stakeholders along axes of potential threat to the corporation's success (high/low) and potential benefit to the corporation (high/low). Stakeholders such as vendors and distributors (high benefit, low threat) are dependent on your organization and you need to pay less attention to these groups – just ensure that your corporation's actions do not really anger these groups. Another type of stakeholders that pose a low threat are minor activist groups; while it is important to monitor these groups, action and communication are not necessarily required. Major activist groups and industry competitors can pose a higher threat, but since these groups also promise less benefit, a corporation should try to reduce its involvement with these groups where possible. High benefit/high threat stakeholders – such as customers, major investors, and the media – should be prioritized for stakeholder communication; the corporation should collaborate with these to introduce interdependence and aim for a win–win outcome to keep them supportive (Kimery & Rinehart, 1998).

CSR communication must be sensitive to the fact that different stakeholder groups have different expectations of the firm's behavior and that those expectations may change over time (Blowfield & Frynas, 2005; Heath & Ni, 2008; Murray & Montanari, 1986). Some people may even exist in multiple stakeholder publics – for example, an employee can also be a consumer of the company's product (Pirsch, Gupta, & Grau, 2007). If a corporation's CSR actions are not properly communicated, these stakeholder publics might not perceive that their expectations for social responsibility are being met (Meznar & Nigh, 1995). The following two sections examine two specific stakeholder publics that a corporation is likely to communicate with about CSR: employees and the local community. A third public, the media, will be addressed in a later section.

Communicating about CSR with employees

Even though CSR is communicated to external stakeholders, the messages also serve to reinforce corporate identity and promote identification with the company by internal audiences (Morsing, 2006). As mentioned previously, CSR can bring a corporation several benefits with respect to employees, including increased job satisfaction, reduced employee turnover, and ease of recruiting quality employees. However, in order for these benefits to be realized, CSR must be communicated to this important internal public in a strategic manner (Birth, Illia, Lurati, & Zamparini, 2008; Du, Bhattacharya, & Sen, 2010).

An active CSR program can also be an asset in attracting potential employees – Vong and Wong (2013) found that this is especially true in the casino gaming industry – but only if this public is aware of it (Sen, Bhattacharya, & Korschun, 2006). When a company participates in CSR, it "signals" to prospective employees that it has positive organizational values; potential employees then wish to identify with a corporation that supports CSR actions (Aguilera, Rupp, Williams, & Ganapathi, 2007; Greening & Turban, 2000). Corporate support of CSR activities also reduces employee turnover, but again, this requires that the employees are aware of the CSR actions that the corporation is taking (Smith, 2003).

In service industries, such as casino gaming, employees are especially important to financial success because of their frequent direct interaction with customers. Thus, the benefits of communicating CSR to employees can translate more tangibly into financial or competitive advantage for the corporation (Lee, Song, Lee, Lee, & Bernhard, 2013; see also Jones, 1999). In addition to outward-facing CSR actions like corporate philanthropy, the creation of employee codes of ethics can also serve as an effective way for a corporation to communicate its socially responsible intentions (Langlois & Schlegelmilch, 1990; Maignan, Ferrell, & Ferrell, 2005).

However, from a moral or ethical standpoint, these CSR actions should be genuine, not simply enacted to boost employee morale (Porter & Kramer, 2002). Although it can be effective, CSR should not be used merely as a tool for short-term gains in employee relations:

> CSR can be helpful in making staff feel much more positively about the company. However, this corporate motivation is in itself a limiting factor, since it renders the very engagement in social initiatives (rather than the long-term developmental benefit) a goal for companies. Simply making charitable donations to an orphanage or a school, for instance, may make staff feel better about themselves, without the need for the firm to ensure that such donations actually have a developmental benefit. Also, as social initiatives undertaken for this reason are to some extent driven by what makes staff feel better about themselves, the developmental priorities are likely to reflect those of the people inside the firm rather than those of the local community.
>
> (Frynas, 2005, p. 586)

CSR also is often used to facilitate a corporation's introduction into a new market by making a positive impression on potential employees (Gardberg & Fombrun, 2006); again, this instrumental use of CSR, while effective, carries the potential for unintended side effects.

A corporation's stance on socially responsible behavior also must be communicated correctly to its employees (at all levels) to ensure that they perceive CSR as a valuable asset to the business (Dentchev, 2004). CSR needs to be built into company codes and policies to ensure that the corporation engages in consistent behavior over time regardless of which employees are involved in decision-making about CSR (Weaver, Trevino, & Cochran, 1999; see also Blumenthal & Bergstrom, 2003 on the value of employing "brand councils" to ensure consistency in CSR actions).

Communicating about CSR with the local community

Corporations, especially larger ones, can have tremendous impact on their local communities. This is true even if they have negative externalities, such as the casino gaming industry – for instance, a casino provides its local community with tax revenue, community development, and a number of direct and indirect jobs for community members (Durham & Hashimoto, 2010). Local communities generally expect that corporations will be "responsible 'citizens'" (Pearce, 1982) and that these corporations will accept a responsibility to improve their local communities (Garriga & Melé, 2004).

Corporations' efforts to fulfill this obligation suggest that local communities should be considered a primary stakeholder for the communication of CSR. A 2000 publication of the World Business Council for Sustainable Development advises companies:

> Be a good guest, but let your story be heard: Your company is a guest in various communities and should behave accordingly. Show respect and consideration for your hosts. At the same time, find the appropriate way to communicate with them openly about your contributions to society. That open relationship will also be an asset if problems arise.
>
> (Holme & Watts, 2000, p. 22)

While this message was intended to address corporations expanding into emerging markets, its message – that corporations should prioritize CSR communication to local communities – seems equally applicable in established markets. However, research by Vong and Wong (2013) and Strauss (2010) finds that this is not always the case in the gambling communities of Macau and Las Vegas, respectively.

In developing countries, multinational corporations have engaged in significant CSR efforts to facilitate their expansion. Reporting these actions is a key part of these corporations' strategic use of CSR (Frynas, 2005). Engaging in CSR communication with the local community in a new market can help familiarize the community with the corporation and "help globalizing companies neutralize their alien features by strengthening community ties" (Gardberg & Fombrun, 2006, p. 343).

However, truly ethical CSR behavior requires that the corporation not merely give handouts to the local community – indeed, as discussed earlier, a purely altruistic approach to CSR is not the answer – but engage in communication with members of this important stakeholder group to learn how the corporation can be an ethical and effective community partner (Du & Vieira, 2012; Wheeler, Fabig, & Boele, 2002). In order to be truly socially responsible, the corporation must address community needs in a way that "its resources can provide the greatest benefit to the community" (Hess, Rogovsky, & Dunfee, 2002, p. 120).

Why or why not? Reasons for and against communicating CSR

Just as definitions of CSR and the corporation's obligation to society are socially constructed, responses to communication about CSR activities may vary across cultures as well, suggesting that CSR communication could potentially open the door for negative impact on the corporation even if its intentions are laudable (Morsing & Schultz, 2006; Starck & Kruckeberg, 2005; Yoon, Gürhan-Canli, & Schwarz, 2006). Potential negative effects could include diverting resources from the business of the corporation, creating a perception that CSR efforts are inadequate, demonstrating conflict with values of stakeholders, or potential damage to corporate reputation "if corporate social performance proves less than stakeholders have expected and managers have promised, or if CSP [corporate social performance]² is perceived as a window-dressing device" (Dentchev, 2004, p. 406).

When corporations communicate about their CSR actions, or their more general intention to enact these behaviors, they establish expectations for their future behavior that might be difficult to uphold (Christensen, Morsing, & Thyssen, 2013; Wagner, Lutz, & Weitz, 2009). For instance, one can imagine that the casino corporations in Las Vegas had to make some difficult decisions and cut back their CSR efforts substantially when their profits plummeted in the late 2000s. Corporations might be loath to communicate additional expectations for CSR behavior beyond what is already expected of them by society, as this would essentially raise the burden on them to meet these higher expectations.

Another factor to consider is the cost of CSR communication. CSR communication must be carefully crafted to have its desired result (Varadarajan & Menon, 1988): Even well-developed messages are subject to interpretation or oppositional reading on the part of stakeholder publics (Suchman, 1995; see also Hall, 1997). Because stakeholder publics can affect the firm in different ways, messages must be delivered strategically to different groups (Kimery & Rinehart, 1998). CSR communication needs to be done with a minimum of expense, so that costs of the communication do not outweigh the costs of the CSR actions themselves; however, this might result in a communication strategy that is ineffective in reaching a wide audience (Yoon, Gürhan-Canli, & Schwarz, 2006). Conversely, excessive communication about CSR may seem like overkill and imply that the company has something to hide.

Consumer skepticism of corporate motives, or the perception that the corporation is being hypocritical in its CSR communication, can undermine the value of not only the communication, but also the CSR actions themselves (Elving, 2013; Yoon, Gürhan-Canli, & Schwarz, 2006). As mentioned earlier, low fit between the corporation and its CSR actions, or even merely advertising for a social cause rather than the corporation's traditional profit-making ventures, can lead to consumer skepticism because consumers are more likely to think about the corporation's motives for its actions (Du, Bhattacharya, & Sen, 2010; Menon & Kahn, 2003; Rim & Song, 2013).

> When there is a good fit between expectations, knowledge, associations, actions and competences of a company and the CSR domain observed by the consumer, it is easily adopted in the existing cognitive structure of that consumer. Congruence is, in general terms, seen as more positive than a lack of congruence. When consumers detect inconsistencies between expectations and the information they are presented with, they think much more critically about the company and its motives than they otherwise would.
>
> (Elving, 2013, p. 282)

Two moderating factors can reduce customer skepticism of companies' CSR efforts: the reputation of the company (Rim & Song, 2013) and the perceived fit between the company and the cause (Bhattacharya & Sen, 2004).

Overwhelmingly, the decision to communicate about a corporation's socially responsible actions can be traced to its desire to earn or keep legitimacy in the eyes of its stakeholders. Legitimacy, or the respect for business as a valuable societal institution, is a concept fundamental to the theory of corporate social responsibility. According to Wood (1991), legitimacy is granted to business by society but can be lost if the corporation acts irresponsibly (see also Moir, 2001; Murphy, Öberseder, & Laczniak, 2013). Therefore, it is important that the corporation act responsibly, both in its operation and communication (including CSR efforts), if the level of legitimacy needed to continue functioning in the business realm is to be maintained (Llewellyn, 2007). Efforts to communicate CSR activities are crucial to the use of CSR to establish the company's legitimacy (Birth, Illia, Lurati & Zamparini, 2008). However, stakeholder skepticism, if it results from CSR communication, can effectively negate the legitimacy created by the corporation's socially responsible behavior (Suchman, 1995).

On a practical level, legitimacy can be extremely valuable to an organization. A corporation that aligns with social norms is likely to be viewed as trustworthy and to gain popular support, and is less likely to be susceptible to undeserved attacks (Suchman, 1995). This may be especially important for corporations in vice industries, which have additional obligations based on the negative externalities they create (Du & Vieira, 2012; Yani-de-Soriano, Javed, & Yousafzai, 2012); however, controversial firms trying to use CSR solely to earn legitimacy will find that these efforts often backfire (Blanco, Guillamón-Saorín, & Guiral, 2013; Elving, 2013; Jo & Na, 2012). Legitimacy is difficult to build but easier to maintain; strategies to gain legitimacy include aligning the organization with social norms, seeking to promote a new set of social norms more in line with the existing organization, or trying to alter the environment to better match the organization's norms (Suchman, 1995).

Companies communicate information about their CSR behavior to various stakeholders in order to remain within accepted societal standards (Williams, 2008). By showing stakeholders that it is socially responsible, the corporation can demonstrate that it conforms to social and industry norms (Du & Vieira, 2012). However, communicating CSR runs the risk of seeming self-promotional and can threaten an organization's legitimacy if it is seen as disingenuous (Wanderley, Lucian, Farache, & de Sousa Filho, 2008). CSR communicators should be aware that publics often see through attempts to utilize CSR for mere image building (Heath & Ryan, 1989; Jo & Na, 2012).

Finally, legitimacy can be granted to (or taken away from) corporations based on coverage of their CSR actions in traditional or new media (Schultz, Castelló, & Morsing, 2013). The next section considers media coverage of CSR as a transition to a discussion about the role of public relations with respect to corporate social responsibility.

Keys to successful CSR communication

CSR communication that is "indirect and subtle" (Morsing & Schultz, 2006, p. 332) may be more successful than overt communication such as press releases.

In a climate of corporate distrust (Porter & Kramer, 2002), any claim of social responsibility that comes directly from the corporation might be perceived with skepticism (Macleod, 2001; Smith, 2003). Corporations can avoid the appearance of hypocrisy by acknowledging that they benefit from CSR initiatives in addition to the positive social impact that these actions generate (Forehand & Grier, 2003).

To succeed, CSR communication must clearly demonstrate that a corporation has created some positive social impact, and it must do so transparently without omitting any details about the corporation's efforts (Frankental, 2001; Graafland, Eijffinger, & Smid, 2004; see also Azzone & Noci, 1998; Webb & Mohr, 1998). For instance, Palazzo and Richter (2005, p. 392) note the inherent danger in CSR communication by tobacco companies:

> In their CSR reporting, corporations normally focus on the positive effects of their engagement, sometimes with smaller aspects of self-critique (in the form of "what remains to be done"). If the social reporting of a tobacco company follows that mainstream approach to CSR reporting, it will not increase its credibility but rather be regarded as the perfect example of window-dressing.

As this example suggests, corporations' self-reporting of CSR efforts needs to truly represent the actions of the company rather than exist primarily as persuasive communication that seeks to boost the company's reputation in order to benefit all stakeholders, not merely the corporation.

Forehand and Grier (2003) found that customers would rather see a firm admit that its CSR activities had some self-serving element; additionally, "a company should emphasize the convergence of social and business interests, and frankly acknowledge that its CSR endeavors are beneficial to both society and itself" (Du, Bhattacharya, & Sen, 2010, p. 12). In order to be effective, CSR communication must accurately communicate both the firm's actions and its motivations, and those actions and motivations must align with the preferences of the stakeholder public for extrinsic (not self-serving) motivations (Du, Bhattacharya, & Sen, 2007).

In order for CSR communication to be effective, companies must take steps to enhance the legitimacy of their messages through the use of tactics such as an educational (not emotional) tone and informative, transparent content (Wanderley, Lucian, Farache, & de Sousa Filho, 2008). Stakeholders might also be less skeptical of communication from third-party sources such as news media (Du, Bhattacharya, & Sen, 2010; Yoon, Gürhan-Canli, & Schwarz, 2006), especially for information about CSR in reaction to to corporate wrongdoing (Groza, Pronschinske, & Walker, 2011). Establishing dialogue with stakeholder publics can also help establish organizational legitimacy (Morsing & Schultz, 2006).

Communicating CSR via the news media

The rise of global media has played a significant role in exposing corporate actions, including involvement in CSR as well as wrongdoing (Frankental, 2001; Lantos, 2001; Smith, 2003; Wagner, Lutz, & Weitz, 2009). Much like nonprofit groups and

NGOs, media can exert pressure on corporations to improve or increase their CSR behavior because media coverage of a corporation can affect its reputation (Campbell, 2007; Christensen, Morsing, & Thyssen, 2013; Weaver, Trevino, & Cochran, 1999). Media can also serve to amplify the messages of nonprofit organizations or activist publics that are pressuring corporations to change their CSR behavior (Azzone & Noci, 1998; Midttun, Gautesen, & Gjølberg, 2006; Munilla & Miles, 2005).

Despite their ability to affect a corporation's reputation, the media are often considered a secondary stakeholder in the communication of CSR (Clarkson, 1995). Although the media are often lower priority than stakeholders such as investors, they are clearly capable of spreading a message with a large reach and should be given special attention in order to harness their ability to help achieve the benefits of CSR such as improved reputation (Zhang & Swanson, 2006). In fact, due to the expansion of media, including the Internet, stakeholders now have access to a tremendous amount of information about a corporation should they decide to seek it out (Murphy, Öberseder, & Laczniak, 2013; Schultz, Castelló, & Morsing, 2013; Wagner, Lutz, & Weitz, 2009). This information can influence not only stakeholder perceptions of corporate reputation (L'Etang, 1994) and societal expectations for responsible corporate behavior (Schultz, Castelló, & Morsing, 2013) but also stakeholder behavior, such as purchase intention (Du, Bhattacharya, & Sen, 2007).

Journalists' perceptions of CSR can vary widely; some will see CSR as a positive development in the relationship between business and society, while others will take a cynical approach and see CSR as simply another way that corporations try to improve their bottom line (Tench, Bowd, & Jones, 2007). American journalists are often hesitant to cover CSR actions by organizations because they are skeptical of seemingly altruistic actions by corporations (Macleod, 2001). However, Smith (1994, p. 112) found that "the media in countries like South Korea, Brazil, Malaysia, Mexico, Argentina, Hungary, and Poland – particularly the newly privatized newspapers, eager to assert their hard-won independence – are often only too happy to give airtime to human interest stories about corporate giving." The ability to gain positive media coverage, while beneficial for the corporation that legitimately engages in CSR behavior for the purposes of social impact, might also lead some corporations to engage in these behaviors simply for the purposes of generating positive media coverage, or even to publicize efforts that were not actually completed (Frynas, 2005; Smith, 1994).

The very discussion of CSR in the media serves to further the conversation – and possibly the confusion – about CSR and the role of the business in society (Carroll, 2011; Guthey & Morsing, 2014). Media play a role in defining societal expectations for socially responsible behavior by corporations (Schultz, Castelló, & Morsing, 2013). Because journalists' news decisions affect which CSR actions are or are not covered by the media, their involvement in deciding what is or is not CSR further confounds the often-ambiguous language used to define CSR when it "refracts these ambiguous and contradictory terms through the prism of the news process in a manner that results in further ambiguity" (Guthey & Morsing, 2014, p. 556; see also Tench, Bowd, & Jones, 2007).

The use of public relations tactics can proactively engage the media in order to reach consumers and other stakeholders with positive CSR messages (Groza, Pronschinske, & Walker, 2011). In research by Tench, Bowd, & Jones (2007), journalists expressed a willingness to portray CSR positively, but also admitted that "bad" CSR made for "a better story." This makes the task of the public relations professional especially difficult in media relations efforts on behalf of corporate CSR.

Kagan, Gunningham, and Thornton (2003, p. 73), in their discussion of environmental performance by mills in New Zealand, talk about a mill that engaged in a proactive public relations and media campaign to combat environmental claims from the nonprofit Greenpeace.

> Mill AT, located in New Zealand, responded to Greenpeace's campaign against it by seeking court injunctions to restrain individual group members and engaging in its own media campaign to counter Greenpeace's arguments. As AT's environmental manager described it: "We decided to take the battle to Greenpeace, and our PR guy enjoyed the scrap. We decided we can win this war. We can visit the schools before they do, and build relationships with indigenous groups. It comes down to individuals and over time, to trust."

This example of a corporation "fighting back" against nonprofit pressure is unusual in the CSR literature; most corporations take a somewhat more subtle approach to CSR communication in order to avoid some of the potential dangers previously discussed.

CSR communication on the Web

Today, most corporations are using the Web to communicate about their CSR efforts (Birth, Illia, Lurati, & Zamparini, 2008). This communication channel has a number of advantages: it allows corporations to reach a wider audience (Wanderley, Lucian, Farache, & de Sousa Filho, 2008) while retaining control over the messages about their CSR behavior; it reaches audiences that are actively seeking information about the company (Moreno & Capriotti, 2009); and it has no temporal or space limitations as do traditional media (Esrock & Leichty, 1998). Using the Web to communicate directly with stakeholders removes the need to bypass gatekeepers in the media (Esrock & Leichty, 1998), but it does also lack the third-party approval that comes with media coverage (Snider, Hill, & Martin, 2003).

Because a corporation's website represents the official voice of the organization, its portrayal of the corporation's policies and attitudes is perceived as representing the formal, approved CSR policy of the organization (Bondy, Matten, & Moon, 2004). It presents a generalized message that is often not tailored to specific stakeholders, which can make CSR communication on the Web especially challenging (Moreno & Capriotti, 2009; Snider, Hill, & Martin, 2003). Due to its reach, however, the Internet can be useful in spreading an organization's CSR messages to a large audience.

The Web can even be used to engage with stakeholders in dialogue about their expectations for the corporation's socially responsible behavior (Miles, Munilla, & Darroch, 2006). However, a great deal of the CSR communication on the Web is monologue, not dialogue (Capriotti & Moreno, 2007; Mishra, 2006), even though technology allows for the latter as well as the former. More two-way Web communications, such as blogs, can help reduce stakeholder suspicion by allowing for conversation with the public and working to alleviate stakeholders' fears of corporate insincerity (Rim & Song, 2013).

Whether a corporation decides to communicate about its CSR behavior using controlled or uncontrolled media, the role of the public relations practitioner is vital in ensuring that communication is strategic and successful. The next section examines the role of public relations, including media relations, in corporations engaging in CSR behavior.

Public relations and its role in CSR

Because public relations is a practice that involves establishing and maintaining relationships with key stakeholders through communication, its use is intricately involved in the practice of CSR, whether it is for ethical reasons or, more commonly, as a strategic investment of business resources (Clark, 2000; L'Etang, 1994). Public relations, which traditionally acts in a boundary-spanning role between the organization and its stakeholder publics, is naturally suited for involvement in the CSR process (Heath & Ni, 2008; Heath & Ryan, 1989; Meznar & Nigh, 1995).

Public relations can add value to a corporation's CSR efforts, which is especially important if the corporation is justifying its CSR behavior using the business case (Heath & Ni, 2008). This value can take a number of different forms. PR efforts can help consumers and other key stakeholders realize that the corporation's values match their own, which could lead to stakeholder identification with the corporation and possible purchase decisions (Llewellyn, 2007; Maignan, Ferrell, & Ferrell, 2005). By promoting transparency, public relations can help portray the corporation as "reliable, non-exploitative, and dependable" (Heath & Ni, 2008, p. 68).

CSR communication can be an involuntary (mandated by legal/industry regulation) or voluntary disclosure; the latter seeks to create value for the corporation including product differentiation and goodwill among stakeholders (Williams, 2008). Public relations strategy can ensure that the corporation's CSR communication effectively reaches stakeholders by selecting the appropriate message and channel to reach the correct stakeholder publics (Du, Bhattacharya, & Sen, 2010; Frankental, 2001).

The rise of CSR has led public relations practitioners to communicate through a number of channels to reach key stakeholders. One of the more popular channels has been the publication of annual reports, which focus on and detail a company's CSR behavior (Frankental, 2001). The Internet is often preferred over other methods of communicating CSR (sustainability reports, advertising campaigns on television, billboards) because it is inexpensive and effective in achieving a wide reach (Wanderley, Lucian, Farache, & de Sousa Filho, 2008).

In a 1994 article titled "Public relations and corporate social responsibility: Some issues arising," Jacquie L'Etang expressed a concern that corporate social responsibility programs would be enacted solely for public relations purposes or that public relations considerations – rather than societal need – would drive the choice of CSR actions (see also Frynas, 2005). L'Etang's article proved rather prescient, and in the 20 years since it was published, a great number of issues have in fact arisen from the intersection between CSR and public relations. In order for public relations practitioners to participate in CSR in good conscience, these issues need to be fully explored and addressed.

Rather than the long-term relationship orientation common to public relations, CSR efforts have tended toward campaigns such as cause-related marketing (CRM), which are short-term CSR programs that tie support of issues or causes to product sales (Webb & Mohr, 1988). Varadarajan and Menon (1988, p. 59) describe CRM as "a manifestation of the alignment of corporate philanthropy and enlightened business interest." Pirsch, Gupta, and Grau (2007) refer to these as *promotional* CSR programs and contrast them with more effective (and ethical) *institutional* CSR programs. The use of institutional CSR is associated with building long-term relationships – the ultimate goal of public relations – where promotional programs are more short-term in nature and not sufficient for the task of relationship building.

Cause-related marketing efforts attempt to join the fortunes of the corporation and a partner nonprofit/issue/cause by tying product sales to a corporation's financial donation to a cause. In this way, CRM campaigns suggest that there is a "win–win" scenario for business and societal interests, something also common to the business case for CSR (Lantos, 2001). CRM efforts are often used by corporations to improve their reputation, but they are met with a variety of responses from consumers, who, as noted above, often view these programs skeptically if they appear to be serving the firm's interest (Murphy, Öberseder, & Laczniak, 2013; Webb & Mohr, 1998).

In fact, some corporations may spend more on publicizing their socially responsible behavior than on the behavior itself (Porter & Kramer, 2002; Varadarajan & Menon, 1988) or look to CSR as a way to build up a stock of reputational capital that can be used in a crisis situation (Porter, Kramer, & Zadek, 2006). These self-involved behaviors, while supported on the face of it by the business case for CSR, fail to balance the interests of the organization and the stakeholders (Heath & Ni, 2008; Schoenberger-Orgad & McKie, 2005). Indeed, as will be discussed later, they may ultimately be bad for society.

Ultimately, responsibility may lie with the public relations practitioners to ensure that CSR is not being used merely to strategic ends. This is in line with previous suggestions that public relations practitioners should act as the ethical counsel or "conscience" of an organization (Bowen, 2008; Ryan & Martinson, 1983). While it is true that "there is no shortage of self-serving philanthropic initiatives that lend themselves to photo opportunities without effecting real change" (Smith, 1994, p. 105; see also González & Martinez, 2004; Palazzo & Richter, 2005), individual practitioners have the ability to resist these inclinations and steer CSR in the direction of true social impact. In this way, they can contribute positively to society, rather than merely managing relationships and placating stakeholders (Heath & Ni, 2008).

CSR as an impetus for stakeholder dialogue

Because of its ability to promote dialogue among stakeholders, public relations is well-suited for learning from key stakeholders what their expectations are for the corporation's socially responsible behavior (Heath & Ni, 2008; Schultz, Castelló, & Morsing, 2013). Understanding stakeholder values can help the corporation align with these values whenever possible (Maignan, Ferrell, & Ferrell, 2005). In addition to providing a way to practice ethical CSR (and effective CSR that benefits the bottom line), establishing stakeholder dialogue through two-way communication might just be the reason why corporate social responsibility should endure as a business concept.

Communication about CSR with stakeholder publics should ideally occur before the actions are planned and carried out (to determine the stakeholders' needs and wants) as well as after, to notify various publics – including but not limited to the stakeholders involved – about the actions that were taken (Hess, Rogovsky, & Dunfee, 2002; Pava & Krausz, 1997; Shocker & Sethi, 1973). Without engaging stakeholders in discussion about what CSR actions are desired and appropriate, "top management runs the risk of intellectual isolation from its stakeholders and its own [employees], creating a 'bunker mentality' that offers a very management-centric, limited perspective of the firm, its capabilities, and potential futures" (Miles, Munilla, & Darroch, 2006, p. 198). Stakeholder communication is therefore needed in order to ensure that CSR benefits society, not just management.

In fact, tailoring CSR efforts too narrowly to fit the business case might end up backfiring on the corporation, as Du and Vieira (2012, p. 424) explain:

> Ironically, it is perhaps oil companies' emphasis on the business case of CSR that is preventing them from deriving maximal benefits such as gaining social legitimacy from their CSR engagement. Only by being transparent and consulting with their key stakeholders to discover their true needs, will oil companies be able to devise authentic and credible CSR programs that, in the long run, transform the public's perceptions of the industry.

Transparency is especially important in controversial industry sectors where products may produce negative externalities, such as oil and also tobacco (Palazzo & Richter, 2005).

In order for corporations to understand stakeholder expectations, they must engage various stakeholders in dialogue about these perceptions, with the understanding that these dialogues must take place frequently to account for changes in the environment and stakeholder perspectives (Miles, Munilla, & Darroch, 2006). Leap and Loughry (2004) suggest that stakeholders expect firms to be accessible, respect their time, be honest and open, welcome their inquiries, accommodate reasonable requests, and provide goods/services that are largely free of defect (and make things right when errors do occur), but the situational nature of stakeholder definition makes it important to evaluate the actual expectations of each group.

Repeated discourses with important stakeholders also facilitate the ongoing discussion of CSR and the role it plays in the relationship between business and society (Guthey & Morsing, 2014). These dialogues allow a business to understand how its stakeholders' expectations may have changed and tailor their efforts accordingly, but they also facilitate the corporation's re-evaluation of its obligation to stakeholders. In this way, CSR is not merely a business strategy, nor is it solely a solution to today's social ills – it is an ongoing conversation about the role of corporations in society (Guthey & Morsing, 2014).

> Responsibility is not only instrumentally manufactured or normatively achieved in separate spheres of society or in a pre-established negotiations [sic], but co-constructed in networks of increasingly undefined publics and power relations in a technologically mediated communication universe . . . CSR becomes a forum for exchange, dissent, and challenge of organizational and societal values via which identities are constructed and realities changed.
>
> (Schultz, Castelló, & Morsing, 2013, p. 689)

However, even when corporations engage in this kind of dialogue, they may still have to prioritize some stakeholders over others due to resource constraints (Pedersen, 2006). Therefore, stakeholder dialogue itself is not a panacea or holy-grail approach to CSR; it must be employed both instrumentally and ethically.

Grunig and Hunt (1984) established two-way symmetrical communication as the most ethical approach to public relations, and similarly a two-way approach to stakeholder dialogue in CSR can help ensure that the stakeholder groups receiving benefits from a corporation are getting what they need (Hess, Rogovsky, & Dunfee, 2002) and do not become dependent on the corporation rather than being improved by the engagement (Frynas, 2005). Dialogue with stakeholder publics is increasingly important in an age where corporations are expanding their global presence, and discussions with these publics about appropriate CSR helps ensure that corporate behavior will prove beneficial to stakeholders other than the corporation (Smith, 1994; Wheeler, Fabig, & Boele, 2002).

Notes

1 Here, the authors define social profits as "the difference between the benefits [the company] receives (higher prices, increased sales, or decreased administrative and production costs) and the costs of producing a certain level of social output" (Husted & de Jesus Salazar, 2006, p. 80).
2 A variant on corporate social responsibility, corporate social performance attempts to measure the degree to which the corporation contributes to society and meets the expectations of its stakeholders.

3 The casino industry grows up

Because "industry maturity" means something as a term in the economic literature, the title of this chapter instead adopts the more colloquial title "The gaming industry grows up." This turn of phrase also serves as a useful descriptive metaphor, as the industry continues to grow significantly, often overly quickly and awkwardly, like a teenager whose clothes are slightly too small and ill-fitting. This chapter looks at some meta-level trends in the contemporary gaming industry around the world; the following chapter dives more deeply into casino history and the current gambling industry in three case study locations – Macau, Australia, and Canada – before the book moves on to its primary case study of Las Vegas, Nevada.

Any attempt to assess the entire gaming industry in one short chapter will inevitably have to gloss over some of the many nuances of this complicated industry. In an attempt to provide enough background on the industry to understand the subsequent discussion of corporate social responsibility by casino corporations, this chapter will begin by looking at aspects of the casino industry that vary across jurisdictions, such as the regulation of gambling and the history of that regulation, characteristics of the communities where casinos are located, the government's involvement in the industry (including the degree to which casino profits are taxed), the ownership structure of casinos in a community, and the community perspective on whether casino revenues should go to public or private interests. For contrast, the chapter will then look at commonalities of gaming communities around the world, including community characteristics, resident perceptions of gaming, opposition to casinos, and lobbying efforts on behalf of casino interests.

The decision to introduce gaming into a community – often as a driver of tourism development – is usually framed as a traditional cost vs. benefit decision (Cotti, 2008; Vong, 2010; Williams & Wood, 2004). The next section of the chapter will unpack the elements of this analysis with respect to casinos and will look at some of the commonly accepted externalities of the casino industry. Academics addressing this topic have attempted to distill this decision down to a simple calculus – if benefits > costs, the casino is a good idea – but most have agreed that the actual calculation is not so straightforward. Another section will look at how public relations has featured in the decisions made by many jurisdictions to allow legalized gambling.

This chapter then turns specifically to the use of corporate social responsibility in controversial or "vice" industries, including gambling. An already complex construct, corporate social responsibility becomes even more complicated when the industry in question raises moral questions about its operations and even its primary product. A wider look at literature in controversial issues writ large – including those whose products damage the environment, such as oil and gas – provides the backdrop for a more specific look at vice industries such as tobacco, alcohol, and gambling.

Finally, the chapter will speak to the specific topic of corporate social responsibility in the casino industry. It will highlight some unique aspects of the industry, including the fact that it is frequently associated with tourism, that make CSR in the casino industry especially challenging. It will then turn to the specific topic of responsible gambling, which has traditionally been associated with social responsibility in the casino industry. The chapter will conclude by proposing a more robust concept of CSR in the casino industry than has traditionally been enacted by casino corporations in the era of rapid casino expansion.

Variations among casino communities

This section explores the characteristics of casino communities that vary between jurisdictions in order to paint a picture of the complexity of the casino industry and the difficult of talking broadly about CSR in the industry as if it was homogenous around the world. It is not intended to serve as a compendium or reference about the casino industry; better sources exist to do that (see Schwartz, 2013b; Thompson, 2001). Instead, this section explores selected aspects of the casino industry that will necessarily affect its approach to CSR.

History and current regulation of casino gambling

While the United States traces its legalized gambling days back to Nevada in 1931 and Macau back to a colonial decree in 1847, the tiny island of Singapore legalized casino gaming as recently as 2005. By Singaporean standards, even Atlantic City, NJ (where gambling was legalized in 1978) has a long history as a casino community. Singapore's long-standing opposition to gambling – its two casinos are referred to as "integrated resorts" because the stigma on the word is so strong (Abbugao, 2010) – eventually crumbled in light of the tremendous profits and economic development that casinos had stimulated in areas such as Las Vegas and Macau.

The actual date of casino legalization varies widely from country to country, and often within countries. For 47 years, Las Vegas, Nevada enjoyed a monopoly on legalized casino gambling in the United States; similarly, the principality of Monaco stood alone as the only European location to offer legal gambling from 1863 until the legalization of gambling in France over 50 years later (Siu, 2007). In 1972, only 15 jurisdictions offered legal casino gambling; by 2003, that number had jumped to 103 countries and 48 of the 50 United States (Siu, 2007).

Some gambling jurisdictions have a historical association with gambling. Although Macau's success as a global gaming destination has evolved relatively recently (the casino industry has existed in its present form only since 2001), its history with gambling goes back several centuries, and gambling has been legal in Macau for over 150 years. In comparison to US states like Ohio, for instance (which legalized gambling only in 2010), Macau has had a considerable length of time to acculturate to being known as a gambling destination, which has likely given the community an advantage as it adapts to the city's success in the casino industry.

The legalization of gambling in a jurisdiction – or the liberalization of existing gaming laws – can almost always be tied to the need for economic development, either by private enterprise or for the purposes of shoring up depleted government coffers (Burnham, 1993; Dioko & So, 2012; Eadington, 1975; Perdue, Long, & Kang, 1999; Walker, 2009). Differing countries and jurisdictions may come to this level of need at different times, leading to differing histories of legalized gambling. The legalization of gambling may also need to overcome significant opposition, leading it to take longer in certain jurisdictions where, for instance, moral obstacles may prevent it (Thompson, Lutrin, & Friedberg, 2012; von Herrmann, 2006).

Perhaps the most fundamental difference across casino communities is the organizational structure of the casino industry. In Canada, as will be described in depth later, casinos operate primarily for the benefit of the government and selected charitable organizations, with private industry receiving some benefit for operating gambling enterprises. Casinos in the United States, in contrast, operate in a more conventional free-market system, with less government regulation and a traditional profit-making motive (Eadington, 2005). European casinos, largely government-owned (or heavily taxed such that government is a de facto partner in the operation), eschew marketing and promotional tactics popular in US and other mass-market casinos (Gu, 2012).

Regulations in different jurisdictions may affect the size of bets patrons are allowed to make, the number of times patrons are allowed to visit, and the acceptable age of casino patrons, as well as the usual labor and employment rules that apply to businesses in other industries. They may even mandate the use of a certain amount of casino profits for social causes or community benefit (Harris, 2005; Wang & Juslin, 2009). Licensing regulations in several countries, most notably the United States, determine which persons and/or corporations are legally permitted to operate casino gambling.

All casinos pay some degree of tax to their government, but the relative size of that tax varies widely across jurisdictions. The success of casino enterprises has encouraged governments to look to them as a source of tax revenue; taxes are further justified as a means to offset the social costs associated with gambling (Gu & Tam, 2011). Taxes on gambling also account for the fact that private casino developments might compete with state-run gambling systems such as lotteries (Grant, 1994). However, these taxes disproportionately affect those in lower socioeconomic classes and this regressivity is accentuated with expansion of the casino industry (Smith, 2000).

The use of casino taxes to fund government programs is inherently controversial. Burnham (1993, p. 155) suggests that casino expansion was approved in the latter half of the 20th century as "influential wealthy citizens saw in taxes on gambling activities an easy method to shift the tax burden off of themselves and onto wagerers at the racetrack, the casino, or the state lottery." The collection of casino taxes (and, for that matter, the regulation of the industry) is itself expensive and diminishes the overall value of casinos to a government (Madhusudhan, 1996). Even the staunchest supporters of casino legalization admit that taxes on gambling are likely regressive, but they suggest that most people accept these taxes because "they are to a great extent voluntary" (Eadington, 1975, p. 55).

There is also some concern that reliance on tax revenues from gambling may impede the government's ability to legislate casinos effectively (Gu, Li, & Tam, 2013; Smith & Campbell, 2007). As McMahon and Lloyd (2006, p. 259) explain:

> On the one hand, it [the government] is determined to make the industry more accessible to the public (with appropriate safeguards to protect vulnerable groups); on the other hand the government asserts the priority of capturing the associated economic dynamic associated with gambling. In particular, it seeks to maximize the potential fiscal contribution from gambling to the national economy.

A government's desire to seek more tax revenue will also necessarily conflict with casinos' desire to produce more profit in those systems where gaming interests are privately owned (Gu, Li, & Tam, 2013).[1] This may lead to corporate interference in gambling regulation via lobbying, which may lead to regulation that prioritizes business interests, not citizens.

The connection in the gambling legalization discourse between casinos and increased tax revenue has caused a number of gaming critics to further highlight these potential conflicts (Skolnik, 2011). The dangers of government reliance on gaming revenue has already been seen in the state of Mississippi, where local governments found themselves scrambling to fund school budgets when several Gulf Coast casinos closed for repairs after Hurricane Katrina in 2005 (von Herrmann, 2006). Similarly, governments that fund gambling addiction programs (and other social programs) through tax revenue can often find those programs in jeopardy if gaming profits (and thus tax revenues) decline (Madhusudhan, 1996).

The role and degree of corporate influence on the casino industry

In gaming markets like Las Vegas and Macau, corporate operators play a major role in the casino industry. The hotels on the Las Vegas Strip, once owned by individuals or small groups of investors, are increasingly owned by one of six major corporations (Binkley, 2008; Eadington, 2012; Strauss, 2010). Of Macau's six authorized casino operators, three – Wynn Resorts, Las Vegas Sands, and MGM Resorts – also hold significant casino interests elsewhere and exhibit a traditional corporate structure.

Other casino markets show more of a mix of smaller and larger business interests. However, as von Herrmann (2006) points out in her discussion of the Mississippi casino industry, smaller casino operators often lack the resources needed to respond to a catastrophic situation, such as a natural disaster. Economies of scale, along with an aggressive push to capitalize on the potential profits in the casino industry, have promoted the aggregation of casino properties (Hamer, 2002).

Corporations have only been legalized to operate casinos in the United States since the late 1960s (Burnham, 1993); most jurisdictions that have legalized gaming since then, however, have allowed corporations to gain casino licenses. Corporations were initially prohibited from receiving a gaming license in Nevada (the only US jurisdiction where gaming was legal in the 1960s) due to concerns about organized crime, which has long been a problem in the Las Vegas casino industry especially (Dombrink, 1996). When Atlantic City legalized gambling in 1978, the market was quickly dominated by corporate interests, which went on to buy properties in a rapid conglomeration effect (Hamer, 2002).

The corporatization of the casino industry in markets like the United States and Macau brings both advantages and disadvantages. Publicly owned companies are more visible and thus might feel more of a compulsion to engage in socially responsible behavior, such as the promotion of responsible gambling (Eadington, 1996). However, the corporation's obligation to shareholders might cause decisions to be made that privilege the corporation's profits over the people it impacts (Gu, 2012). The chief executive of Christchurch (NZ) Casino, in a 1999 article in the *Journal of Gambling Studies*, suggested that

> a casino's social responsibility to the community is inextricably linked with its financial responsibility to its shareholders.
>
> The two cannot and must not be allowed to become incompatible. Too much emphasis on financial imperatives risks alienating the community and losing public support along with business – a lose/lose scenario. Conversely, working to keep the local community on the side of the casino operator leads to goodwill, fewer social downsides and more opportunities for business growth – a win/win situation.
>
> (Pitcher, 1999, p. 155)

While these sentiments sound ideal in theory, in practice it may be somewhat idealistic to believe that casinos would take such a big-picture approach to long-term success that focuses on non-financial elements such as goodwill and reduced social costs.

In fact, Stokowski (1993, p. 39), in a study of two rural gambling communities in the United States, showed that the undesirable "lag effects" following the construction of a casino clearly demonstrated "the adoption of a development approach that advances economic goals at the expense of social considerations." Where casinos are run by profit-driven corporations, and permitted to do so by governments that reap similar financial rewards from tax revenues, there is a strong inclination toward making decisions that promote financial profits.

The danger that casino corporations' decisions are being made with economic profit superseding social cost is one of the prime concerns generated by corporate ownership of casinos.

Characteristics of casino communities and their residents

Differences across jurisdictions in the legal structure of gambling affect casinos (and their communities) in a number of ways (Hsu, 2000). A great deal of research has examined these communities, looking at the actual economic change generated by casinos (Eadington, 1975; Kearney, 2005; Madhusudhan, 1996; Walker, 2009), the number and quality of jobs created by casino development (Back & Lee, 2012; Cotti, 2008; Kearney, 2005; Zeng, Forrest & McHale, 2013), the ways that casino development can affect community identity (Shannon & Mitchell, 2012), the negative externalities generated by casinos (Stokowski, 1993), and quality of life in casino communities (Perdue, Long, & Kang, 1999; Roehl, 1999; Stokowski & Park, 2012), among others. Griswold and Nichols (2006), in looking at casinos in New Zealand, found that social capital[2] was significantly reduced in communities within 15 miles of a casino.

A great deal of research on casino communities has addressed residents' perceptions of casino development (Caneday & Zieger, 1991; Kang, Lee, Yoon, & Long, 2008; Kang, Long, & Perdue, 1996; Lee & Back, 2009; Lee, Kang, Long, & Reisinger, 2010). Understanding residents' perceptions of how gaming has impacted their community is important in understanding how their quality of life has been affected – either positively or negatively – by the casino(s) in their community (Stokowski & Park, 2012). Residents' perceptions can also be important in driving public policy by setting parameters for acceptable regulation and legislation of casino gambling (McAllister, 2014).

In principle, casino development should engage local residents in decision-making processes that will have an impact on the community (Black & Ramsay, 2003; Chhabra & Gursoy, 2012; Perdue, Long, & Kang, 1999; Tam, Tsai, & Chen McCain, 2013; Yu, 2008). This kind of engagement can help both government and industry officials better understand what makes residents support or oppose the casino development (Kang, Lee, Yoon, & Long, 2008). Residents may be uniquely qualified to ensure that a cost–benefit analysis of a casino's future impact accurately evaluates the situation in the community (Lee & Back, 2009).

However, efforts to engage residents often superficially focus on the advantages that a casino can bring – namely, tax revenues that can support social programs (Ham, Brown, & Jang, 2004) – but ignore the real need for residents to contribute ideas and opinions about the implementation of the casino development plan. Casino interests often seem to think that listening alone fulfills their social obligations to communities (Pitcher, 1999), but in fact it is what they do with this information that truly matters. Many discussions of community engagement in the academic literature (Back & Lee, 2012; McKechnie, Grant, Sadeghi, Khan, & Taymaskhanov, 2009; Pitcher, 1999) seem to evoke Grunig and Hunt's

(1984) model of two-way asymmetrical communication, where communities are engaged only to the extent that they can be more effectively persuaded to adapt to the organization's benefit (Wan & Pinheiro, 2014).

One concern with corporate control of casino enterprises is that gambling profits may be unfairly distributed or, even worse, will leave the community entirely (Roehl, 1999). Because many casinos are operated by corporations located in other states (and sometimes other countries, as in the case of Macau; see Balsas, 2013; Wan, 2012; Wan, Li, & Kong, 2011 for more on the amount of foreign investment in Macau's casino market), the casino corporation contributes only a percentage of its profits as tax revenue to the community – other profits "leak" out to the corporation's home location (Lee & Back, 2009; Tam, Tsai, & Chen McCain, 2013).

Although academics theorize that the casino community should ideally be able to export the social costs of gambling by catering to out-of-town tourists (Eadington, 1975; see also Garrett & Nichols, 2008; Walker & Jackson, 1998), casino communities may also see some negative effects of gaming. These negative impacts, common to many casinos, are often categorized as environmental, social, and economic (Lee & Back, 2009). Although casinos are promoted as drivers of economic prosperity, their success can lead to higher property prices and a raised cost of living, as well as a higher tax burden. Social impacts include a possible increase in crime (see also Friedman, Hakim, & Weinblatt, 1989) and the divorce and suicide rates as well as the potential for gambling addiction in the community. Negative environmental impacts include noise, traffic, and air pollution (Lee & Back, 2009; Zheng & Huang, 2012).

Communities can also be affected by privatization in the casino industry, which advantages privileged classes and disadvantages those at the lower levels of society. This has been especially true in Macau, where the government's process to legalize casinos led to a significant worsening of the divide between social classes (Sheng & Tsui, 2009b). As Thompson (2001, p. xxvii) describes it, the casino industry is "at best a neutral economic phenomenon overall. Wealth changes hands through gambling, but wealth is not created through gambling." Corporate control of casinos can lead to a situation where certain segments of the community – those outside the friendly confines of the corporation and its employ – are affected differently by the negative externalities of casino gaming (Stokowski & Park, 2012).

Casino industries with strong ties to the government are more likely to take measures to ensure responsible gambling because their obligation to the people of the community is so direct (Blaszczynski, Ladouceur, Nower, & Shaffer, 2008). Purely profit-driven companies operating casinos, such as are found in the United States and increasingly in Macau, ultimately have a responsibility to shareholders and a financial bottom line. This may cause the possibility of a "trade-off" between people and profits (or, just as problematic, the appearance of such a trade-off), forcing casino corporations to make tough decisions that can ultimately have a negative impact on the casino community.

The cost–benefit framework for evaluating casino proposals

Eadington (1975) suggests that in order for communities to minimize costs and maximize benefits from casino gaming, the costs must be exported to other communities – that is, the gamblers at the casino must be tourists (see also Garrett & Nichols, 2008; von Herrmann, 2006). The necessary connection between gambling and tourism may have led to the frequent use of social exchange theory in analyses of gaming's effect on a community (Friedman, Hakim, & Weinblatt, 1989; Ham, Brown, & Jang, 2004; Lee & Back, 2009). Popular in the tourism development literature, the social exchange theory posits that communities are willing to accept some negative externalities of tourism development as long as they perceive the benefits to the community will exceed the costs (Ap, 1992).

This cost–benefit analysis framework dominates the literature on casino gaming and its global expansion and drives the discourse about gaming toward a traditional economic framework (Stokowski & Park, 2012; Wenz, 2014), probably because casino proponents often promote potential economic development to dubious communities (Perdue, Long, & Kang, 1999). As such, most expansion in the casino industry is justified by its potential as a driver of economic success for governments, corporations, and their communities. However, this justification often minimizes the social costs generated by casinos, which are difficult to calculate (Madichie, 2007; Stokowski & Park, 2012). Additionally, while this cost–benefit analysis usually precedes the decision to build a casino in a community, this analysis often lacks the follow-up needed to monitor any changes in the social costs that might ultimately grow to outweigh the benefits (Hsu, 2000; Lee & Back, 2009).

It is certainly tempting to try to ground decisions about casino development in the familiar rhetoric of costs vs. benefits. However, there are some key problems with this approach. Primarily, the many negative externalities across economic, social, and environmental dimensions (Lee & Back, 2009) often defy the ability to be translated directly into monetary cost (Wenz, 2014). Even benefit issues such as increased tax revenue and greater job opportunities can be more complex than they might appear: Because expenditures on gambling may have been spent elsewhere in the absence of a casino option, the tax revenue increase might not be as substantial as it initially appears (MacDonald, McMullan, & Perrier, 2004). Jobs created by casino development might not be of a high quality (Reith, 2003) and the number of jobs created by casinos often levels off a few years after the casino is opened (Forrest, 2013). Also, these jobs can be threatened if the economy sours and the casino industry contracts, as was the case in Las Vegas in 2008–2010 (Eadington, 2012).

In some cases of casino expansion, the traditional cost–benefit framework may fail in its attempt to assess whether casinos bring value to a community. Speaking to the issue of Native American tribal casinos in the United States, Kearney (2005, p. 288) notes that while tribal affiliation and employment numbers may rise in the wake of a casino opening, "the question remains as to whether this [casino gambling] is the most efficient policy to improve economic circumstances on reservations." In other words, although casino gaming has improved economic conditions in some circumstances, it is certainly not a panacea for the social problems of Native Americans, nor is it the only possible way to improve reservation economies (see also Evans & Topoleski, 2002).

The traditional cost–benefit discourse also breaks down in the context of gaming because certain members of a community may benefit more than others from the introduction of a casino, and those people are more likely to assess the casino positively because they have benefited personally (Caneday & Ziegler, 1991; Chhabra and Gursoy, 2012; Lee & Back, 2003; Roehl, 1999). The fact that members of the same community may come to a different conclusion on the casino's value to the community may lead to dissension between community groups, which could diminish their bargaining power with respect to corporate-owned casinos and government interests. Groups within the community could also disagree over the way that costs and benefits of casinos should be distributed (Roehl, 1999), which could lead to further discord in a community.

The introduction or expansion of casinos, especially as part of a larger tourism strategy, is ostensibly linked to an attempt to improve residents' quality of life in a community (Hsu, 1998). In order to truly do this, the discussion about casinos must not be limited to economic concerns and the quantification of costs and benefits:

> Tourism development strategies are typically promoted to local residents on the basis of the related jobs and income benefits. *Although these economic benefits are clearly necessary conditions, they are just as clearly not sufficient.* Both communities and businesses must take a broader perspective, providing opportunities and support for programs that focus on community social environments.
>
> (Perdue, Long, & Kang, 1999, p. 174, emphasis added)

In fact, if casinos are not designed to improve residents' quality of life, it would appear that they are intended instead to benefit corporate interests and government coffers – quite possibly to the detriment of the community members.

Contraction in the casino industry

On a cautionary note against the looming specter of unchecked capitalism which arises from casino expansion (Grant, 1994; Simpson, 2012), it seems appropriate to turn to the illustrative example of Russia, which actually constricted its gaming regulations in 2006. In 2000, the Russian casino industry employed over 120,000 people in 2700 casino establishments (Vasiliev & Bernhard, 2012). The industry was lucrative for the Russian government, as it collected 90% of the casinos' profits in tax revenues (Shapiro, 2010).

In 2009, the new regulations took effect and gambling was effectively banished to four remote tourist-oriented destinations (Vasiliev & Bernhard, 2012), causing drastic contraction of the industry. The government cited rampant expansion of gambling facilities (which it had previously declined to regulate) as driving the need for the new legislation (Skopchevskiy, 2008). The new legislation approved the creation of four "gambling zones," which it defined as "part of the territory of the Russian Federation which is designated for organizing and holding risk-based events with an uncertain outcome" (Skopchevskiy, 2008, p. 7). Two casinos did open in Russia in 2010 (Shapiro, 2010), but the closing of casinos in 2009 left around 350,000 Russians unemployed in what was already a weak economy (Harding, 2009).

The Russian move was not entirely without economic motivation, as the government pledged funding for infrastructure projects in hopes of promoting investment opportunities in the newly designated gambling zones (Skopchevskiy, 2008). These tourist destinations were preferred for gambling locations because it was thought that they would attract primarily those with enough money to travel – and hence gamble – in contrast to casinos in poorer neighborhoods where residents gambled in spite of their financial situation (Vasiliev & Bernhard, 2012).

The legislative change was primarily motivated by ideology: Because of gambling's traditional association with the capitalistic profit motive, and its role in widening the gap between social classes through regressive taxation, casinos simply were not in line with Russian values and political thought (Vasiliev & Bernhard, 2012). And so, in spite of tremendous financial detriment, Russian President Vladimir Putin acted to significantly reduce the profile of casinos in Russian culture.

The radical change in legislation had significant financial consequences for the Russian government. In the wake of the sudden move, Russian gamblers began to explore online options for gambling. This resulted in the tax revenue from gambling going not to the Russian government, but to offshore interests and governments; the government had to act quickly to make such gambling illegal (Shapiro, 2010).

If "casinos should not be treated differently than other businesses," as the lobby organization American Gaming Association argued in a 2014 document,[3] what might explain the Russian decision to, in fact, treat casinos quite differently by sending them into exile? A later section details the unique topic of CSR in the casino industry and identifies the ways in which, from the perspective of social responsibility, casinos are in many ways quite different from other businesses.

Public relations in the casino industry

As the stakes of casino gaming grow ever higher, both proponents and opponents of gambling have turned to public relations in order to advance their positions. It is becoming increasingly difficult to remain neutral on the idea of legalized gaming, as "the debate becomes increasingly polarized between those who regard it as a legitimate commercial business and those who see it as a harmful social activity" (Reith, 2003, p. 14). Both casino corporations and the governments that hope to legalize gambling (and reap the associated tax benefits) have needed to use strategic communication to convince and mobilize proponents and stave off the attacks of critics (Grinols & Mustard, 2001).

Gambling has traditionally been opposed for moral reasons and due to its fundamental nature as a seemingly unproductive activity (Burnham, 1993). Eventually, however, more practical concerns, such as the historical association of gambling with organized crime (Hing, 2005; Lee & Park, 2009; Siu, 2006; Thompson, 2012; Vasiliev & Bernhard, 2012; Verona, 2012), gradually replaced moral opposition. Eventually, the potential benefits of gambling – and the tax revenues it promised to bring with it – became irresistible even in the face of lingering moral concerns (Thompson, Lutrin, & Friedberg, 2012).

Once initiated, the push for legalized gambling is usually driven by a combination of involved parties, such as governments seeking to increase tax revenues, community leaders seeking additional economic development, and the casino corporations themselves. Supporters of casinos often engage opponents and those who are undecided about gaming with persuasive communication intended to garner support. As an example, those who supported opening casinos in several mining communities in Colorado waged an organized public relations campaign to gain community support:

> Throughout the [legalization] campaign, promoters of the gambling amendment highlighted the recreational nature of the proposed developments. Brochures described limited stakes gambling as "a few slot machines in every local business." In terms of wager levels and spatial distribution in the communities, gambling was to be an "added attraction" rather than an "industry." The overall image was one of harmless entertainment for tourists and substantial benefits for community businesses and residents.
>
> (Stokowski, 1993, pp. 37–38)

However, Stokowski (1993) suggests that this approach may have actually set the Colorado communities up for failure by eschewing a thorough analysis of data in favor of persuasive rhetoric. Without a consideration of costs, residents were unprepared for them and felt that they had been uninformed about them by casino advocates.

Elements of strategic communication for public relations purposes abound in the literature about casino development. Chhabra and Gursoy (2012) suggest a traditional public relations approach of segmenting publics who may support or oppose casino development and addressing specific concerns of each public individually (see also Yoo, Zhou, Lu, & Kim, 2014). Kang, Lee, Yoon, and Long (2008) suggest that research is needed to examine these publics' motivations for supporting or opposing casino gambling. Certain publics in the community, such as the highly educated and those more likely to be opinion leaders, can be targeted for assistance in generating support (Hsu, 1998). In order to be successful, casino proponents may also need to broaden their persuasive arguments beyond the traditional economic framework and proactively address negative externalities, such as crime, as well as identifying non-economic benefits of casino development (Perdue, Long, & Kang, 1999).

Effective communication is also needed to ensure that communities are receiving accurate information about casino effects in the community. For instance,

Hsu (2000) found that riverboat casinos and local governments in the US Midwest were not adequately promoting benefits of these casinos to the local population, leaving the community to see only the negative impacts of the casinos (see also Harrill, Uysal, Cardon, Vong, & Dioko, 2011). However, this need poses a challenge to the casino industry: If stakeholders receive communication about casino benefits from the corporations themselves (or the governments that benefit from the tax revenue), they may be skeptical about its veracity or any potential ulterior motives (Suchman, 1995).

Ultimately, the use of public relations in advocating for or against legalized gambling can raise some ethical issues for practitioners (Harris, 2005). Because public relations efforts necessarily require a certain amount of resources, they are often undertaken by more powerful groups (Edwards, 2006); this has a definite effect in the casino industry:

> The dependency on gambling monies by special interest groups exerts a gravitational pull that makes it hard to alter gambling policy. In part, it's simple economics – those who benefit from gambling largess have more money to lobby to keep it in place. Moreover, while the social and economic costs of gambling have only a general effect on all taxpayers, the financial rewards of gambling are highly concentrated which results in opposition to gambling being diluted and diffuse while support for the activity is intense.
>
> (Smith et al., 2011, p. 75)

These corporate interests can also drive the discourse about a topic (Motion & Leitch, 1996) – here, legalized gambling as a driver of economic development. This display of corporate power through the use of public relations efforts can result in the expansion of legalized gambling, or the maintenance of current gambling standards, even if the local community experiences significant social costs as a result.

CSR in the casino industry

Significant precedent for philanthropy and charity from the gaming sector can be seen throughout various cultures' histories. Australian gaming operator George Tattersall donated considerably to charitable causes during his life and even provided for them in his will (Harris, 2005). In Macau, operators of monopolized gambling interests were frequent donors to the community throughout the 20th century (Siu, 2006). In fact, the frequent donations by early casino monopoly holder Stanley Ho may have fueled Macanese concerns about overhauling that country's gaming system: If the philanthropist lost his monopoly on the gaming industry, he might not contribute as generously to community causes. Throughout Macau's history, as long as casino owners contributed to charitable causes, government was less likely to crack down on any illegal operations that might be funding these donations (Eadington & Siu, 2007).

This section unpacks the concept of corporate social responsibility in the casino industry. It begins by looking at unique aspects of the casino industry, including the strong connection between casino gaming and tourism. A theoretical consideration of the two approaches to corporate social responsibility, moral and functional, lays the groundwork for consideration of CSR in the so-called "vice" industries, which include gambling. An examination of responsible gambling efforts, a traditional element of casino CSR, is followed by a more well-rounded concept of what corporate social responsibility in the casino industry would look like.

Unique characteristics of the casino industry

A great deal of CSR literature offers broad, general suggestions about the role of CSR and the way that it can be most effectively deployed to a corporation's strategic advantage. But corporate social responsibility in the casino industry has a different nature than CSR in other industries, in large part because the casino industry has a set of unique characteristics that influence the role and execution of CSR efforts (Vong, 2010). These characteristics need to be examined before a discussion of CSR in the gaming industry can be properly undertaken.

As an industry that is focused on consumption not production, of goods, gambling fits in well to the 20th-century evolution of a growing consumer culture (Burnham, 1993; see also Simpson, 2012). It is also a service industry, reiterating its consumption focus (Siu, 2007). In fact, some suggest that gambling is a supply-, rather than demand-driven industry, where consumer interest in gambling rises with the expansion of casino facilities (Marshall, 2005; Mellen & Okada, 2005); however, gambling proponents argue that expanding casinos are only meeting consumer demand (Livingstone & Woolley, 2007).

Casino gaming is a heavily regulated industry, and due to its expected social costs, it often requires that certain publics (citizens, governments) be convinced that it should be introduced into a community (Breen, Buultzens, & Hing, 2012). Often, casino proponents tie in their attempt to introduce gambling into a community with a suggestion that the presence of a casino will benefit the community's attempts to draw tourists, who can presumably offer a host of economic benefits to the community. However, the link between casino gaming and tourism has some unique elements that affect the concept of casino CSR.

Casino gaming and tourism

Gambling expansion often goes hand-in-hand with efforts to promote tourism development[4] (Hsu, 1998; Perdue, Long, & Kang, 1999; Siu, 2007), and this historical association between the two renders some interesting nuances in the casino industry. As with other forms of tourism, the introduction of a casino can have a significant impact on the community in which it is located (Caneday & Ziegler, 1991; Eadington, 1986; Kang, Long, & Perdue, 1996). A central concern is that tourism development might benefit business and local government (via tax revenues), but not the people of the community (Stokowski, 1993; see also Hsu, 1998).

The example of casino development in former mining towns in Colorado and South Dakota in the United States helps illustrate this last point. Casinos were opened in Deadwood, SD and in three towns in Colorado (Central City, Cripple Creek, and Black Hawk) as a way to revive the crumbling economies in these locations by promoting joint tourism and gambling development (Nickerson, 1995; Stokowski, 1993). Casino development in these communities was tied into existing efforts to promote heritage/tourism development of these frontier towns and level out visitor numbers across all months of the year, rather than just the traditional summer months (Blevins & Jensen, 1998).

Consistent with the tourist development literature, these Colorado and South Dakota communities experienced several negative side effects from casino openings, but residents' concerns were often suborned to the ostensible economic benefits of gaming (Nickerson, 1995). Some of these externalities were consistent with the development of "boomtowns" that had experienced sudden growth, such as in natural resource extraction (Perdue, Long, & Kang, 1999). Casino gaming, in particular, has the potential to vastly disrupt communities, with a fear that it will "displace local residents, squeeze out neighborhood businesses, and steamroll indigenous culture and heritage" (Hannigan, 2007, p. 968).

Literature in the area of tourism development has tried over the years to understand the complex interchange between a community and its efforts to develop as a tourist location, often using the conventional cost–benefit framework discussed previously (Roehl, 1999). But these traditional measures might not suffice, as "the success of a tourism growth strategy . . . should be gauged by how well the needs of all community members are served, not only by the aggregated wealth accumulated, which may not be evenly distributed" (Stokowski & Park, 2012, p. 657). Additionally, community impacts might vary widely based on characteristics of different communities, making it difficult to talk generally about tourism impacts and cost–benefit analysis for casino development (Hsu, 1998).

Recent literature in the field of sustainable tourism, which suggests that the economic development motives of tourism need to be balanced with the social costs created in order for progress generated by tourism to be viable in the long run (Wan, 2012), can help inform casino/tourism development. Although this concept is especially applicable to casino locations with natural resource limitations such as Las Vegas and Macau (Du Cros, 2009; Sheng & Tsui, 2009a), elements of sustainable tourism align nicely with discussions of corporate social responsibility in the casino industry.

> As suggested by Swarbrooke (1999), tourism development needs to be economically viable but should not destroy the resources on which the future of tourism will depend, notably the physical environment and the social fabric of the host community. Casino development has important links to the tourism industry; an understanding of the triple bottom line impacts of casinos is essential for the sustainable development and management of many destinations with casinos in them.
>
> (Wan, 2012, p. 738)

Issues related to sustainable tourism will be highlighted in later discussions of Macau (chapter 4) and Las Vegas (chapter 5), where environmental issues are especially significant.

Moral vs. functional CSR in the casino industry

The debate over CSR in the casino industry might be more accurately reflected in the degree to which one believes the casino corporation has a moral obligation to take actions that benefit society, especially to provide recompense when its actions damage a certain sector of the public (Black & Ramsay, 2003; Lantos, 2001; Lindorff, Prior Jonson, & McGuire, 2012; Margolis & Walsh, 2003; Swanson, 1995; Wood, 1991) or, ideally, cease the harmful behaviors entirely (Kilcullen & Kooistra, 1999; Pava & Krausz, 1997). Unlike adherence to legal regulations on gambling, which fulfill a functional obligation, these efforts may be voluntarily undertaken to fulfill moral obligations. Barring the corporation's willingness to fulfill this moral obligation voluntarily, government regulations can be imposed to force it to do so (González & Martinez, 2004). The variety of negative externalities generated by the casino industry, including but not limited to an increase in problem gambling, produces a moral obligation that is especially keen.

In theory, the consequences may be serious when a casino corporation abandons its moral responsibility to society. Buchanan and Johnson (2007, p. 1) suggest that gaming operators who do not engage in an adequate level of CSR "abrogate their duty of care thereby forfeiting their legitimacy." Although moral opposition to gambling itself has largely faded in light of the tremendous tax and other economic benefits that the casino industry can create (Madichie, 2007; Thompson, Lutrin, & Friedberg, 2012), this does not absolve casino corporations from a responsibility to behave morally. Similarly, casino corporations must not ignore social costs of gambling that are exported to other locations simply because they do not see their effects directly (Gu, Li, & Tam, 2013).

Considering CSR in vice industries

A great deal of research has looked at CSR in so-called "vice" industries of tobacco, alcohol, gambling, etc. (Blanco, Guillamón-Saorín, & Guiral, 2013; Buchanan & Johnson, 2007; Buchanan, Elliott, & Johnson, 2009; Cai, Jo, & Pan, 2009; Jo & Na, 2012; Lee & Park, 2009; Palazzo & Richter, 2005; Yani-de-Soriano, Javed, & Yousafzai, 2012) as well as the effects of CSR behavior on companies with bad reputations across a variety of industries (Yoon, Gürhan-Canli, & Schwarz, 2006). Scholars disagree whether the genre of vice industries should be defined primarily by the products produced by companies in this sector, which can be harmful, or the processes used in the industry (De Colle & York, 2009; Du & Vieria, 2012), but the gaming industry will be considered as a vice industry here because its product is undeniably capable of producing harm, and there is certainly some concern that the way that casinos market their product leaves something to be desired from an ethical perspective (Hing, 2002, 2012a; Kingma, 2004). This section looks at some of the industry-specific aspects of CSR that should be considered when discussing the casino industry.

Companies in vice industries are likely to face higher expectations for participation in CSR from a variety of stakeholders (Wood, 1991). These industries often generate significant negative externalities in pursuit of economic success, an approach that is justified by the stakeholder primacy perspective (Boatright, 1996) but leads to additional ethical responsibilities to stakeholders (Laczniak & Murphy, 2007). In fact, it may not even be possible for corporations in this kind of industry to be socially responsible "while producing products harmful to human being, society, or environment" (Cai, Jo, & Pan, 2012, p. 467; see also Lee & Park, 2009; Lindorff, Prior Jonson, & McGuire, 2012; Yani-de-Soriano, Javed, & Yousafzai, 2012).

However, a pure business case for CSR would support the use of CSR as a strategy by any industry, regardless of its product, in order to reap the purported benefits of CSR such as improved reputation, product sales and differentiation, lower firm risk, etc. (Cai, Jo, & Pan, 2012; Jo & Na, 2012). Given the expansion of legalized gambling and the amount of (legal) revenue that the industry now generates, it bears considering that gambling may no longer be considered a vice industry by a majority of the world's population (Yani-de-Soriano, Javed, & Yousafzai, 2012; see also Schwartz, 2003). Certainly, a blanket perception of the entire casino industry as socially irresponsible due to its vice product is unlikely to encourage much expansion of CSR efforts among casinos (De Colle & York, 2009), and no one wants to entirely discourage these firms from engaging in CSR.

In order to exceed stakeholder expectations and generate benefits based on their CSR efforts, vice companies will likely need to engage in more such activities than companies in other industries (Bhattacharya & Sen, 2004; Wan, Li, & Kong, 2011) due to perceptions that these companies are falling short of their obligations; this added effort may cost more to the company than it is expected to benefit from engaging in CSR (Blanco, Guillamón-Saorín, & Guiral, 2013; Lee & Park, 2009). Given the number of negative externalities generated by gambling, it is likely that CSR in the casino industry will parallel the findings of Palazzo and Richter (2005, p. 388) who suggest in their examination of the tobacco industry that "CSR in the tobacco industry must be conceptualized differently from the mainstream understanding of the debate." This would suggest that a conventional business case for CSR might not be applicable to the tobacco industry or, by extension, the casino industry.

Vice companies may decide to engage in socially responsible activities as a form of reputational insurance (in the event of some sort of public, negative backlash), but this rationale "risks confusing public relations with social and business results" (Porter, Kramer, & Zadek, 2006, p. 83). Additionally, stakeholder sentiment might turn against a vice corporation if its actions are perceived as merely strategic and not based in any kind of moral grounding (Jo & Na, 2012). However, the fact that these companies' products are controversial does not mean that they are incapable of contributing to the common good, and for the sake of societal progress and wellbeing, they should be encouraged to do so (Lindorff, Prior Jonson, & McGuire, 2012).

CSR efforts by companies in vice industries need to be carefully communicated to important stakeholders (Clark, 2000; Du & Vieria, 2012; Lewis, 2001). This challenging communication task requires corporations to exude authenticity and genuine concern so that stakeholders do not assume that the corporation is engaging in socially responsible actions merely to make a good impression – known as the "window-dressing hypothesis" (Cai, Jo, & Pan, 2012, p. 467; see also Blanco, Guillamón-Saorín, & Guiral, 2013; Buchanan, Elliott, & Johnson, 2009; Dentchev, 2004; Palazzo & Richter, 2005; Weaver, Trevino, & Cochran, 1999). Perception of CSR efforts as merely "window dressing" will likely damage stakeholders' evaluation of the corporation's reputation, thus negating any benefits accrued from the CSR activities.

Additionally, companies in vice industries may find charitable organizations unwilling to accept their donations because they fear being stigmatized for their association with the corporation (Palazzo & Richter, 2005). However, most charitable organizations are not in a situation where they can refuse donations, as is shown by the prevalence of philanthropic endeavors throughout the history of the global gaming industry (Harris, 2005; Siu, 2006; Strauss, 2010). The use of gaming revenues for charitable donations once again emphasizes the regressivity of casinos' effects in their communities and uses money for philanthropic donations that have been effectively contributed by those in the society who are least able to do without it (Harris, 2005). Communicating the corporation's philanthropic efforts – promotion of CSR being a crucial part of ensuring its strategic effectiveness – also allows the corporation to further profit from these donations in the form of an improved reputation (Harris, 2005).

The predisposition of many stakeholders, especially skeptical ones, to ascribe to the window-dressing hypothesis generates a particular challenge for the gaming industry. If a casino corporation gives money to a related philanthropic cause (e.g. programs that promote responsible gambling, as will be addressed below), it is merely seen to be fulfilling its obligations to remedy harms that it has caused. However, if a casino chooses to support an unrelated charity, stakeholders may perceive this to be an act of window dressing and an attempt to distract them from the harm being caused by the casino industry (see Palazzo & Richter, 2005). And, of course, if the casino corporation ceases to contribute to philanthropic efforts, a number of important social organizations will lose the funding they often desperately need (Harris, 2005).

CSR and responsible gambling (RG)

The need for socially responsible corporations to take efforts to remedy harms they may have caused has special weight in the case of the casino industry (Song, Lee, Lee, & Song, 2014). Like the tobacco industry, the casino industry promotes a product that lowers a person's ability to control his or her actions, an effect that is compounded over time (Doughney, 2007). If the corporation's product renders the customer unable (or even less able) to control his or her behavior, it follows from a moral perspective that the casino corporation bears some responsibility for instituting controls to prevent harms to the consumer, a concept known as responsible gambling.

However, when it comes to the idea of promoting responsible gambling, casino operators may feel that any effort in this direction would be "tantamount to madness, as it would be seen as fundamentally challenging their *raison d'être*" (Buchanan, Elliott, & Johnson, 1999, p. 92; see also Yoon, Gürhan-Canli, & Schwarz, 2006). This inherent contradiction seems emblematic of the deeply problematic nature of CSR in the casino industry: True social responsibility may, in fact, entail the end of casino corporations.

Corporate social responsibility in the casino industry was initially synonymous with responsible gambling, but over time it became clear that responsible gaming was only one piece of the corporation's CSR profile (Song, Lee, Lee, & Song, 2014). Although many corporations like to take credit for responsible gaming endeavors (Pitcher, 1999), they were unlikely to address these concerns to any great degree unless such efforts were mandated by government regulation (Hing, 2012b) or as an attempt to respond to public outcry (Campbell & Smith, 2003; Hing, 2002; Korn, 2000) due to the prioritization of economic competitiveness and, eventually, profit. When the negative social impacts of casinos began to surface in the public discourse, casinos began to nominally contribute to responsible gaming efforts; however, their efforts were still primarily geared toward treatment, rather than prevention (Fong, Fong, & Li, 2011).

Summarizing the extensive literature on problem gambling certainly lies outside the scope of this book; however, some aspects of responsible/problem gambling research are pertinent here, notably aspects of the phenomenon that are likely to vary across jurisdictions. This further emphasizes that corporations' attempts to be socially responsible in the gaming industry must be targeted rather than generalized.

It is hard to draw too many firm conclusions from the body of problem gambling research because the condition manifests itself differently under different conditions. For instance, individuals' relationship with gambling is often culturally located (Raylu & Oei, 2004; see also Bellringer, Perese, Abbott, & Williams, 2006), and thus research findings about problem gambling often contradict each other. Perspectives that advocate an individual gambler's responsibility to behave sensibly (Blaszczynski, Ladouceur, Nower, & Shaffer, 2008; Hing, 2002) clash with viewpoints which hold that casino operators are facilitating behavioral compulsions that might have otherwise gone unexercised (Skolnik, 2011). Even the most adamant proponents of the casino industry's viability, however, will acknowledge that problem gambling is a possible, if not probable, outcome of the rapid expansion of casino gaming (Eadington, 2003).

But even financial contributions by casino corporations to promote responsible gambling, as an aspect of the corporation's social responsibility and in fulfillment of moral obligations to remedy harms that it might have caused, can be problematic. Problem gambling, the condition that these efforts are intended to address, has been described primarily as an individual medical issue similar to alcohol addiction (Borch, 2012; Hing, 2002). This trend, however, has an unintended side effect, as explained by Skolnik (2011, p. 143):

> This is the theory of gambling critics: the casino industry created the NCRG [National Center for Responsible Gaming, an industry-funded research center] to try to establish the idea that pathological gambling is caused by gamblers who mostly suffer from addictive "personalities." Under this theory, casinos and other gambling operators aren't responsible in any way for getting gamblers hooked. This not only aids the industry in its state-by-state legalization fights, but it establishes a ready-made defense against potential lawsuits.

This approach, therefore, locates the "problem" in problem gambling in the individual, and not in the casino industry that provides opportunities for that person to gamble (and profits from his or her actions) or the government that legalizes gambling in order to reap the associated tax benefits (Burnham, 1993; Campbell & Smith, 2003).

Ironically, then, the more money casino corporations give to fund research on problem gambling (under the auspices of the NCRG or otherwise) or to treat those who have been affected by it, the more the discourse describes problem gambling as an individual failing and not a societal concern. Discourse about this issue almost never locates the problem in the corporations that profit from gambling and, having done so, continue to expand their casino operations in hopes of increasing their financial gain. Thus, one of the most common ways for casino corporations to engage in CSR – by funding problem gambling research and treatment – actually serves to absolve the corporations of any responsibility in fostering the existence of problem gambling. Further, research by Turner, Wiebe, Falkowski-Ham, Kelly, and Skinner (2005, pp. 109–110) showed that residents in Canada tend to believe that "the responsibility to avoid problems is entirely in the hands of the players, not the gambling industry," suggesting that this discourse is having its desired effect.

When considering the role of casinos in the promotion of responsible gambling as a part of their CSR efforts, comparisons between gambling and tobacco as vice products are instructive because both industries' products have the potential to cause direct harm to the customer if not used responsibly (Doughney, 2007). For this reason, Palazzo and Richter's (2005, p. 397) conclusion on the potential for CSR in the tobacco industry speaks especially well to the issue of CSR in the gaming industry:

> In some cases, integrity would even demand proactive behavior: Tobacco companies should make dilemmas transparent that are not yet in the public awareness. They should have a closer collaboration with governments to create effective tobacco regulation. They should do this in transparent discourses clearly accessible to civil society.

Applied to the casino industry, this normative prescription would manifest itself as responsible gambling: making casino customers aware of the potential harms of gambling and instituting controls on their gambling behavior (Black & Ramsay, 2003; Wan, Li, & Kong, 2011). However, such proactive efforts occur infrequently in the gaming industry and treatment options are more prevalent (Hing & McMillan, 2002), perhaps because these remedies align better with the casinos' profit motive.

CSR in the gaming industry: a more robust concept

Ultimately, the greatest challenge for CSR in the gaming industry may align with one of the ongoing debates in the CSR literature: what should be considered corporate social responsibility in this context? Research by Buchanan, Elliott, and Johnson (2009, p. 92) suggests that there may be a disconnect between perception of CSR on the part of gaming operators and other stakeholders.

> In sum, we found that operators of electronic gaming machines (EGMs) surveyed, particularly those in Nevada, considered that they operate within the tenets of corporate social responsibility. Evidence exists however to indicate that EGM operators may not be as socially responsible as they believe. Although the majority of operators satisfy legal/regulatory compliance, we found that very few go beyond this to incorporate voluntary ethical and philanthropic/discretionary principles into their marketing and other business function processes and programs.

Without a clearly explicated definition of CSR in the gaming industry – one that is far more robust than a mere promotion of responsible gambling and funding of treatment for problem gamblers – this kind of misunderstanding will likely perpetuate, frustrating all involved and hampering efforts to produce positive social change.

Government intervention may be needed to ensure that casino operators participate adequately in CSR activities and that the responsibilities are evenly distributed among operators (Siu, 2007). When CSR is not mandated by government regulation, casino operators risk little by abstaining and in fact may keep as revenue those resources that would have been invested in CSR. If none of the casino operators in a particular market become involved in CSR, casinos do not suffer a comparative reputational disadvantage if they also do not participate in CSR. This leads to a sort of reverse prisoner's dilemma[5] situation: As long as all casinos in a market avoid participating in CSR, none are comparatively disadvantaged. However, once any casino engages in CSR, others in the market may have to follow suit or risk suffering damage to their reputations.

As will be explored further in chapter 7, the jurisdictions in which gambling has been legalized as a driver of economic development and tax revenues pose a particular problem to efforts to establish the correct role of CSR in the gaming industry, because approaches to gambling expansion based on economic principles may be too focused on financial gain to account for negative social externalities (Hing, 2012a). However, even in jurisdictions where gambling was initially licensed so that its proceeds can promote social benefit (e.g. Australia), the expansion of casino gaming has led to economic competition and a diversion of focus from the initial intention of social good (Hing, 2012b).

Recommending a broad but inclusive concept of CSR in the casino industry, Hing (2012b) suggests that true social responsibility in gambling needs to include commercial, regulatory, and social considerations: Casinos should make money, yes, but they also need to follow the law and ultimately have a net positive impact on society. Any failure in these three areas threatens the long-term sustainability of the enterprise, and thus casino corporations should be willing to engage in CSR from a position of enlightened self-interest (Eadington, 1996; Kingma, 2004). However, the broad construct of CSR that benefits the company's long-term, overall best interest – incorporating intangible benefits such as reputation – is often incompatible with a business case for CSR that looks narrowly at profit and evaluates CSR in a costs vs. benefits framework.

Notes

1 To be fair, in the United States, the use of gambling taxes as a crucial component of state budgets evolved in the latter part of the 20th century as a result of the federal government's abdication of a number of social welfare obligations. State governments tried to raise taxes, but faced a significant backlash, leaving them to find alternate sources of revenue (Blevins & Jensen, 1998). Into this void, the prospect of tax revenue from casinos must have seemed like an opportunity that was too good to pass up.
2 As defined by Griswold and Nichols (2006, p. 387), based on the work of Putnam (2000), "Social capital is a networking process that translates into an individual's effectiveness in the community and workplace, and binds communities together."
3 This document is available at http://gettoknowgaming.org/sites/default/files/AGA_ G2KG_ExecutiveSummary_natlpoll.pdf.
4 In fact, Dimanche and Speyrer (1996, p. 97) said of gambling, "The recent changes related to this recreational activity that have taken place in the past few years represent without doubt the most significant phenomenon affecting the tourism industry in this country."
5 According to Axelrod (1980, p. 4): "The distinguishing feature of the Prisoner's Dilemma is that in the short run, neither side can benefit itself with a selfish choice enough to make up for the harm done to it from a selfish choice by the other. Thus, if both cooperate, both do fairly well. But if one defects while the other cooperates, the defecting side gets its highest payoff, and the cooperating side is the sucker and gets its lowest payoff. This gives both sides an incentive to defect. The catch is that if both do defect, both do poorly. Therefore the Prisoner's Dilemma embodies the tension between individual rationality (reflected in the incentive of both sides to be selfish) and group rationality (reflected in the higher payoff to both sides for mutual cooperation over mutual defection)."

4   Understanding the global casino industry

This chapter looks at three illustrative case studies in the contemporary global casino industry. These three cases were chosen for very specific reasons: Canada, to showcase its unique gaming industry with strong government involvement; Australia, to show an industry that has evolved and changed with a particular focus on balancing the social costs of problem gambling with using its revenues to generate social benefit; and Macau, because no discussion of the contemporary casino industry would be complete without a thorough analysis of this burgeoning gaming enclave. It is to this "Las Vegas of the Orient" (Yu, 2008, p. 670) that we turn our attention first.

Macau: evolution of a casino giant

Nearly every journal article in the 21st century about Macau (also spelled Macao), a former Portuguese protectorate that now exists as a Special Administrative Region (SAR) of China, and its gaming industry has started with an impressive description of the industry's astronomical growth relative to the city's small size and population. Although the obvious comparison of Macau to Las Vegas is inevitably made, in just a few short years, Macau's casino industry has actually eclipsed Las Vegas's as the largest in the world, in profit though not in size. The history of gaming in Macau is far more complicated than Las Vegas's, and much longer; however, Macau's capitalistic narrative – the triumph of competition over monopoly – perhaps contributes to its popularity.

As mentioned previously, many jurisdictions have looked to gaming to address economic stagnation and generate additional tax revenues for the government. While Macau falls into this group as well, Macau marks a diversion from the traditional narrative because this happened in the mid-19th century, not the recent past. As traditional manufacturing in Macau declined (Hao, 2011), the Portuguese government decided to legalize two popular Macanese games, fantan and papacio, in the 1840s to address government shortfalls (Godinho, 2013). The decision was especially strategic given that gambling was illegal in nearby Hong Kong and mainland China, giving Macau a very favorable economic position as the only location in the region where legalized gambling was available (Eadington & Siu, 2007).

The evolution of Macau's legalized gaming industry, a roughly 150-year history, contains several notable turning points. In order to further regulate the industry (and also to improve its performance as a tax generator), the government licensed the Tai Xing company in 1934 to be the sole gambling provider in Macau (Hao, 2011; Hing, 2005).[1] When the initial monopoly contract expired, the government licensed Macanese businessman Stanley Ho to run the monopoly gaming franchise in Macau (Hao, 2011).

Ho's influence on Macau's casino industry cannot be overestimated. His Macau Tourism & Entertainment Company operated gambling in a monopoly market from 1962 until the government granted licenses to two other concessionaires in 2001 (Ho's company received the third) (Hao, 2011). During his monopolistic reign over the casino industry, Ho's company (STDM, for the Portuguese Sociedade de Turismo e Diversões de Macau) also made non-casino investments in Macau's economy such as hotels and transportation (Hing, 2005; Siu, 2006).

It was Ho's decision in the late 20th century to subcontract the operation of casino VIP rooms to third-party operators that ultimately led to massive changes in Macau's gaming industry. Because government regulation did not speak to the issue, STDM was able to generate substantial additional profit by subcontracting operation of VIP rooms to outside interests (Hing, 2005). Ho did not choose his subcontractors discerningly, however, and organized crime infiltrated the operation of Ho's VIP rooms. Ultimately, the social costs from organized crime's involvement in gambling – loan sharking and revenge attacks were particularly visible problems – led to enough public disapproval that the government stepped in to regulate the industry (Siu, 2006).

As had been previously arranged, the right to rule Macau was given back to China in 1999 (Hao, 2011). After the handover, very little changed in the everyday governance of Macau, which operates on a policy of relative self-governance that is referred to as "One Country, Two Systems" (Sheng & Tsui, 2009a, p. 422; Thompson, 2012, p. 81). Seeing the success of Macau's gaming industry and its potential for growth, China decided in 2001 to move the system from monopoly to oligopoly, permitting two more operators (in addition to Stanley Ho's STDM) to enter the market (Hing, 2005). This move "struck a balance between preserving its history and identity and allowing new entrepreneurs to bring fresh ideas and a wave of new construction to the city" (Schwartz, 2013a, p. 319).

China's decision to open Macau's gaming market – albeit in a limited manner served a number of strategic purposes (Siu, 2006). The rise in gaming-related crime had elevated perceptions about gambling's social costs, and thus it was believed additional regulation could help diminish some of these effects (Hing, 2005). After years of monopoly, the casinos were perhaps not being run as efficiently as possible, due to a lack of competition (Siu, 2006); the change from monopoly to oligopoly has benefited the casino industry notably in terms of economic efficiency (Eadington & Siu, 2007), although its effects on social impact are still unknown.

The timing of Macau's handover to China seemed to align well with a decision to liberalize Macau's gambling regulations and also marked the first time that governmental interests had considered Macau's long-range interests, rather than a short-term extraction of resources (Siu, 2006). Because of its location next to China and its Portuguese government, Macau has long served as a sort of bridge between Eastern and Western cultures (Eadington & Siu, 2007; Yu, 2008), and prior to the handover to China, its Portuguese government worked extensively to ensure that this image was preserved.

> In the years just prior to the handover, the Portuguese state's project became one of convincing both its own residents and observers around the world that Macau's history and culture should be sources of pride to its current residents. Macau was the earliest and most enduring site of respectful, amicable relations between Chinese and Westerners. It was an exemplar of multicultural tolerance and peaceful coexistence. Its residents were not abjected and corrupted by centuries of collaboration with the forces of European imperialism; instead, their experience of Portuguese rule had made them the bearers of a kind of Chineseness that was at once more rooted and more cosmopolitan than any other.
>
> (Clayton, 2013, p. 26)

In the years since the handover, Macau's international success has indeed raised the international profile of the small city – and by extension, the country of China – considerably (Wan, Li, & Kong, 2011; Wan, 2012).

This process of gaming liberalization was unique in Macau because it was a reorganization of an existing industry, as opposed to the establishment of an entirely new industry (McCartney, 2005). This afforded government officials some power in choosing licensing partners and setting ground rules for their participation. The financial opportunity in the Macau market (Simpson, 2012) made it attractive enough to potential operators that they were willing to play by the government's ground rules, such as hiring locals to fill casino jobs and supporting schools and charities (Hing, 2005).

Macau's development as a casino destination has also been affected by its designation in 2005 as a UNESCO World Heritage Site. With over 400 years as a Portuguese colony, Macau has a significant physical history that has value in its preservation (McCartney, 2005; Yu, 2008). As Du Cros (2009, p. 74) explains, "Caring for cultural heritage assets is important because our society has a responsibility toward present and future generations to manage such heritage assets to the best of our ability." Preserving Macau's cultural heritage has proven exceptionally challenging as the city simultaneously attempts to deal with rapid casino expansion and the attendant issues, many of which focus on environmental impact (Yu, 2008). Much like casino development, management of cultural heritage assets in a tourist-driven location also requires a great deal of stakeholder engagement, which is often challenging (Du Cros, 2009).

In order to modernize the Macanese gaming industry, government officials looked to the world's most impressive example of casino gaming: Las Vegas, which was at the end of an unprecedented 20-year building boom (Hing, 2005;

Siu, 2006). Comparisons between the two cities are nearly omnipresent in both academic literature (Balsas, 2013; Loi & Kim, 2010; Luke, 2010; Rose 2013; Simpson, 2012; Wong, 2012) and the popular press (Dreier, 2013; Rapoza, 2013; Riley, 2014). Government officials traveled to Las Vegas to learn from that city's success (Hing, 2005; Sheng & Tsui, 2009b) and licenses to operate casinos in Macau, after a competitive bidding process, were eventually awarded to corporations that had previously opened Las Vegas-style casinos (Simpson, 2012).

Macau's inspiration by Las Vegas led to the introduction of Western-style management practices at Macanese casinos (Wan, 2010) and also prompted government officials to support the development of facilities for meetings and conventions in order to diversify somewhat from Macau's dependence on tourism and gambling (Dioko & So, 2012; Harrill, Uysal, Cardon, Vong, & Dioko, 2011). However, there is some question as to whether these applications are in Macau's best interests: Wan (2010) notes that Western management styles are often incompatible with Macanese and Chinese cultural attitudes, and Loi and Kim (2010) and Gu (2004) suggest that the development of Las Vegas-style convention facilities may actually hurt Macau, rather than benefit it, by diminishing its uniqueness.

Wang and Juslin (2009) also suggest that a Western conception of CSR may not be appropriate in Chinese culture, which is especially important to consider in a discussion of casino CSR in Macau. While principles of morality, fairness, and benevolence can be traced back to China's Confucian heritage, those principles were largely dissociated from business in the latter half of the 20th century. When CSR was introduced in its traditional Western form, it was largely scorned as antibusiness, but Chinese companies – especially those that do business around the world – eventually adopted these principles in their own self-interest.

Instead of a Western approach to CSR, Wang and Juslin (2009, p. 446) propose that a culturally sensitive approach, framing CSR as an attempt to create harmony between business and society, might be more effective.

> Simply, the Chinese harmony approach to CSR means "respecting nature and loving people". Modern enterprises should carry on their business in a harmonious way, and cultivate virtues and to become a "superior enterprise", in this way to contribute to the construction of a harmonious society.

This concept will be considered later in the discussion of CSR in Macau's gaming industry.

In some gaming jurisdictions, casinos are for tourists only, and residents are not allowed to enter (e.g. Korea, see Lee & Back, 2003, 2009). In contrast, Macau relies heavily on the citizens of China for its patronage, especially since gambling remains illegal in mainland China (Hao, 2011; Wan & Pinheiro, 2014). However, the Chinese government does have the right to restrict Chinese nationals' travel to Macau, and in 2008 it did so, based on the drastic rise in problem gambling seen among Chinese mainlanders (Gu, Li, & Tam, 2013). As mentioned in chapter 3, casinos are at their most productive for a community when they export social costs (i.e. are patronized largely by tourists); this was certainly true for Macau in the early days of its casino industry, as Macau's monopoly on gaming in China kept "tourist gaming money incoming, casino tax burdens outgoing, and domestic social welfare intact" (Gu & Tam, 2011, p. 603).

Macau's casinos largely draw patrons from outside of the city; there are still, however, negative impacts from the large casino industry. The city's size is a tremendous limitation; Macau is so small that it could "fit inside the [US capital city] District of Columbia six times over, with room to spare" (Rose, 2013, p. 397). The negative side effects of Macau's casino industry largely fall into three categories: natural resources, human resources, and problem gambling.

Already a city with a high population density, Macau's growing pains during the era of casino expansion have been significant (McCartney, 2005). Space-related concerns, such as traffic congestion, have been an inevitable byproduct of casino development (Wan, Li, & Kong, 2011; McCartney, 2005). Gaming interests have used their considerable resources to purchase existing land in Macau, and efforts to increase the amount of available land by reclaiming an area called the Cotai Strip have resulted not in more housing and retail options for residents, but in more casinos and hotels for tourists (Wan & Pinheiro, 2014). Macau imports 95% of its water from mainland China, and increased water use by hotels, casinos, and tourists has tested this resource supply, without much involvement from the casino industry in reducing water use[2] (Li & Chen, 2014).

Macau provides a classic example of the economic phenomenon known as "Dutch disease," when the overwhelming strength of a particular industry allows that industry to attract the most capable workers in a labor market, putting other industries at a disadvantage and threatening their continued existence (Gu, Li, & Tam, 2013; Sheng & Tsui, 2009a, 2009b). Lured by attractive casino jobs, workers might leave their jobs at other companies, and students may even drop out of school (Hao, 2011). Thus the ripple effects of the Macau casinos' success is not all positive, as small businesses struggle to recruit qualified workers and the overall level of education drops.

Macau's casinos rely heavily on imported labor because the population of Macau has not been large enough to supply the demand for skilled and semi-skilled workers (Loi & Kim, 2010; Sheng & Tsui, 2009a, 2009b; Zheng & Hung, 2012). When the industry faced cutbacks in the wake of the 2008 global recession, many Macanese employees had their hours and pay cut or were made redundant entirely, while imported laborers in low-skilled jobs were retained (Loi & Kim, 2010). This caused many of Macau's residents to doubt the social responsibility of these corporations (Vong, 2010).

The jobs created by Macau's growing casino industry have benefited some of Macau's residents, but not all; those in the working classes may find that the casinos dismiss them as lacking the necessary skills for casino jobs (Zheng & Hung, 2012). Those who have found work in Macau's casinos have not necessarily been the beneficiaries of the casino industry's boom. Salaries have increased, but not by very much (Sheng & Tsui, 2009a), and casino workers face challenges finding affordable housing in an economy with an increased cost of living (Zheng & Hung, 2012).

As the casino industry in Macau has grown rapidly, the specter of problem gambling has naturally loomed over the city (Wan, Li, & Kong, 2011). Because most of the Macau casinos' patrons came from mainland China, the city itself saw relatively few social impacts in the early days of the casino boom (Gu, Li, & Tam, 2013). Eventually, residents began to perceive negative social impacts from problem gambling including excessive borrowing of money for gambling and inter-family arguments about gambling (Smith et al., 2011).

Because tourism and gaming make up what is unquestionably the largest industry sector in Macau (Gu, Li, & Tam, 2013), this industry is often given preferential treatment in government legislative decisions, sometimes at the expense of residents (Wan & Li, 2013). This dominance of the casino industry has significant effects on both the negative externalities of the industry and on the way that the industry should consider approaching CSR. (More on the nuances of CSR in a dominant industry can be found in chapter 2; see also Kagan, Gunningham, & Thornton, 2003.)

Because the casino industry in Macau is so economically beneficial to the community, residents may not feel like they can complain about its negative externalities (Smith et al., 2011; see also Rowley & Berman, 2000). But research by Vong (2010) among teachers and students in Macau found that there was very little belief among these populations that casino corporations were participating in the community at an appropriate level. This suggests that Macau's residents may disapprove of the current approach to CSR being taken by casino corporations that operate in the city, but feel unable to properly address the topic in a productive and public manner.

A responsible gaming approach by Macau's casinos, and an overall broad conception of corporate social responsibility, could address a number of these negative impacts by considering the effects on various stakeholders (e.g. customers, suppliers, the government, the community, the environment) and taking steps to make sure that employees are treated fairly and customers are proactively warned about the potential for problem gambling (Hao, 2011; Wan, Li, & Kong, 2011). In keeping with the principles and practices of sustainable tourism, as discussed in chapter 3, true corporate social responsibility in gaming in Macau would need to pay attention to the environmental impacts of gaming and adjust industry practices to promote environmental sustainability.

Government-run gaming in Canada

According to the country's criminal code, gambling in Canada is still technically illegal and has been so since the latter part of the 19th century (Campbell & Smith, 2003). However, through passing a series of exceptions allowing provincial governments to "conduct and manage" a variety of gambling operations, Canada's government has given its 10 provinces the right to engage in gambling for public benefit – and to an ever-increasing degree, the provinces have taken advantage of these opportunities (Patrick, 2000, p. 118). Perhaps as a result of this regulatory uniquity, the government is involved more directly in gaming in Canada – which takes a variety of forms including standard casinos, video lottery terminals (VLTs) in bars and lounges, racinos (racetracks with casino elements), and lotteries – than in perhaps any other jurisdiction, making this an important case study. What happens to CSR in the gaming industry when the corporations are largely secondary and social responsibility is addressed by the government instead?

In a series of amendments to the criminal code from 1969, Canada has increasingly widened the ability of provincial governments to operate gambling enterprises, ostensibly for public benefit (Belanger & Williams, 2012). In a watershed moment, the Canadian government authorized the use of electronic gaming machines (EGMs) in 1985, placing the authority for regulating and operating gambling with the provincial governments (Henriksson, 2001). Due to the immediate financial success of these machines, they expanded rapidly across most of Canada's provinces (Smith & Campbell, 2007).

The focus on Canada's gaming industry as a force to generate public revenues (for both provincial governments and charitable organizations) emerges as a unique characteristic of the Canadian gaming system and a motivating rhetorical structure for the discussions of gaming in Canada (McMillan, 1996). Canada evoked arguments for legalizing gambling that were at some level similar to other countries – it would reduce illegal gambling, and therefore crime (Campbell & Smith, 2003; Smith et al., 2011); it would benefit the tourism industry; it would prevent gambling revenues from "leaking" out to other countries (Smith & Campbell, 2007) – but it relied heavily on the proposed use of gambling revenue for public good in making its case for support of legal gambling (Campbell & Smith, 1998, 2003; Smith et al., 2011). In this way, "the link between legal gambling and worthy causes turned out to be an effective strategy for helping to transform gambling from a vice into a respectable pastime" (Smith & Campbell, 2007, p. 96).

In a mid-1990s campaign to support the continued use of video lottery terminals (VLTs), the rhetoric around gaming in Canada displayed further elaboration of the philosophical grounding of its opponents and proponents. Those who supported the continued use of the gambling machines – often the government, the operators of establishments where VLTs were placed (who received a 15% cut of the profits), and those who feared removing VLTs would create higher taxes – told a story of individual freedoms and the government's financial limitations: Gamblers should be given the freedom to decide whether or not they play VLTs, they argued, and without the revenue generated by the terminals, higher taxes and program cuts would be imminent (Smith & Campbell, 2007).

Opponents of VLTs (who were many) argued that the social costs of gambling, though difficult to formally measure, had become significant during gambling's rapid expansion in Canada (Smith & Campbell, 2007). Opposition to gambling in Canada, mostly based on moral/religious grounds, has been visible since the early 20th century (Campbell & Smith, 2003). Perceiving strong negative externalities from the proliferation of VLTs, the opposition remobilized in the 1990s, making some progress in halting the spread of the machines and making the government fund programs in responsible gambling (Campbell & Smith, 2003).

Although the measure to eliminate VLTs was defeated and the machines remained, the emergence of an opposition to the government's use of gaming to generate public revenue was a significant moment in Canada's gaming history (Campbell, 1994; Campbell & Smith, 1998). Since then, the history of gaming in Canada has been marked by continued citizen opposition to the use of gambling to generate revenue for provincial governments (Henriksson, 2001). This opposition often centers on social costs and negative externalities, but also complains that the public is not usually consulted on gambling expansion, and even when residents oppose gaming, the public is often overruled by provincial governments seeking gambling revenue (Campbell & Smith, 2003).

Responding to public outcry about gambling's negative externalities, provincial governments began to establish (albeit slowly) programs to treat problem gamblers (Campbell & Smith, 1998, 2003; Korn, 2000). As in many other gaming jurisdictions, problem gambling in Canada has been framed as a public health issue, with a medical perspective on gambling addiction (Campbell & Smith, 2003; Korn, 2000). This rhetoric has pervaded both treatment and prevention efforts, all of which have been led by the provincial governments (Campbell & Smith, 2003). As was discussed in chapter 3, however, this approach to gambling addiction tends to stigmatize and blame the individual (i.e. problem gambling is an individual failing) while uncritically ignoring the role of the gambling provider – here, the Canadian provincial governments – in the problem (Skolnik, 2011).

Canada's governance of the gambling industry takes on a new complexity when one factors in the many recognized First Nations tribes, primarily in Alberta, that have tried to take advantage of gambling's proclivity to generate revenue. However, Alberta's provincial government (the one to which the request was made) denied the First Nations' petitions to directly conduct their own casinos for the purpose of revenue generation and increasing jobs for First Nations members. Instead, the provincial government required the First Nations tribes to apply as charities under the previously established scheme (Belanger & Williams, 2011).

As First Nations casinos opened, some irregularities persisted. First Nations casinos were required to pay a flat 30% of revenues to the province, in exchange for being allowed to operate the casino enterprise (Belanger & Williams, 2012). Rather than providing revenue solely for the First Nations tribes, these casinos also generate revenue for the Alberta provincial government. The new casinos have brought some benefits to the First Nations tribes, such as lowered debt and raised employment (Campbell & Smith, 1998). However, the neocolonial manner in which these casinos were allowed to come into existence further alienated the First Nations from the mainstream Canadian economy (Belanger & Williams, 2011) and subjugated them, in effect, to the provincial government, putting off tribal hopes of increased self-governance (Campbell & Smith, 1998).

The Canadian government's unique position as both provider of gambling services and protector of citizens' wellbeing makes its role in the gaming industry especially complicated.

One constraint facing responsible gaming coalitions arises from the fact that in Canada, agencies mandated to deliver problem gambling treatment and prevention programs are often affiliated with government, and in some cases, funded directly from gambling revenues. If not in reality, at least in public perception, this presents a potential conflict of interest.

(Campbell & Smith, 2003, p. 141)

This conflict of interest (which is arguably very real; see Gu, Li, & Tam, 2013; Henriksson, 2001; Williams & Wood, 2004) between the government's social obligations and its desire to generate revenue with gambling facilities is a significant one, especially since most customers in Canadian casinos are residents, not tourists (MacDonald, McMullan, & Perrier, 2004).

An example of how the government's vested interest in casino gaming can affect its policy can be found in the province of Ontario, where a large casino operated by Caesars Entertainment was licensed to operate just across the border from the US city of Detroit. Canada has chosen not to tax gambling winnings, in part to improve its competitiveness again the similar "product" of gaming in other jurisdictions, such as the United States, that do tax winners' windfalls. Although the province could clearly raise additional revenues for public services by taxing casino winnings – such a procedure is very profitable for US state governments – it opposes efforts to do so in order to protect the viability of its gaming "product," even though the citizens of Ontario may need to make up the disparity in revenue (e.g. through taxes) or may have less access to necessary services (Campbell & Smith, 1998).

This casino, Caesars Windsor Hotel and Casino, also provides a good example of the provincial government's movement toward engaging private enterprise in the production of state-sponsored gambling. In 1993, the Ontario government chose Caesars Entertainment (then Caesars World, Inc.) to build a state-run casino ("Caesars, Circus Circus and Hilton in casino deal," 1993). Private companies have successfully engaged with public gambling in Canada by operating and managing gambling endeavors, especially in Western provinces where charitable and/or temporary gambling is popular (Campbell & Smith, 1998). Some provinces have created so-called Crown Corporations, businesses designed to serve the revenue generation interests of the provincial government, to run their casinos (Campbell & Smith, 1998; Smith & Campbell, 2007). The affiliation of government-run gambling with private, corporate interests has undoubtedly brought a more profit-driven attitude into the Canadian gaming industry (Smith & Campbell, 2007).

Some theoretical concerns arise in situations where governments function in the role of corporations, as is arguably the case in Canada's gaming industry. Acting "out of character" in this way "creates a tension between two primary government gambling policy objectives: revenue generation and social responsibility. The tensions are manifold: If citizen welfare concerns come first, revenues may be sacrificed; conversely, if financial exigency prevails, community well-being could well be jeopardized" (Smith & Campbell, 2007, p. 90). The consequences of governments acting like corporations can be dire; according to Smith and Campbell (2007), they can include policies that focus on profits, not people; negative externalities felt by people (citizens) who never agreed to legalize gambling in the first place; and incomplete and oversimplified cost–benefit analyses which lead to errant decisions on whether gaming brings value to a community.

Succinctly, "the dilemma facing provincial governments is that EGMs provide the most lucrative source of gambling revenue – but also the most contentious" (Smith & Campbell, 2007, p. 89). As VLTs proliferated, Canadian residents across the provinces began to express their opposition to such widespread gambling and the effects were felt in local government and media; in Alberta alone, 41 referenda were called to determine the future of VLTs (Smith & Campbell, 2007). Having become somewhat dependent[3] on gaming revenues, provincial governments felt they had no other way to replace those revenues should they scale back or eliminate gambling completely (Henriksson, 2001; Patrick, 2000). They retrenched with classic addiction symptoms of denial and disavowal of blame (Smith & Campbell, 2007).

Feeling their livelihoods threatened, these governments then hired professionals to promote their pro-gaming mantras to the public: addiction is not really a problem, gaming is beneficial to social causes, people will just go elsewhere to gamble if it's outlawed here, we need the revenue (Smith & Campbell, 2007). The role of public relations in the Canadian gambling industry is especially troubling and fraught with potential for unethical behavior (see Harris, 2005). At the very best, the messaging on legalized gambling is likely being controlled by governments, which stand to make the most from a pro-gambling sentiment, and would thus see it as beneficial to fund such a campaign. At the worst, these messages may be deceptive, as the government desperately struggles to preserve its gaming revenue and private interests seek to maintain the profitable position they have carved out.

It is difficult to define a prescription for corporate social responsibility in Canada's gaming industry because, by and large, the drivers of casino expansion in this jurisdiction have been Canada's provincial governments (Henriksson, 2001). However, there does seem to be a clear path forward for Canada's gaming industry if a socially responsible approach is truly desired. Smith and Campbell (2007, p. 99) summarize that path thusly:

> Although it may perhaps represent an oversimplification of the healing process, some immediate steps that might help include admitting that EGMs may be more dangerous than other gambling formats and adopting more rigorous EGM harm minimization strategies. This means committing to an organizational priority shift whereby Canadian provincial gambling operations are blatantly transparent and social responsibility and community well-being become the paramount objectives of all Canadian gambling policy.

There is also a great need for the type of community engagement and consultation about gambling in the provinces, and additional research[4] about gaming's impacts in the community, in order to make sure that decisions are made with Canada's residents – not its revenues – in mind.

The spread and containment of gambling in Australia

While it seems likely that some sort of gambling has been part of most world cultures, gaming holds a special place in the history and culture of Australia (Reith, 2003). The story of the Australian gaming industry is one of balance, or the attempt at balance: balancing an obvious cultural inclination toward gambling among the Australian people with a desire to ensure that this gambling did not cause social harm while channeling gaming revenues to appropriate recipients (Nisbet, 2005). Technology in the form of electronic gaming machines – known to Australians as poker machines, or "pokies" (Smith & Campbell, 2007; Valenzuela & Fisher, 2012) – has allowed this kind of gambling to make its way into Australian communities via the location of these machines in Australian social clubs (Eadington, 2003).

Electronic gambling in Australia spread rapidly, as was the case in Canada (Forrest, 2013; Marshall, 2005), and the Australian case stands out for the way that problem gambling as a result of these machines was identified and explored by an active community of gaming researchers (Doran & Young, 2010; Hing, 2002, 2012a, 2012b; Livingstone & Woolley, 2007; Marshall, 2005; Nisbet, 2005; Pickernell, Keast, & Brown, 2010; Pickernell, Brown, Keast, & Yousefpour, 2009; Scull & Woolcock, 2005; Storer, Abbott, & Stubbs, 2009). The Australian government struggled to provide the treatment services necessary for those who developed gambling problems as a result of access to the "pokies," negotiating a complicated landmine of cultural issues that arose from Australia's diverse population (Doran & Young, 2010; Scull & Woolcock, 2005; Young, Barnes, Stevens, Paterson, & Morris, 2007).

But, much like in other jurisdictions, the Australian government saw great potential in gambling, not only to generate tax revenue (as was previously mentioned, this is one of the primary reasons for gaming legalization and expansion) but also to raise funds for social programs and charitable organizations that might not otherwise be funded (Grant, 1994; Hing, 2012a; Pickernell, Keast, & Brown, 2010; Pickernell, Keast, Brown, Yousefpour, & Miller, 2013). As a result, the placement of electronic gaming machines (EGMs) in Australia's social clubs created a powerful lobby that became invested in protecting the legality of gambling in Australia (Hing, 2012a; Hing & McMillan, 2002).

The use of EGMs to generate revenues for social clubs is a feature of Australia's gaming industry that makes this an especially complicated policy decision (Pickernell, Keast, & Brown, 2010). The government benefits to the tune of A$300 million from EGMs in social clubs in New South Wales alone, and these clubs direct 50% of their own revenue to fund a variety of social projects (Hing, 2012a). Any decision to restrict gambling or reduce the number of EGMs would necessarily be controversial because it would decrease the amount of funding for these social causes.

In order to demonstrate their social utility, social clubs in the state of Victoria submit a Community Benefit Statement (CBS) to demonstrate that at least 8.33% of their revenue from gaming is redistributed to meet community needs. This includes making donations to community charities, providing employment to community members, and sponsoring local sports teams (Pickernell, Keast, & Brown, 2010). Ironically, it is these social donations and sponsorships that allow the clubs to market their gambling product as a responsible venture, since a portion of profits from the EGM machines are reinvested in the community (Harris, 2005; Hing, 2012a; Pickernell, Keast, & Brown, 2010).

Club managers in Australia revealed in research by Pickernell, Keast, and Brown (2010) that they believe themselves to be contributing significantly to their communities, not only by funding community causes but also by providing an outlet for building social connectivity. This suggests that gaming operators in Australia may also have a misperception about their level of social responsibility, or at least a view of the term that focuses a little too narrowly on the benefits they are providing without a consideration of the attendant costs.

However, small social clubs – usually operated on a membership model – often do focus on the interests of their communities, not merely because it gives them some assistance in marketing their gambling product. Larger casinos and non-membership clubs, however, may not be as focused on community needs (Pickernell, Keast, & Brown, 2010). Additionally, competition between social clubs for patrons has caused these clubs to stray from the initial social benefit of EGM machines and has led to a prioritization of economic competition among social clubs instead (Hing, 2012a; Hing & McMillan, 2002).

An already complex situation of government-run gaming became more complicated when private industry began to enter the Australia gaming industry. In 1994, the state of Victoria privatized its Totaliser Agency Board, the entity in charge of operating the state's gaming interests (Hoye, 2005). The ensuing private company has become immensely profitable to shareholders and has streamlined the operations of the gaming enterprise (Hoye, 2005), but it has also brought more of a profit focus to gaming in Victoria, taking focus from the social benefit that had previously motivated Australia's gaming enterprises (Hing, 2002).

Proponents of legalized gaming in Australia have taken what Marshall (2005, p. 67) calls a "consumer sovereignty" approach, which "implies that providers of gambling facilities are passive agents in the supply chain, responding only to increased consumer demand." Much like the medicalization of problem gaming, which locates the "problem" in the individual gambler, this rhetoric absolves gaming operators (primarily social clubs) and the governments that permit their functioning (and expansion) from any responsibility for social costs associated with gambling. This approach ignores structural factors, including the findings by many researchers that EGMs are statistically more likely to be found in low socioeconomic areas, resulting in a higher level of gambling in those areas and a further regressivity in deriving public funds from gaming (Doran & Young, 2010; Harris, 2005; Livingstone, 2001) and a higher prevalence of problem gambling in these low-income communities (Storer, Abbott, & Stubbs, 2009).

But if gamblers are sovereign consumers, then as consumers they must also be protected, by preventative measures such as education and awareness, in-play options to restrict or slow down gambling on EGMs, and treatment options for those who do develop gambling problems (Nisbet, 2005). Operators are less likely to implement options, especially for in-play modifications, that will result in lowered gambling wagers and thus lowered revenues (Valenzuela & Fisher, 2012).

Because gaming operators do not often take these measures, it appears that these operators have abandoned their responsibilities (Livingstone & Woolley, 2007).

In addition, due to the immense revenues generated for the government by these gambling machines, it is often difficult for the government to make clear-headed decisions about gaming regulation to ensure that consumer protection is in place (Livingstone & Woolley, 2007). This leads to what Livingstone and Woolley (2007, p. 362) call a "discourse of business as usual," where government regulation allows for the unfettered spread of gaming into communities. In this discourse, individuals who develop gaming problems are stigmatized and isolated for treatment of an individual failing without acknowledging the role that the industry might have played in creating their dependence.

Because the government played a major role in facilitating gaming in Australia, it was willing to step in and provide some treatment services and problem gaming prevention programs, although some would argue whether its efforts were sufficient (Hing, 2002; Livingstone & Woolley, 2007). Hing (2002, pp. 104–105) argues the need for a wider conception of social responsibility in the Australian casino industry:

> Redefining problem gambling to focus on harm and to recognise that its impacts extend beyond individual gamblers has helped propel problem gambling into the public arena as an issue of social concern. It invites further research into the social impacts of gambling and strategies that might minimise harm and protect consumers of gambling products, rather than ways to cure pathological gambling behaviour, as previous medical and addiction models have done (AIGR 1997:17). *As such, this redefinition extends the onus of responsibility to address problem gambling from individual gamblers, to gambling operators and governments who largely control the context in which legalised gambling is operated, managed and marketed*, although it is acknowledged that individual gamblers must ultimately assume responsibility for making personal changes.
>
> (Emphasis added)

Without addressing a community's concerns about gaming and meeting the expectations of all stakeholders for responsible behavior, gaming interests fall short of meeting their social responsibility threshold (Breen, Buultzens, & Hing, 2012). Thus is it increasingly important that the Australian government step in to regulate this behavior and prevent harm to its citizens – even though such an action may cause a decline in gambling revenues (Livingstone & Woolley, 2007).

Postscript: gambling's fall from grace in Atlantic City, New Jersey

The most notable thing about the casino industry in Atlantic City, New Jersey, USA is that it failed. When New Jersey legalized gambling in 1978, hopes were high for the seaside resort on the Jersey Shore: Given the city's proximity to population centers in the Northeast US such as Philadelphia and New York, leaders of the legalization effort believed that Atlantic City could follow in Las Vegas's footsteps and develop a gaming industry that could provide much-needed economic development (Braunlich, 1996).

But in the summer of 2014, two of Atlantic City's casinos were preparing to close, and a third was entering bankruptcy for the second time (Mikle & Diamond, 2014). City leaders began talking about diversification and tourism development strategies that eschewed gambling for a more family-friendly approach. The Atlantic City experiment, it seemed, was over. And it had not ended well, with estimates that the city was $2 billion in debt from years of trying to make casino gaming work in Atlantic City (Mikle & Diamond, 2014).

In hindsight, Atlantic City's 40-year experiment with gaming has taken the city to dramatic heights, but also plunged it to a low that will be hard to recover from. New Jersey voters chose to legalize gambling in Atlantic City only (a previous measure to legalize gaming in the entire state had failed), perhaps in hopes of reviving the faded seaside resort, which had enjoyed great success in the early 20th century (Stansfield, 2006).

It is difficult to know why Atlantic City's experiment with casino gaming failed. Proponents of a free-market approach to the casino industry frequently criticized New Jersey's rigorous gaming industry regulations (Eadington, 2005): as an example, the state revoked the MGM Resorts corporation's license to operate casinos in New Jersey when it found that MGM had partnered with Macau's Pansy Ho on a project in Macau, citing Ho's ties to organized crime (Rose, 2013). Competition from other jurisdictions that legalized gambling was a factor, of course. Atlantic City may have even become too focused on making money with its casinos and lost sight of the need to continue promoting the destination itself (Hampson, 2014) – something that Las Vegas has always done, and done well (Strauss & Maxian, 2014).

In 2006, Stansfield predicted a rosy future of development for Atlantic City:

> The casino industry has big plans for Atlantic City. Huge new "megaresorts" are planned for vacant land on the bayside. These future mammoth hotels will out-glitz the city's existing casinos – no small challenge there. They will feature "total resort environments", more family-oriented, with amusement rides, video games, shopping areas, lavish showrooms, continuous entertainment and, of course, a slot machine or two.
>
> (Stansfield, 2006, p. 304)

So what happened in eight years? The global recession in 2008 dealt a crippling blow to the growth of the casino industry as potential gamblers cut back on discretionary spending and access to credit to fund expansion projects dried up (Wells, 2009b). At the same time, gambling was legalized in neighboring states such as Pennsylvania, West Virginia, and Maryland. In spite of opening glitzy, high-profile casinos Borgata (in 2003) and Revel (in 2012), Atlantic City struggled to stay relevant in the casino landscape of the United States.

Ultimately, however, it failed.

Notes

1 As a point of reference, Schwartz (2013a) notes that Macau's establishment of a monopoly for casinos was nearly contemporaneous with Nevada's decision to legalize "wide-open" gaming as a means of economic development, primarily in Las Vegas and Reno, although the two are unrelated.

2 Water use in this context involves not only direct use of water for operating hotel/casino facilities (such as would be reflected in conventional statistics about water usage), but also the water that goes into products used in the industry (e.g. producing plastic bottles of water). It also includes water that is used by employees, some of whom come to live in Macau to work in casino jobs, thereby increasing the city's overall water usage as well.

3 Some gaming critics like to claim that governments are "addicted" to gambling revenues (Buchanan & Johnson, 2007; Skolnik, 2011), in order to establish a pretty symmetry with the notion of individual gambling addiction and further emphasize the negative externalities of gambling when it comes to addiction. However, Campbell and Smith (2007, p. 97) suggest that while "it is a misnomer to label governments 'gambling addicts,' it is accurate to say that EGM-friendly governments have a gambling revenue dependency," adding that "although less debilitating than an addiction, a dependency may still indicate misaligned governance."

4 The repetition of the same three or four names in this section's citations speak to the fact that the Canadian gaming industry is woefully under-researched.

5 Casino city in the desert

History and context of Las Vegas, Nevada

The following two chapters dive deeply into the casino industry in Las Vegas, Nevada in order to locate this research in a particular social and economic context. The ability to ground research in a physical, historical, and economic location is a particular characteristic of the case study approach (Stake, 2005; Yin, 1998), which here will allow for contextualized understanding of not only the casino corporations but also the environment in which they operate.

Single-case studies often raise concerns about generalizability; however, the goal in this situation is not to attempt to generalize about CSR in all casino industries, but to draw conclusions about this situation that may be applicable to others with similar characteristics (Stake, 2005; Yin, 1998). This is what Stake (2005, p. 447,) refers to as an *intrinsic case study*, the research on which "is not undertaken primarily because the case represents other cases . . . but because, in all its particularity *and* ordinariness, this case is of interest" (emphasis original). It is unlikely that any other city in the United States – or, for that matter, any other city in the world – can claim the particular combination of historical background, dominance of a single industry in its economy, and diverse and dynamic population that is found in modern-day Las Vegas. It is precisely this quality that makes the topic of corporate social responsibility in the Las Vegas casino industry intrinsically interesting.

Las Vegas has emerged as a cultural icon, a symbol of greed and excess loved by some and hated by many, but known by almost everyone. But beyond its status as "America's adult playground," Las Vegas is a community much like any other: It has underfunded schools, a significant population in need of social services, and an arts community that constantly struggles to stay afloat. In 2014, Las Vegas has recovered somewhat from the global recession, but the city still faces the challenge of a flagging economy and attempts to reinvent itself as a more sustainable economy. As its community groups scramble to adapt to a reordered world (Urevich, 2008), they are doing so with the help of an unlikely ally: the casino corporations whose business operations seem to many to be the very opposite of socially responsible.

Established in 1905, the city of Las Vegas was an unremarkable town centered around a small train depot in the middle of an unrelenting desert. One hundred years later, Las Vegas is a controversial icon of US success and excess. More importantly, though, Las Vegas has grown into a community that as of 2014 is home to over 2 million people (Taylor, 2014).

Las Vegas: history of a gambling town

Originally a small Mormon settlement, and later an equally small railroad town, Las Vegas began to grow as workers on the Boulder Dam (later the Hoover Dam, built from 1931 to 1935) came to its friendly environs to escape the strict regulations of the workers' residence town, Boulder City. Gambling was legalized in Nevada by the state legislature in 1931, but both gambling and drinking were strictly forbidden in Boulder City. Dam workers would frequently pick up their paychecks and head straight for Las Vegas, where both vices were legal (Land & Land, 1999). Almost since the town's inception, Las Vegas's economy has been based on gambling and associated with vice.

The city of Las Vegas has long needed the assistance of nonprofits to provide social services for its residents. A 1931 wire-service article, written just before construction began on Boulder Dam, described problems with homelessness that ensued when unemployed laborers showed up in the city hoping to find work on the dam. The article was accompanied by a picture of Salvation Army workers providing food for three homeless men who had come to Las Vegas in hopes of finding employment (NEA wire service, 1931).

Las Vegas eventually experienced its long-awaited boom once dam construction got underway in late 1931, but this was just the beginning of a long cycle of boom and bust that would mark Las Vegas's economy. When the steady stream of gamblers from the dam project dried up after the structure was completed in 1935, many thought the town of Las Vegas would dry up as well. But several far-sighted entrepreneurs saw in Las Vegas a potential tourist destination for those drawn by the lure of legalized gambling.

Some of the early hoteliers and casino owners who built on the Strip were legitimate businessmen, often from the West Coast, but many of them came from places as far away as Chicago, Cleveland, and New York and had ties to those cities' largest Mafia families. As the building boom began and hotel-casinos began springing up along Highway 97, later to be known as the Las Vegas Strip, city residents welcomed the prosperity and turned a blind eye to the Mafia connections of the casinos' owners (Ferrari & Ives, 2005).

Many of these Mob-connected casino owners were colorful, iconic characters whose presence dominated the early history of the town. In the 1940s and 1950s, they were not unwelcome; in fact, many believed that the unofficial "system" of mob justice helped discourage crime and petty theft in the town (Land & Land, 1999). Moreover, these mobsters were good for business and for the development of Las Vegas into a viable city rather than a railroad-stop town. By building increasingly large hotel-casinos on previously undeveloped land, they brought jobs and tax revenue into the local economy (Rothman, 2002). Many Las Vegans welcomed even the dubious notoriety these mobsters' presence and prominence in the local economy brought to the town (Land & Land, 1999).

Legendary mobster Benjamin Siegel (more commonly known, and celebrated in film and folklore, as "Bugsy") was the first notable organized crime figure to come to Las Vegas, opening the Flamingo hotel-casino in the late 1940s. However, a more typical Las Vegas mobster/casino owner arrived on the scene in 1950 when Cleveland's Moe Dalitz provided capital and financing for the completion and opening of Wilbur Clark's Desert Inn (Gottdiener, Collins, & Dickens, 1999). Over his years as a Las Vegas fixture, Dalitz became a leading community figure, building shopping centers, a hospital, and a country club – additions that helped Las Vegas gain legitimacy and credibility as a city (Smith, 2004).

Dalitz was a noted philanthropist, and although his ties to organized crime were not in doubt, he was considered a community leader (Rothman, 2002). He was so generous in donating to local charities that decades later discussions about philanthropy in Las Vegas were still invoking the name of Moe Dalitz and holding him up as a shining example of a community patron (Andersen, 1994; Gorman, 2001). Today, a display (titled "Mr. Las Vegas") at the National Museum of Organized Crime and Law Enforcement (popularly known as the "Mob Museum") refers to Dalitz in glowing terms:

> Later in life Moe Dalitz was honored for his philanthropy and contributions to the growth of Las Vegas.
> UNLV [University of Nevada at Las Vegas] called him the "Grand Patron of the Arts" for his generosity. The mayor gave him the Trendsetter aware for making Las Vegas the home of lavish, spectacular show, and city leaders named him "Mr. Las Vegas." Joan Rivers presented him with the Torch of Liberty from the Anti-Defamation League. Others referred to him as "the Godfather of Las Vegas."
>
> (National Museum of Organized Crime and
> Law Enforcement, 2013)

On his 80th birthday, Moe Dalitz was presented with the ceremonial key to the city. Regardless of the philanthropic accolades he received, however, Moe Dalitz is rarely mentioned in Las Vegas history without reference to his criminal past and the suspicions about possible continued connections to organized crime during his years as a civic leader in Las Vegas (Schwartz, 2012; Smith, 1999).

Many of Dalitz's contemporaries became active members of the community, much as Dalitz had (Ives, 2005). This was no mere coincidence. In their pre-Vegas lives, men like Moe Dalitz had been considered criminals and were outcasts in their communities, living on the wrong side of the law. In Las Vegas, they were legitimate businessmen running legal gambling operations. Moving to Las Vegas gave Dalitz and his contemporaries the opportunity to leave their criminal lives behind, and many aspired to do so (Ferrari & Ives, 2005).

Active participation in the community was one step in these early casino owners' transformation from underworld crime bosses to legitimate businessmen. Early philanthropy in Las Vegas was fueled by these mobsters' desire for legitimacy, but it was funded by socially questionable gambling profits. As Las Vegas's reputation grew and spread beyond the borders of Nevada, the city became known for ties to organized crime and not strong civic values (Rothman, 2002). In the 1950s, Senator Estes Kefauver targeted Las Vegas's casino industry with his public hearings on organized crime; ultimately, though, Kefauver's efforts may have served more as a publicity stunt than an actual attempt to eliminate organized crime from the casino industry (Bernhard, Green, & Lucas, 2008).

As officials looked to clean up their city's image in the wake of the Kefauver hearings, the mobster/casino owners like Dalitz eventually wore out their welcome in the city. In their place rose Las Vegas's next larger-than-life figure – reclusive billionaire Howard Hughes, who purchased the Desert Inn from Dalitz in 1967. Although a respectable businessman like Hughes seemed to be an answer to city leaders' prayers, by that point he was already a bit of an oddball.

However unconventional Hughes's personal and business practices might have been, though, this era in casino ownership provided a transition to later phases of corporatization and conglomeration. Hughes's impact on Las Vegas was swift and significant. After he purchased the Desert Inn, he continued to purchase surrounding casino properties, making it clear that he intended to stay in Las Vegas for an extended time. Local leaders must have been delighted at Hughes's grandiose vision for Southern Nevada:

> Less than a year after he set up quarters in the Desert Inn, Hughes issued a statement to Southern Nevadans. He was going to improve the face of the Silver State. He promised to help diversify the economy by creating industry of the sort that had made him rich and famous.
>
> Hughes painted a future in which Las Vegas would become a clean, bright, shining city in the sun. "We can make a really super environment: no smog, no contamination, efficient local government, where the taxpayers pay as little as possible and get something for their money," Hughes wrote in a memo.
>
> (Smith, 2004, pp. 80–81)

Due in part to Hughes's declining health and increasing eccentricities, his vision for Las Vegas was never realized. In contrast to Dalitz and the mob-connected owners who preceded him, Hughes was not generous with philanthropy – in fact, no record exists that he contributed to local charities during his four years as Las Vegas's most prominent resident. Perhaps because of his mental state (and his immense wealth), Hughes was unconcerned with his image in the community. His money allowed him to wield great power, and he never encountered obstacles with local or state governments.

When Hughes departed Las Vegas in 1970, the city once again suffered from a void of forward-thinking leadership. Into the void of power created by the absence of Hughes's overwhelming influence came a new breed of casino owners: entrepreneurial businessmen looking to cash in on Las Vegas's ability to draw tourists willing to part with their money (Smith, 2004). Although brief, Hughes's involvement in the evolution of the Las Vegas casino industry noted a shift in the amount of capital that developers were able to access for building improvement and expansion, construction of new casinos, and purchase of existing casinos. This change foreshadowed the coming trend of casino ownership by corporate interests, which were able to access far more capital than their predecessors from organized crime.

The 1970s also saw the beginnings of the corporatization of the gaming industry in Las Vegas. Hilton Hotel owners Barron and Conrad Hilton successfully lobbied the Nevada Gaming Commission to change its rules on casino ownership, paving the way for corporations with multiple stockholders to acquire gaming licenses without requiring background checks for every investor (Ferrari & Ives, 2005). Many hotel chains, such as Holiday Inn and Ramada Inns, tried their hands at the Las Vegas hotel-casino business, but ultimately most were not well suited to gaming endeavors, and they sold their interests in Las Vegas (Gottdiener, Collins, & Dickens, 1999).

However, the face of the Las Vegas gaming industry was irrevocably changed by this revision to the Gaming Commission's regulation. Potential casino owners now had the option of raising capital by offering stock shares in a publicly held corporation rather than relying on private financing. This ability to raise large amounts of capital made the old model of casinos funded and run by organized crime "financially obsolete" (Rothman, 2002, p. 22; see also Schwartz, 2003). In addition, once they had been approved for a gaming license, public corporations could purchase casinos, and having done so once, many corporations continued to buy and sell casino operations in Las Vegas and elsewhere (Gottdiener, Collins, & Dickens, 1999). The post-Hughes era of development in Las Vegas showed a strong trend toward incorporation and conglomeration.

Corporate investment in casinos escalated slowly because of the stigma of casino gambling: crime-ridden, mobbed-up, and socially unacceptable to the mainstream. To put it another way, "The general view on Wall Street was that the casino industry wasn't *nice*. Investors would rather buy tobacco stocks" (Binkley, 2008, p. 22). Loans given by the Teamsters' Union in the 1970s to casino-hotel operators to build large resorts including Caesars Palace and Circus Circus laid the groundwork by "legitimizing" these endeavors as worthy of investment, even though there was some shadiness with respect to the dealings between casino operators and notorious Teamsters' Union president Jimmy Hoffa (Schwartz, 2003, p. 110).

It would be the 1990s, though, before Wall Street investors caught on to the potential for profit in Las Vegas gambling stocks, later sanitized and called "gaming" stocks to reflect a greater mainstream acceptance of gambling as an acceptable recreational pastime (Rothman, 2002). Some also attributed this greater acceptance to a somewhat misguided attempt, early in the city's mega-resort development era, to turn Las Vegas into a family-friendly vacation destination (Binkley, 2008). Once the gaming industry became corporatized, it paved the way for the staggering growth in the Strip casino-hotels, and by extension in the city, of the period beginning with the opening of the Mirage in 1989. In this way, "the publicly accepted truism that the corporations had driven out mob interests and made gaming respectable, which is a powerful idea that itself served to legitimize the industry, camouflaged the true crisis that corporations had solved, that of capital" (Schwartz, 2003, p. 163).

Corporate ownership brought pressure on the gaming corporations to generate the steady, predictable profit streams acceptable to investors and shareholders

(Binkley, 2008). This has led to significant changes in the casino industry as gaming corporations attempted to create more consistent cash flows through non-gambling expenditures (Stein, 2009). This change in emphasis led to the creation of thousands of service jobs in the hotel and restaurant industries, filled by workers represented by Las Vegas's powerful Culinary Union.

Founded in the 1950s, Culinary Workers Local 226 is one of the strongest and most powerful unions in the nation, and the high percentage of hotel jobs that are unionized means that wages in Las Vegas average $3 per hour higher than comparable jobs in cities with less union representation (Meyerson, 2004). Prior to the economic downturn of 2008, Las Vegas was often called the "last Detroit" for its high percentage of unionized labor and the ability of middle-class, unskilled laborers to make a decent wage (Rothman, 2002). In modern-day Las Vegas, the Culinary Union still serves as the "counterbalance to gaming's wealth and clout" (Alexander, 2002, p. 174), ensuring that the immense financial success of casino gaming in Las Vegas does not come entirely at the expense of the workers who make the industry possible. A discussion of labor issues in Las Vegas follows in chapter 6.

In early 21st-century Las Vegas, the trends towards corporatization and conglomeration first seen in the 1970s have reached a high point. As of 2014, three corporations primarily own the casinos that make up Las Vegas's Strip: MGM Mirage, Caesars (formerly Harrah's) Entertainment, and Wynn Resorts (Binkley, 2008). A fourth, Shelden Adelson's Las Vegas Sands Corporation, owns two of the Strip's largest high-end properties, the Venetian and the Palazzo, in addition to other gambling properties overseas. Two other gaming corporations own a number of casino properties in Las Vegas: Boyd Gaming, which also owns properties in Atlantic City and the Midwest, and Station Casinos, which owns and operates 18 casinos in the Las Vegas metropolitan area that largely cater to a local audience.

When the global economy took a downturn[1] in 2008, some of its victims were more obvious than others. In Detroit, Michigan, automobile giants Ford and General Motors laid off workers and closed long-standing production plants, leaving many to wonder how a city that had revolved around the auto industry would survive in its absence. Although Las Vegas was not at the forefront of US attention the way the auto industry was, it was suffering almost as badly.

Large-scale construction projects, which had fueled the Las Vegas economy from roughly 1988 to 2008, dried to a trickle and unemployment rates skyrocketed. Heavily leveraged gaming corporations began to have trouble meeting their debt payments, and several smaller companies filed Chapter 11 bankruptcy (Green, 2009). Tourism to Las Vegas plummeted as the economy plunged into a state of uncertainty and Americans abruptly tightened up their discretionary spending, forcing layoffs in the city's casinos and hotels.

Just when it seemed things couldn't get worse for Las Vegas, an offhand remark by President Barack Obama in a town hall meeting suggested that the town was an unsuitable business travel location for "responsible" businesses, especially those receiving federal bailout funds. This remark threatened the city's thriving convention trade, which had helped fuel the recent growth and development – the number of convention delegates visiting Las Vegas had increased by almost 350% between 1988 and 2008 (Las Vegas CVA, 2009). Las Vegas mayor Oscar Goodman publicly called out President Obama, saying his comments were "harmful" to the city's attempts to extricate itself from a financial situation that was, in many ways, every bit as perilous as Detroit's.

The situation in Las Vegas was dire. From January 2007 to that same month in 2010, the number of jobless claims in Nevada doubled from around 15,000 to over 30,000 (Associated Press, 2011). At first, job seekers continued to flock to the city – over 30,000 people moved to Las Vegas between July 2008 and July 2009 – still lured by its years of prosperity and the opportunities it offered even the least educated workers (Robison, 2009). This confluence of in-migration and lost jobs created an even larger population of residents who were subject to the effects of the economy's downturn.

Las Vegas has long been known as a land of opportunity for job seekers both domestic and foreign. In the city's early days, African-Americans from the American South, seeking better opportunities than those afforded to them at home, flocked to Las Vegas to work in its hotels, primarily in service roles (Geran, 2006). The strong presence of labor unions in Las Vegas in the latter half of the 20th century made it a place where one could earn wages as a dishwasher, cocktail waitress, or line cook and still earn a respectable salary (Meyerson, 2004).

But jobs at all levels in Las Vegas disappeared quickly during the Great Recession. With the economy uncertain, potential tourists tightened up on their budgets and postponed or rescheduled their trips to Las Vegas. From a high of 39 million in 2007, the number of visitors to Las Vegas dropped 4% in 2008 and another 3% in 2009 before rebounding in 2010 and the years beyond. Perhaps most crucially, gaming revenue in Clark County, after reaching a high of $10.8 billion in 2007, declined every year through 2009; as of 2014, it had yet to rebound fully ("Historical Las Vegas Visitor Statistics," 2012).

Due to the plunging customer base, casinos tightened up on staffing in defense of their bottom line, laying off workers from casino dealers to housekeeping. In addition to contributing to the rising number of Las Vegas's unemployed, these were also community members who owned homes and patronized local businesses. When they found themselves unemployed, they tightened their own purse strings, sending economic ripples throughout the community. Many lost their homes to foreclosure (Wells, 2009a).

As the global impact of the recession became clear, things got worse for Las Vegas. Credit markets tightened, and large casino projects like Boyd Gaming's Echelon and the aspirationally named Fountainbleu were halted because their owners could no longer pay the bills without the expected infusion of credit. MGM Resorts, which opened its massive CityCenter complex in December 2009, only completed the project due to an influx of cash from investors in Dubai (Wells, 2009b).

As the economy worsened, the dominos continued to fall. The sudden stop in construction projects already in progress, and the delay on nearly all new construction, caused unemployment numbers to spike. Construction had been one of Las Vegas's more reliable and higher-paying industries for many years as the city added mega-resorts almost yearly from 1989 to 2009. From a high of 96,000 in 2006, the number of Las Vegas residents employed in construction dropped to 48,000 by April 2012 (Green, 2012c).

Housing prices, which had soared due to demand in the mid-2000s, plunged and Las Vegas briefly became the foreclosure capital of the United States, taking that dubious title from Stockton, CA in 2008 (Christie, 2008). Compared to other US housing markets, Las Vegas's dropped most precipitously in the Great Recession, with houses losing on average over 50% in value (Wells, 2009a). Thousands of Las Vegans found themselves unemployed and underwater, owing more on their houses than they were worth. Foreclosures and repossessions turned entire Las Vegas neighborhoods into ghost towns.

The recession changed the labor landscape of Las Vegas significantly. Even as the city's overall population grew in the period 2007–2010, its pool of employed workers fell by nearly 200,000 (Associated Press, 2011). Las Vegas's economy recovered more slowly than most other US cities (Green, 2012b). Las Vegans in search of jobs had to contend with competition from an average of 4.47 unemployed residents per job vacancy, compared to a national average around three (Green, 2012b). A 2012 report suggested that Las Vegas would not regain all jobs lost during the recession until 2017 (Green, 2012c).

Las Vegas's struggles in recovering from the recession are often blamed on lack of diversity in its economy (Green, 2012b). The casino gaming and tourism industry generates a significant portion of Las Vegas's jobs and tax revenue; without significant improvements in this sector, the city would be hard-pressed to return to pre-recession levels. Some city leaders did champion diversification projects that led the Las Vegas economy away from its gaming core. In one high-profile example, online retailer Zappos, through by the efforts of its CEO Tony Hsieh, moved its headquarters to downtown Las Vegas, and Hsieh spearheaded an attempt to develop the city's urban core into an innovation and technology hub.[2]

But recovery in tourism and gaming was hamstrung by an unfortunately timed series of events: Just as visitor numbers dipped in the wake of the recession, several of the city's hotels completed a massive expansion, bringing 16,000 new hotel rooms online and adding to what was already a significant oversupply of hotel room product ("Historical Las Vegas Visitor Statistics," 2013). This caused significant declines in two of the city's leading economic indicators, hotel room occupancy and average daily room rate. It was only in the early 2010s that this imbalance steadied somewhat, as both occupancy and average daily rate increased in 2011 and 2012 (Green, 2012a).

Las Vegas has come to rely heavily on foreign tourists, who make up roughly 17% of the city's visitors (Kennelly, 2013). These visitors, primarily from Asia, Europe, and Canada, tend to stay longer, gamble more, and spend more on non-gaming activities (Velotta, 2012), making them a valuable target for casinos. On the whole, visitors to Las Vegas are spending less since the recession than they did before: Overall spending declined, on average, about 22% in the five years after

2007, and a visitor to Las Vegas in 2013 likely budgeted only $480 for gambling, down from $650 before the recession (Nagourney, 2013).

Las Vegas, no stranger to the boom and bust of economic cycles, has, on the whole, thrived on its largely undiversified economy when the big picture is considered. In 1955, the city's relatively new casino industry was feeling the effects of a nationwide economic downturn (Whitehair, 2009). In spite of the national economic climate, however, 1955 saw six hotels open in Las Vegas, three of which (Dunes, Frontier, and Riviera) would remain open for over 35 years (Binkley, 2008; Bybee, 1999).

Not immune to the recession that affected the United States in the early 1980s, Las Vegas saw jobs in the city drop by 4.5% over an 18-month period (Robison, 2010a). The city's economy also saw a significant downturn after the 9/11 terrorist attacks, and 15,000 lost their jobs in the casino industry when visitor numbers fell precipitously (Fletcher, 2001; Ramstack, 2001). But construction of new casinos continued unabated, and the next seven years saw the opening of three additional mega-resort hotels (Palms, Wynn, and Palazzo) and the expansion of several others.

As Las Vegas's economy has ebbed and flowed, it has experienced many of the same growing pains of other cities, such as underfunded local government, crowded schools, and the need for social services. The next section examines the current landscape for Las Vegas's roughly 4,000 nonprofit organizations as they attempt to adjust to the city's recent hard times and address the challenges faced by its residents.

The challenge for Las Vegas's nonprofits

In times of economic crisis, nonprofits are often called upon to step forward and fill the gaps that emerge in a financially troubled community. Although local and state governments provide some services to the homeless and the jobless, for instance, much of this responsibility increasingly falls on the various local and national nonprofit organizations established to address needs in their communities (Jamali & Mirshack, 2007). Nonprofit organizations address a wide range of community needs, from providing basics such as food and shelter to beautifying parks and recreation areas, providing education and training, and advocating for the rights of those who are often unable to do so themselves.

Nonprofit organizations in Las Vegas find themselves in an unusual position. Like many, these organizations are expected to fill a substantial hole in service provision caused by limited help from the local government, a result of lower tax revenues (Gose, 2005). Unlike other organizations, however, Las Vegas nonprofits face additional challenges. For example, an ever-changing resident population makes it difficult for nonprofit organizations to form and maintain lasting relationships with donors and volunteers (Gorman, 2001; Miller, 2005).

Additionally, the nonprofit organizations in Las Vegas exist in a community whose primary corporate citizens are companies in gaming and tourism – two industries that have not historically prioritized community involvement and philanthropy (and of which little in the way of community involvement is actually expected). Early casino owners in Las Vegas, many of whom moved to the city to leave behind their past lives in organized crime, became generous and involved members of the community, perhaps in an attempt to overcome their checkered pasts and establish themselves as legitimate businessmen (Ives, 2005). But as casino ownership became largely corporate toward the end of the 20th century, the old tradition of community stewardship gradually waned.

In August 2001, a *Los Angeles Times* article on philanthropy in Las Vegas quoted Southern Nevada United Way president Garth Winkler making a bold statement: The casino corporations in Las Vegas were not pulling their weight (Gorman, 2001). Rather than engendering discontent among these corporations, which included most of the city's largest employers, Winkler's statement seemed to serve as a call to action. As the casino corporations continued to expand their Las Vegas operations at a staggering rate, they began to increase their involvement in the community through both corporate giving and nonprofit partnerships.

The gaming and tourism industry suffered a brief economic setback in the wake of the 9/11 terrorist attacks, but in the mid-2000s, gaming corporations such as Harrah's Entertainment, MGM Mirage, Wynn Resorts, and Sands Corp. continued to expand both their properties on the Las Vegas Strip and their involvement in the Las Vegas community through volunteerism and philanthropic donations. In the period of Las Vegas's most recent significant growth, from 2003 to 2008, these gaming corporations increased hotel occupancy in the city by almost 10,000 rooms and the city saw visitors (both leisure and business) increase by almost 15% (Las Vegas CVA, 2009).

Community in Las Vegas

Local gaming corporations Boyd Gaming (Sam Boyd) and Station Casinos (Frank Fertitta, Jr.) were founded in Las Vegas by men who became iconic figures in the Las Vegas community, much like their Mob-connected predecessors. When Fertitta died in August 2009, local papers' obituaries referred to him as a "philanthropist" in their headlines and noted his contributions to local charities, schools, and medical research (German, 2009). Before his death in 1993, Sam Boyd donated to local organizations, including the University of Nevada-Las Vegas, which named its football stadium in his honor (Associated Press, 1993). Both founders' commitment to community issues reflects the tradition of community involvement in the Las Vegas community that was, oddly enough, originally started by transplanted mobsters.

In the mid-1990s, Andersen (1994) suggested that Las Vegas had come to represent the typical American city. However, there are some distinct differences in Las Vegas residents' sense of community and civic spirit. For most of its lifetime, Las Vegas has existed as a "company town" in the vein of Detroit, Michigan or Pittsburgh, Pennsylvania. During the 1950s and 1960s, the casinos were the only industry in town; "what was good for the industry was good for the town, and nearly everything that these communities had or became stemmed directly

from their industry . . . The difference in Las Vegas was that the industry was sin"
(Rothman, 2002, p. 135).

The development of Las Vegas as a gaming and tourism destination was influenced by a number of larger societal trends, and its evolution as a physical community has wide-ranging implications for the city today. Gambling as an industry
in Nevada emerged as a last-ditch effort to recover from the economic valley of
the Great Depression, and the organizing forces in this effort centered on Las
Vegas as the location for their development of this industry.

> Throughout America, citizens became increasingly anxious about the explo-
> sion of gambling in the cities. In the state of Nevada, hard economic times
> gave the business and political elite a license to construct the most ambitious
> regime of legal, regulated gambling ever seen in the United States. At the
> southern corner of the state, cunning operators hoped to take advantage of
> Las Vegas's relative proximity to Los Angeles by introducing a new kind
> of tourist experience centered on gambling in self-contained resorts outside
> of the city. Finally, as more Americans called the suburbs home, they natu-
> rally found appealing a gambling environment that reflected the suburban
> order. These factors combined to create the conditions needed for the new
> casino resort industry to prosper.
>
> (Schwartz, 2003, p. 16)

By creating an "oasis of gambling" in a far-flung location where it could be seen
as harmless and unable to influence most of the country, the developers of Las
Vegas's early casino resorts were able to not only play into societal fears about
the potentially harmful effects of gambling, but also harness the obvious interest
in participating in organized gambling in a safe, sanctioned manner.

The fact that most of the city's casino resorts were developed on the Las Vegas
Strip, a geographic area that has never actually been included in the boundaries of
the city of Las Vegas, is crucial to understanding the factors that influenced Las
Vegas's growth as a city. In addition to the isolation that Las Vegas enjoyed from
the rest of "polite society" – the largest nearby city, Los Angeles, was several
hundred miles away – the casinos on the Strip were physically separated from the
city itself, furthering the idea that they were an isolated "haven" that those interested in participating in Las Vegas's vice industries could retreat to (Schwartz,
2003). This has significant implications for modern-day Las Vegas, which has
developed around these large casino-hotels on the Strip, rather than the city and
its other industries.

Today, Las Vegas's gaming corporations employ tens of thousands of
residents – it is estimated that one large casino-hotel employs approximately
4,000 people, most of these in blue-collar service jobs rather than white-collar,
managerial-level positions (Gottdiener, Collins, & Dickens, 1999). As the city's
largest employer, these corporations' fortunes are often reflected back onto the
community. These corporations have also drastically affected the population
of Las Vegas by drawing tens of thousands of people to the area: When three

large casino-hotels (MGM Grand, Luxor, Treasure Island) opened in 1993, they recruited employees not just locally, but nationally (Parker, 2002). This brought a large number of residents to Las Vegas who had previously lived elsewhere, and the opening of several more large casino-hotels in the next decade established Las Vegas as a nationally known destination for improving one's job prospects.

For a city of its size, Las Vegas has relatively little public meeting space or green space for residents to use and enjoy. Community groups often meet in the commercial space provided by restaurants and facilities at large "neighborhood" casinos, located off the Strip in Las Vegas's suburban areas (Rothman, 2002). Las Vegas has long lacked the infrastructure of local government and social organizations that has allowed communities to thrive in some other locations.

Instead of integrating into their community, Las Vegas's residents – most of whom have arrived in town only recently seeking better job prospects – have remained largely individualistic (Rothman, 2002). This hyper-individuality has led to a lack of support for tax bond measures to support improvements to public facilities such as roads, schools, and libraries (Andersen, 1994). This lack of community support for needed improvements and expansion is especially problematic for a city where the population has grown so quickly that resources such as roads and water/sewage systems are overburdened.

Social impact of casino gaming and a tourism-based economy in Las Vegas

Las Vegas residents endured a number of adverse effects from rapid population growth from the late 1980s to the 2000s. Many of these negative impacts can be attributed directly to the population growth and not specifically to the nature of economic expansion in Las Vegas (Parker, 2002) – they would have ensued had the city's economy centered around industries such as information or manufacturing instead of casino gaming and tourism. In addition to infrastructure strain, rapid population growth has also taxed Las Vegas's welfare system with an influx of job-seeking residents, many of whom end up unemployed or underemployed and in need of services such as welfare and food stamps (Parker, 2002).

Negative social impacts attributable to the casino gaming industry's dominant presence in Las Vegas fall into three main categories: problem gambling, over-population, and an inhospitable housing and business climate for locals. Many identify the predominance of gambling in Las Vegas, and to some extent the city's short-lived attempt to market itself to families, as potential causes of compulsive/problem gambling as well as underage gambling (Parker, 1999). The rapid population and commercial growth in Las Vegas in the 1990s and 2000s, which was a direct result of the success and expansion of the casino industry, caused a host of problems in the city: Reduced air quality, traffic congestion, lack of green space, and an overextended criminal justice system could all be attributed to the fact that Clark County's population reached 1.3 million by the year 2000, up from 463,000 in 1980 (City of Las Vegas, 2009; Parker, 2002). Finally, Las Vegas's growing prominence as a tourism-based city created many of the problems such cities face, including a lack of affordable housing and the failure of small, locally owned businesses (Parker, 1999).

Many studies have attempted to draw direct links between the prevalence of casinos and negative social impact (Grinols & Mustard, 2001; Oh, 1999; Pizam & Pokela, 1985; Stokowski, 1993). Such research has become increasingly important to Las Vegas residents as casino development expands beyond the Strip to the suburban areas of the Las Vegas Valley, where many people make their homes and raise their families (Thompson, Schwer, Hoyt, & Brosnan, 1993).

However, drawing definite conclusions about linkages between casinos and social costs poses methodological and practical challenges. Thompson (1999) suggested that the results of such research might be moot because the potential costs of casinos could not come close to matching their astounding financial success; however, this suggestion was made during one of Las Vegas's strongest boom times. When the gaming industry produces substantial profits and creates tax revenue and job opportunities, the local community can more readily accept the possible negative impacts of tourism and casino gaming. The balance between casino profits and social costs in Las Vegas during an economic downturn is more complex.

The city of Las Vegas is fundamentally affected by its orientation as a tourism-based city. Subject to the whims of changing trends in tourism, it must constantly reinvent itself in order to generate new interest and attract tourist attention and dollars (Fanstein & Judd, 1999; Rothman, 2003). Although some tourist cities accentuate their history as a means to attract tourism, Las Vegas has thus far done much the opposite, imploding "historic" casinos to build new mega-resorts in their place. The constantly changing landscape of Las Vegas gives tourists a continually refreshed vision of the city, but it may also prevent residents from forming permanent or longer-term connections with the city in which they live. This trend toward dynamism also implies that job security may not be high for those in the tourism industry (Easterling, 2004).

Orientation as a tourist city carries with it a great number of benefits. The largest, of course, is financial: In several situations, a tourism-based economy has helped offset job losses in agriculture and industry (Fanstein & Judd, 1999). Tourist cities often see benefits such as economic growth, job opportunities, a higher standard of living, and possible revenue for infrastructure improvements (Easterling, 2004), although the latter has not yet been seen in Las Vegas (Parker, 1999). Tourist cities can also enjoy benefits such as increased cultural exchange and understanding by exposure to visitors from other cultures, preservation of local traditions and art/crafts, and strengthened cultural identity and community pride (Easterling, 2004).

Although the tourism industry in Las Vegas may benefit the community, negative impacts can also result from a city's attempts to generate revenue through tourism. Many of these, as mentioned above, appear quite evident in Las Vegas: overcrowding and traffic/parking congestion, negative environmental impacts, and increased cost of living and consumer prices (Easterling, 2004; Parker, 1999). Tourism can also accentuate and aggravate race and class differences within the local community (Easterling, 2004); this is especially problematic when tourists are confined to a particular area of town, as they are in Las Vegas (Judd, 1999). Tourism can also lead to an unstable economy where job opportunities may only be temporary or seasonal and economic success is tied to larger economic forces that influence consumer spending on tourism and travel (Easterling, 2004); Las Vegas saw this very clearly during the Great Recession.

Las Vegas as cultural icon

Although just over 100 years old, the city of Las Vegas has come to play a prominent role in US culture. There are many possible reasons why Las Vegas as a cultural symbol is significant in our 21st-century society: its globally diverse architecture that takes one on a mini-world tour including a replica of an Egyptian pyramid, an imitation Bavarian castle, and a faux Eiffel Tower; its well-known advertising tagline "What happens in Vegas, stays in Vegas," exalting the desires of the individual and condoning the shameless pursuit of those desires; and its postindustrial economy centered around the production and consumption of lifestyle and experience (Firat, 2001). Las Vegas is considered the epitome of the postmodern city, "a combination of space and form in light and dark that owes nothing to its surroundings and leaves meaning in the eye of the beholder" (Rothman, 2002, p. xi).

The development of a small frontier town into the fast-growing city whose amazing growth *Time* magazine profiled in the mid-1990s (Andersen, 1994) parallels and highlights many of the changes in US society in the last century. Las Vegas thrived financially in the post-World War II era even though it did not share in the governmental largesse that fueled the growth of states such as California (Rothman, 2002). The never-say-die story of Las Vegas is quintessentially American: The town has rescued itself from a certain demise not once, but twice, by reinventing itself in a way that would capture the popular attention and attract elusive tourist dollars (Rothman, 2002). Over the course of less than a century, Las Vegas transformed itself from a railroad town on the verge of extinction into an entertainment destination that draws millions of visitors from all corners of the globe.

Because the city of Las Vegas developed primarily in the postindustrial era (as a city it was founded in 1905, but its greatest growth took place after 1950), the economy of the city was never based around the production of goods or the commodification of natural resources (Rothman, 2002). Instead, Las Vegas has always focused on the production and consumption of information and experience, reflecting the larger trend in the US economy away from manufacturing and industrial production (Rothman, 2002). What Las Vegas "makes" is not something that is packaged, shipped, and sold in the way of refrigerators or high-definition TVs. Its goods – hotel rooms, dining, entertainment – are consumable; they are experienced and used up and must be purchased again if one wishes to continue "consuming" Las Vegas.

Although Las Vegas's economy is not centered around "production" in the traditional sense of the world, the city is inextricably linked to one of the most

American ideas of them all: capitalism. Every decision that has shaped the evolution of Las Vegas, most notably its constant reinvention by implosion and reconstruction, is motivated by the desire for profit.

> Unlike other tourist towns, Las Vegas has no illusions about itself; it is what it is and despite the mask of glamour and glitz, it offers no illusions. In Las Vegas, it is always about money, and in late capitalist postmodern America, there's nothing unusual about that except the frankness in acknowledging it.
>
> (Rothman & Davis, 2002, p. 14)

Las Vegas also reflects the US trend toward gigantism, where bigger is better and it is important to be the best. When merged with Las Vegas's capitalist preoccupation, this results in mega-resort hotels that are almost offensively large (the MGM Grand opened in 1993 with over 5,000 rooms), each built to be bigger than the last. Nine of these hotels opened between 1989 and 2009, the last two of which were opened during the nationwide recession that began in September 2008. In December 2009, MGM Grand opened CityCenter, a mega-megaresort consisting of three large hotels, high-end shops, and several condo buildings, the construction of which nearly bankrupted the corporation in summer 2009 (Stone, 2009).

Las Vegas's peculiar sort of excess has come to typify the US image, especially in the early part of the 21st century. Las Vegas of the late 2000s is an exemplar of the larger problems in the turn that US capitalism has taken over the past few years – think big, borrow big, build big; don't worry about who you might step on along the way. Hijackers involved in the 9/11 terrorist attacks allegedly came to Las Vegas beforehand to be reminded of the evils of capitalism in its US incarnation (Fletcher, 2001).

Noted Las Vegas historian and commentator Hal Rothman (2003, p. 229) suggests that "The new Las Vegas is different, a function not only of the change in the city itself but in the mores, manners, and values of Americans." The focus of the city's tourism machine has shifted from gambling to entertainment and includes examples of low and high culture, from topless reviews to Guggenheim-branded museums with priceless works of art. The evolution of Las Vegas represents a shift in US morals that has been evident in changes in US media; the city in its current incarnation would have never risen to such prominence without a significant relaxing of the rigid morals of mid-20th-century America (Rothman, 2003). Ironically, it was those very values that allowed Las Vegas to first flourish as a slightly dangerous, lurid rebellion against the rigid societal expectations of post-World War II America (Firat, 2001; Schwartz, 2003).

Harkening back to an era where gambling was strictly regulated and illegal in most states, the casino has long existed as a symbol of Las Vegas's reputation for vice and permissiveness. Although legalized casino gambling is now allowed in many countries and other US states, the casino as a cultural icon continues to be largely associated with Las Vegas. After a period of conglomeration and corporatization, the casinos in Las Vegas are now primarily owned by six large corporations, many of which are publicly traded on the same stock exchanges as consumer goods such as sneakers and big-screen televisions. The predominance of large casino corporations in the Las Vegas community, along with the potentially damaging social impact of their gambling operations, calls into question the social responsibility of these corporations and their obligation to the Las Vegas community.

Notes

1 As Rampell (2009) discussed, the term "Great Recession" has become popularized in describing this economic event that features prominently in Las Vegas's history, as well as in the global casino industry, with a significant impact on CSR in the casino industry. This term will be used henceforth.
2 Hsieh's Downtown Project is discussed in additional research by this author (Strauss, 2015).

6   CSR in Las Vegas

Evidence of the casino industry's presence physically dominates Las Vegas. On local television channels, traffic and weather cameras are sponsored by Caesars Entertainment. Billboards and advertisements for the MGM Resorts casino-hotels line the streets. Even the buildings themselves, such as the Wynn, bear the names of the casino corporations that operate them.

Porteous (1970, p. 127) described the company town as "a settlement completely owned, built and operated by an individual or corporate entrepreneur," adding that the company town "is a device, especially suited to conditions obtaining in nations undergoing rapid development. In economic pioneering the town is used to open up previously unexploited territory." While Las Vegas does not fit this definition exactly – at least six large corporations are represented in Las Vegas's casino industry – many would argue that Las Vegas is indeed a classic example of the modern casino company town (Littlejohn, 1999).

Company towns are knit together by commonalities: the joint employer of many residents, for starters, leads to a populace whose fortunes rise and fall with the corporation's. In Las Vegas, this has especially been true: The five years following the start of the Great Recession saw terrible hardships for many Las Vegans, even those not directly employed by the casino industry. Many early company towns had a social engineering purpose (Porteous, 1970), and in this light, the donations of volunteer hours and financial support to Las Vegas's schools and nonprofit organization can be seen not only as a charitable endeavor but as a canny act of enlightened self-interest.

This chapter looks at CSR in the Las Vegas casino industry with a focus on local community impacts, although the effects of these corporations' actions often stretch beyond the confines of the city. However, considering the context of the Las Vegas community holds special importance here because CSR is very much defined by the expectations of various corporate stakeholders and how well those expectations may or may not be met by the corporation (Heath & Ni, 2008; see also Wood, 1991). Additionally, the prominent role of Las Vegas's casino corporations in the city's economy gives them a special role and importance in meeting societal expectations for responsible behavior.

The chapter begins by discussing the results of qualitative research with nonprofit managers in the Las Vegas community (Strauss, 2010) that demonstrate how casino corporations in this community engage in CSR primarily motivated by a business case and not a moral obligation. The chapter then considers other elements of CSR, such as environmental sustainability and labor relations, before discussing how an approach to CSR based on moral obligation would look in Las Vegas. Finally, the chapter considers how such an approach to CSR would impact casino corporations' efforts to address problem gambling and other negative externalities created by the casino industry.

Casinos in the community

As discussed in chapter 5, Las Vegas as a community has several unique characteristics: Youth sports teams may be sponsored by a casino, community groups may meet at a restaurant next to a gaming floor, and families might go bowling or take in a movie at an off-Strip "locals" casino. For this reason, this chapter begins by examining elements of casino CSR that address the corporation's obligation to the Las Vegas community.

In previous research, this author conducted a series of qualitative in-depth interviews with managers and executive directors at Las Vegas nonprofits in order to ground the research in the specific context of the community (Strauss, 2010). McCracken (1988, p. 9) refers to the long-form, in-depth interview as "one of the most powerful methods in the qualitative armory" for its ability to understand the world from another's perspective. Using qualitative methods such as the in-depth interview allows the researcher to understand the cultural context of a phenomenon (McCracken, 1988), which is especially important in this case because of the strong cultural basis of the perceived need for corporate social responsibility.

Participants were selected to provide the maximum amount of information on the possible range of experiences that nonprofit managers have had in their relationships with gaming corporations. Weiss (1994, p. 23) suggests that a sample that intends to maximize range should "select respondents purposively so that we obtain instances of all the important dissimilar forms present in the larger population," especially in studies where the sample size will be small (Weiss, 1994). Nonprofit executives were selected through recommendations and snowball sampling methods.

The decision to ask nonprofit managers about communication, rather than casino corporations' CSR managers, was strategic as well as practical. On a practical level, it is difficult to get "in" with many of these casino corporations; many have strict corporate policies that prevent them from participating in academic research. This may be a reason why CSR research involving the casino industry, especially in the United States, has thus far been sparse.

This research, which focused on the relationship between nonprofit managers and casino corporations, found some inherently problematic elements in the way that casino corporations engage with community nonprofit groups. In interviews, nonprofit managers portrayed a rather bleak picture of the lengths to which many of them had to go to receive support (primarily financial) from casino corporations. They suggested that being able to communicate with CSR representatives at casino corporations was, in the words of one recipient, "all about who you know."

Most of the nonprofit managers interviewed described a situation where they had approached a casino corporation for support and received absolutely no response to their queries. Beyond the issue of unresponsiveness, several nonprofit managers expressed a concern that employees responsible for casinos' CSR activities were uninterested in learning more about the missions of nonprofit organizations and the services they provide in the community. The concerns of nonprofit managers in this situation might suggest that corporations have a previously undiscussed responsibility in terms of CSR: to become educated about the community's needs and allocate their corporation's support appropriately so that these needs can be addressed as completely as possible. Expectations that casino corporations will be proactive about how their support can promote the health of the community, rather than reactive to the specific requests for support by nonprofit organizations, redefine CSR as a more complex engagement with a community.

Nonprofit managers described how many of the casino corporations' CSR efforts – such as donations and executive board participation – were tied to personal relationships and networking. Many described the challenge of navigating the labyrinthine corporate structure of casino corporations in trying to identify the appropriate person to approach for support as a part of the corporation's CSR efforts. Ultimately, nonprofit managers believed that their organizations expended a great deal of their resources in attempting to establish relationships with casinos, often unsuccessfully.

Interviews with nonprofit managers also revealed the extent to which a nonprofit's mission might affect its ability to engage with casino corporations' CSR efforts. Several of these corporations have established giving priorities in an effort to align with the sort of strategic CSR that was described in chapter 2. However, these standards necessarily exclude certain nonprofits whose missions fall outside the scope of these proscribed priorities. Even without a formal set of giving priorities, casino corporations might choose (or exclude) certain nonprofits from receiving CSR benefits because of perceived concerns about fit, as discussed in chapter 2.

The author's prior research intended to assess whether nonprofit managers' expectations of CSR by casino corporations was affected by the gambling nature of the corporation's product. Although this research was qualitative in design, and therefore does not allow for generalization to a wider audience, the nonprofit managers interviewed here indicated that, with one exception, these corporations' involvement in the business of gambling did not affect nonprofit managers' perceptions of them. Most of these nonprofit managers considered casino gaming to be an industry like many others, in which the producer of goods or services will endeavor to promote consumption of those goods and services (here, the gambling/Vegas experience). Several of them compared casino gaming to other industries such as manufacturing.

Nonprofit managers expressed a strong desire for gaming corporations to play an active role in the community as a committed partner with nonprofits and other community groups. They cited the role of casinos as Las Vegas's "leading" industry as justification for their expectation of this high level of involvement. Most managers suggested that casino corporations should ideally take a proactive stance toward learning organizations' missions and assessing the community's needs; however, most of them acknowledged that this was not likely to happen. Still, a few of the managers implied that this sort of hands-on approach to CSR was needed to ensure that casino CSR efforts were actually benefiting the community and that dollars were being directed to the organizations that most needed them. In the absence of an open research and vetting process, many nonprofit managers wondered if casino CSR efforts were instead being directed merely to organizations with which someone in the corporation had a personal connection.

Environmental issues in a desert oasis

In 2009, the casinos on the Las Vegas Strip first turned off their iconic neon lights in celebration of Earth Hour. This event, sponsored yearly by the nonprofit nature advocacy group WWF, started in Sydney, Australia in 2007 and since then has evolved to involve over 7000 cities in 162 countries (WWF, 2014, p. 2). In 2014, Las Vegas's casinos once again participated in the event, which is designed to draw attention to energy use issues and motivate action through what WWF refers to as "the power of the crowd."

Their participation in Earth Hour has offered Las Vegas's casinos the opportunity to widely promote their participation in this symbolic environmental effort, which they have frequently done through the use of press releases and other promotional tools such as websites. Participation in Earth Hour dovetails nicely with these casinos' continuing efforts to promote their environmental endeavors, which have increasingly become part of their CSR activities. These efforts have garnered Las Vegas's casinos very positive coverage in media outlets around the world (e.g. "Millions of people worldwide," 2014; Posner & Kiron, 2013).

But the casinos' participation in Earth Hour is symbolic, leaving one to wonder what actual efforts these casinos are taking to reduce their environmental impact. A review of the websites and CSR reports of these casino corporations does reveal that some actual efforts to mitigate environmental impact have been taken: Reduction of greenhouse gas emissions, programs to reduce water and energy use, and enhanced recycling programs are all mentioned as examples (Caesars Entertainment, 2014; Las Vegas Sands, 2014; MGM Resorts International, 2014). Other actions, such as the aforementioned Earth Hour and the installation of electric car chargers by MGM Resorts, seem to be more of the "window-dressing" discussed in chapter 2 – efforts designed to make the corporation *appear* to be socially responsible. Given that the strength of the LEED (Leadership in Energy and Environmental Design) building designation can be considered debatable ("In U.S. building industry," 2013), efforts by corporations Las Vegas Sands and

MGM Resorts to build according to these supposedly environmentally friendly standards might not be as significant as they first appear.

In their discussion about corporate environmental policies and greenwashing, Ramus and Monteil (2005) get to the heart of the concern over casinos' efforts to enact environmentally sustainable behavior as part of their CSR actions: Are these policies enacted in true pursuit of environmental sustainability, or are they merely intended to present an appropriate face of a socially responsible corporation? Highly publicized statements of environmental philosophy, such as are found on most[1] of Las Vegas's casino corporations' websites, raise the stakes on this issue because these statements, presented as fact, may influence stakeholders' perceptions of the corporations' CSR actions. This may affect customers' decisions on which hotel to patronize during their Las Vegas visit, shareholders' evaluation of the company's social responsibility, and government/regulators' perception of the corporation's benefit to society.

The impact of the casino industry's growth on the Las Vegas physical environment has been significant in a number of ways (Sun, Tong, Fang, & Yang, 2013). Drastic population growth in the Las Vegas area has generated a number of externalities, such as increased water use and generation of wastewater, and even some indirect effects such as increased salinity in the Colorado River, which is linked to the Las Vegas watershed (Venkatesan, Ahmad, Johnson, & Batista, 2011). Air quality has been affected by the increased number of vehicles in use and even from the increased use of plants for landscaping due to the growth and development of suburbs (Papiez et al., 2009). Even the efforts to ameliorate the effects of excessive water use in Las Vegas exact a significant carbon footprint (Shrestha, Ahmad, Johnson, & Batista, 2011).

Water conservation and reuse efforts are key to offsetting the tremendous population growth in the Las Vegas Valley (Sun, Tong, Fang, & Yang, 2013; Venkatesan, Ahmad, Johnson, & Batista, 2011). In this vein, some of the casinos' CSR efforts seem admirably aligned with needs for environmental sustainability: For example, most hotels in Las Vegas offer guests the option to decline a new towel or change of sheets every day (Levy & Park, 2011). This endeavor seems genuine to consumers because the policy also generates an economic benefit to hotels in terms of reduced laundry and water bills (Ramus & Monteil, 2005). However, it seems very possible that even these efforts will be insufficient to reduce water use to sustainable levels, especially if outdoor water use and population numbers continue to rise (Qaiser, Ahmad, Johnson, & Batista, 2013) – both of which are likely if the casino industry continues its pattern of growth.

The efforts by Las Vegas's hotel-casinos to communicate their environmentally oriented CSR behavior require careful scrutiny. Certainly, the casinos have improved a number of environmental practices, although often they do so at some considerable financial benefit to themselves. However, the use of environmental messaging in marketing, often done to attract potential patrons and not because of personal beliefs of the corporation or its employees (Dief & Font, 2010), can be problematic from an ethical perspective. If Las Vegas's hotel-casinos are attracting patrons because they project an image of environmental responsibility, while at the same time imparting negative impacts on the city's natural environment, then they are deceiving these customers in the name of corporate profit.

Las Vegas: a disappearing workers' paradise

During much of Las Vegas's history, workers held the upper hand in Las Vegas; casinos were expanding so quickly that they were unable to easily acquire competent employees, leading to the overall strength of the unions (Kraft, 2010). However, the corporatization of Las Vegas's casinos led to a couple of prominent union defeats in bargaining in the 1980s and 1990s, as "management became concentrated in the hands of corporate officers elected and responsible to stockholders. Corporate leaders focused not on daily operations but on long-term policy and planning and on the bottom line of profitability" (Kraft, 2010, p. 29).

The last two decades of the 20th century proved turbulent for Las Vegas's labor unions (Greenhouse, 2004). As casinos were purchased by corporations, their policies became more regulated and impersonal (Kraft, 2010). A union strike against the Frontier hotel-casino, which refused to recognize the union, began in 1991 and lasted for six years (Meyerson, 2004). Smaller strikes continued through the 1990s and 2000s (Komenda, 2013).

With the unions already weakened, the beginning of the Great Recession in 2008 dealt a further blow to workers in Las Vegas. Suddenly, almost 200,000 Las Vegans, many of them former casino workers, were out of work (Robison, 2010b). Casino corporations took advantage of the recession to streamline their workforces and eliminate some job positions (Green, 2012c). On average, the out-of-work Las Vegas resident faces about 150% more competition for every position than do job-seekers in other cities (Green, 2012b).

The unions in Las Vegas still have significant strength in numbers – today, the Culinary Union Local 226 represents about 55,000 service-industry workers in Las Vegas (Culinary Union Local 226, 2014). However, economic conditions have given casinos the upper hand in labor relations, making CSR in labor relations especially important because workers in Las Vegas casinos now lack the bargaining power they have traditionally enjoyed.

Las Vegas's casino workforce has several unique qualities. Many of the jobs in this sector are low-skill jobs with accompanying low pay (Kraft, 2010), although the prominence of labor unions in Las Vegas has driven up the expected pay for jobs there, even at lower income levels (Greenhouse, 2004; Meyerson, 2004). Most of the jobs in the casino industry are service jobs, placing Las Vegas in a rather enviable position where its jobs cannot be exported, as has often been the case in the manufacturing sector (Kraft, 2010).

Front-of- house workers in casinos (in Las Vegas and elsewhere) are crucial to the casino's success because of their frequent interactions with customers (Lee, Song, Lee, Lee, & Bernhard, 2013). For this reason, casino corporations do spend a large amount of time on employee issues because it serves a functional purpose. However, because their efforts are primarily directed toward the ultimate goal of increasing casino profits, rather than improving the conditions for workers for the sake of the workers, the choice of CSR actions taken by the casino corporations ultimately is driven by a strategic purpose.

As an example, workers in Las Vegas casinos face significant challenges from their continued exposure to secondhand smoke. Nevada is one of the last US states to allow smoking in public places (Nagourney, 2013) and many would argue that the vast numbers of employees in Las Vegas's casinos jeopardize their personal health just by doing their jobs ("Despite health risks," 2010). Casino workers have reported that requests to be removed from smoking environments have jeopardized their continued employment, and the power dynamic between casino employees and employers suggests that employees are unlikely to proactively seek advances in workplace safety in this realm.

That smoking remains legal in Nevada's casinos, in spite of popular support for a smoking ban as well as significant efforts by workers' groups and the American Heart Association (Nagourney, 2011), stands as a testament to the lobbying power of the casino corporations. In an interview conducted as part of the qualitative research mentioned earlier, the executive director of a regional health advocacy association reported that his nonprofit did not accept financial contributions from casino corporations due to their opposition to the smoking ban. Although the nonprofit obviously needed such financial support, this executive director ultimately believed that the nonprofit could not forfeit its principles for financial reasons.

> There's some policies, especially with casinos . . . if they're – because of some of our advocacy work, our policies really need to be aligned, to make it a mutually beneficial relationship . . . If it's a year round cause partnership that they're branding all of their messaging with [our organization], but yet the next ad that they place they're saying "Smoke all you want! We love it in our casinos." Or "We're not going to eliminate smoking in our casinos," then it kind of contradicts each other.
>
> (Kent,[2] Personal interview, 2010)

These casino corporations' decision to support smoking in their casinos clearly advances their profit-making motive: Because Nevada is one of the few places gamblers can smoke, this offers a unique selling proposition to those customers who like to smoke while they gamble. Just as clearly, the health of front-line service employees is jeopardized by their exposure to the smoke generated by customers ("Despite health risks," 2010).

The work done by casino workers often has a negative physical impact. A 2005 study by Krause, Scherzer, and Rugulies found that housekeepers in Las Vegas casinos often had neck and back pain as a result of their work. More significantly, this study found that these housekeepers self-reported a rise in their workload over the past five years, suggesting that their responsibilities have been increased in the name of corporate efficiency (Krause, Scherzer, & Rugulies, 2005). Other job positions in Las Vegas casinos, such as blackjack dealers, involve sitting for long periods of time and repetitive musculosketal motions, which inherently bear danger for injury over the long term.

Labor issues are an important topic of discussion for casinos because the increased number of jobs they promise often leads as a justification for opening a new casino or expanding an existing casino enterprise (Perdue, Long, & Kang, 1999). However, Zeng, Forrest, and McHale (2013) point out that these jobs might not be ones that employees are particularly satisfied with. Employees cite several negative aspects of the casino industry, such as the need to work unsocial hours (night shifts, etc.), the fact that casino jobs often are not challenging, perceived inequality between pay for managers and lower-level employees, and the frequent interactions with unpleasant patrons as negative aspects of their jobs (Zeng, Forrest, & McHale, 2013). In Macau, Wan (2010) found that rapid expansion of casinos had caused a situation where employees felt inadequately trained and ineffectually communicated with by management, and this has likely also been the case in Las Vegas in the past at similar times of rapid growth. In addition, employees are often subject to the many negative externalities of casinos such as higher cost of living and increased traffic and congestion (Lee & Back, 2009; Zheng & Huang, 2012).

In this context, CSR efforts with a focus on improving employees' work conditions are especially important. CSR websites of Las Vegas casinos tout programs that support employee health and wellness and many have established programs to allow employees to engage with local nonprofits they support, often with matching donations from the corporation or with time off to volunteer. However, an interview with a nonprofit manager in 2010 revealed that these efforts might be counterintuitive from the employee's perspective:

> I think another thing, the way things have been going here, people's morale – it's down. You know, jobs are lost, hours are being scratched. They're asked for more responsibility for the same amount of pay. And this is just me personally, but the last thing some people might want to do is, you know, volunteer for something on a Saturday, or you know, this company's asking me to donate money.
>
> (Kevin, Personal interview)

This example shows how casinos' attempts to promote socially responsible behavior among employees, as a sort of partnership in helping the community, might actually appear different to employees, who may perceive it as a burden or even as an implicit condition of their continued employment. Several nonprofit executives suggested that corporations could be more helpful in terms of promoting community involvement by helping them educate employees about nonprofits and community needs.

In general, the way that Las Vegas's casino corporations engage in CSR with respect to community involvement, environmental sustainability, and labor relations evidences some of the key problems with CSR that is enacted as a business strategy. The next section will summarize some of those inconsistencies between a moral and a functional approach to CSR before applying this rubric to the gaming industry's promotion of responsible gambling.

CSR in Las Vegas: a moral vs. functional approach

Table 6.1 summarizes elements of CSR found in Las Vegas that adhere to a functional approach to CSR, which sees these actions as a strategic step to improve financial output. It then contrasts them to a hypothetical moral approach to CSR, which sees CSR more generally as a way for businesses to contribute to the society that allows them to operate and expects them to make up for any negative externalities they may have generated and help those with less power.

The final section of the table considers the difference in communicating CSR from a moral vs. a functional perspective. The next section explores the complexity of communicating casino CSR efforts in the Las Vegas community as found by interviewing nonprofit managers in the area.

Communicating CSR in Las Vegas

Reflecting trends found in the literature (e.g., Wanderley, Lucian, Farache, & de Sousa Filho, 2008), the casino corporations in Las Vegas do not widely communicate with external audiences about their CSR activities. Their efforts to do so are usually limited to their corporate websites and to annual reports, especially for those corporations that are publicly traded. In contrast, nonprofit managers mentioned that corporations in other industries in Las Vegas, such as banking and telecommunications, often highlight their CSR efforts through television commercials, newspaper advertisements, and more wide-ranging and proactive types of communication.

Nonprofit managers interviewed in previous research believed that outside of the nonprofit community, Las Vegas residents have little chance of finding out about the casino industry's CSR actions. These managers do not perceive a high level of awareness of casino CSR among average Las Vegas residents. Many of the nonprofit managers attribute this lack of information to the low involvement of the local media in covering the partnerships between casino corporations and nonprofit organizations, noting that this leads to a lack of public knowledge about the CSR efforts of casino corporations (and other industries) in the Las Vegas community.

When nonprofit managers were asked for their perspectives on why these corporations did not more actively promote their CSR activities outside the realm of media relations, they almost universally referred to the expense of such actions, especially within the context of the economic situation created by the Great Recession. Even though they perceived that efforts at external communication might generate some benefits for the casino corporations, nonprofit managers still balanced this benefit against the potential cost of the communication. They also placed external communication of CSR as a low priority that was often overlooked in a climate of reduced executive workforce and increased employee responsibility at that level.

Managers also mentioned that casino companies might receive little benefit from advertising their CSR efforts to the Las Vegas community because the corporations' target customer base is primarily out-of-town tourists. Once again, this reflects a bottom-line approach to the communication of corporations' CSR efforts and frames these efforts solely as functional, profit-driven endeavors.

Table 6.1 Comparing functional and moral approaches to CSR in the case of Las Vegas

Functional approach to CSR (actual)	*Moral approach to CSR (ideal)*
1 Community engagement and support	
Donations from casino corporations are nominal, often superficial, and based on personal connection or some sort of grant process. Some nonprofits are excluded because they lie outside the prescribed giving priorities established by the corporation. Nonprofits expend a lot of resources trying to make connections with gaming corporations and/or participating in formal grant processes.	Corporations actively research nonprofits and distribute donations fairly (procedural justice) so as to do the best job of addressing community needs to the best of their ability.
Because corporations engage in CSR as a means to generate reputational advantage, territorialism and turf battles prevent nonprofits from engaging with or benefiting from the CSR of multiple corporations.	Corporations are more interested in helping the community than in benefiting from the CSR actions, so they disregard these issues and assist multiple nonprofits as needed.
Casino executives sit on boards as part of personal networking and to ensure that the corporation appears engaged in the community.	Casino executives participate on nonprofit boards based on personal interest and to provide the benefits of their expertise to nonprofits.
Nonprofits compete for limited resources from casino corporations; managers feel powerless to speak out against corporations because they are dependent for vital resources and the "stamp of approval" that casino funding implies.	Casino corporations donate enough money to adequately address needs in the community, especially those needs that are in some part generated by the business activity of the corporations.
2 Environmental sustainability	
Changes to hotel/casino operations largely mimic trends across the industry, such as increased recycling and giving guests the option to decline fresh sheets/towels each day.	Casinos present new ideas in environmental sustainability that are more suited to the particularities of the industry. For instance, the slot machine system known as "ticket in ticket out" (TITO), where a paper voucher replaces a payout in cash or coin, generates a great deal of waste but could be replaced with a paperless system. However, the installation of this kind of system would require substantial financial investment on the part of the casinos.

Messaging on environmental issues can be inconsistent: Messages emphasize the casino's commitment to the environment in ways previously mentioned, but some aspects of casino operation generate tremendous amounts of waste in very visible ways. For example, the Monte Carlo Hotel and Casino touts its "Green Key" rating for sustainability, but it provides its guests with a one-cup coffeemaker that uses disposable Keurig pods, which can only be used once before generating unrecyclable waste.

Casino actions on environmental issues would be consistent with their messages on the topic.

Efforts are largely symbolic, such as participation in Earth Hour activities, and are widely promoted through casino messaging.

Environmental sustainability efforts involve direct action that may or may not be in line with the casino's financial best interests.

3 Labor relations

Decisions about casino policy on issues such as smoking and worker efficiency are based on the ultimate ability to affect profit, not workers' health issues.

Casino policies prioritize the health and well-being of employees by banning smoking and reducing workload on employees with physically demanding jobs.

Because there is an oversupply of workers and a limited number of jobs for them to fill, casino corporations know they have the upper hand when bargaining with unions and their efforts to negotiate prioritize the casino's profit-making and attempt to exact the maximum concessions.

Casino corporations bargain with unions in good faith and attempt to find a fair middle ground even though workers have considerably less power; they are willing to make some concessions for workers even when it is not directly tied to their (the casino's) bottom line, especially considering that casino jobs are not always satisfying for employees.

Casino employees are encouraged to donate time/money to nonprofits selected by the corporation.

Casinos facilitate nonprofits' access to and education of employees, who give time/money as they feel personally connected to nonprofits and compelled to do so.

4 General principles for casino CSR

Casino corporations engage in a certain level of CSR based on their cost–benefit analysis of these actions' ability to benefit the corporation.

As an industry leader, the casino corporations in Las Vegas engage in CSR at an extremely high level in order to set a high bar/standard for other businesses in the community.

(continued)

Table 6.1 (continued)

Functional approach to CSR (actual)	Moral approach to CSR (ideal)
Casino corporations' participation in CSR is limited by economic concerns because CSR behavior in this industry is not legislated or legally required.	Regardless of the lack of regulation, casino corporations engage in CSR at a high level.
Casinos participate in CSR because it benefits their bottom line (the "business case" for CSR).	Casinos participate in CSR because they have a moral obligation to assist those with less power/resources (e.g. nonprofits, the environment, employees) and also to address the social costs of their business operations (e.g. problem gambling).
5 Communicating CSR	
CSR is communicated on an as-needed basis to obtain the financial benefits afforded by strategic CSR; decisions about whether to do this are made in the cost–benefit framework; corporations expect/encourage nonprofits to publicize CSR efforts, further straining nonprofits' resources.	Robust CSR communication by the corporation engages local stakeholders, employees, and media in addition to shareholders without regard to cost.

Additionally, some managers believed that CSR behavior might not have any impact on potential customers' decisions on which casino they would patronize. By this logic, then, gaming corporations have no financial motivation to promote widespread understanding of their CSR efforts.

Many nonprofit managers also expressed a concern that if gaming corporations communicated their CSR activities to external publics, it might make them a "target" for other nonprofit groups seeking funding. As previous literature has suggested, the gaming corporations also may not be communicating their CSR efforts widely because of a concern that those efforts will be perceived poorly by the general community. One executive director summed up the inherent clash between the desire to spread knowledge of CSR efforts and the concern over seeming self-promotional.

> Yeah. It's a Catch-22, you know. You don't do it, and nobody knows . . . I don't necessarily see it as a negative when I see an organization highlighting the contributions that they made or that their employees have done, because I see where they're coming from. They need to get that out there. But I think those that aren't necessarily benefiting maybe from their investment see it as, they're just patting themselves on the back, and putting themselves out there as, we're great corporate citizens.
>
> (Kent, personal interview)

In sum, nonprofit managers believe casino corporations may be dissuaded from communicating their CSR efforts to the general community because of four simultaneous influences – the added financial cost, low priority placed on these efforts, concern about becoming a "target" for nonprofits seeking funding, and concerns about seeming authentic in their efforts.

Addressing social costs and negative externalities of casinos

Few would argue that casinos, whether run by governments or corporations, have a responsibility to address the negative externalities caused by their endeavors and, when possible, to prevent them from happening altogether. The final section in this chapter addresses the difference between functional and moral approaches to CSR from the perspective of the industry's efforts to promote responsible gambling, considering how these approaches influence the way that casinos treat problem gamblers and the negative social costs these problems can create.

Casino operators talk at length about their efforts to promote responsible gambling. They fund treatment programs and research about gambling addictions and join industry groups, such as the American Gaming Association's National Council on Responsible Gaming, to show their support of these efforts. Governments that operate casino interests, in countries such as Australia and Canada, run problem gambling treatment programs, usually out of the same offices that treat chemical dependencies such as alcoholism and drug addiction.

As mentioned previously, however, the medicalized approach to problem gambling "treatment" and "diagnosis" locates the blame for gambling's social costs in the individual, not in the system that allows and promotes legalized gambling. Although these efforts might appear to address the problems that casinos are generating – and in this particular case, the appearance of an effort is almost as significant as the efforts themselves – they do so without accepting any responsibility for the problem, something that is instrumentally necessary for their continued, legal existence. In this way, casinos' promotion of responsible gaming, although it may appear at first to be a moral attempt to address negative externalities the industry itself has caused, is in fact more of a functional CSR effort to ensure that casinos can continue to generate revenue for public and private interests.

Casinos promote their responsible gambling efforts widely on casino websites and pamphlets about problem gambling are located, albeit discreetly, throughout the casino. In many casinos, these brochures are located near ATM machines, ostensibly because problem gamblers would use these machines to withdraw additional funds to feed their gambling addiction. However, if these casinos wanted to be truly responsible from a moral perspective of beneficence, they would eliminate ATMs from the property entirely, which would require patrons to plan a cash budget ahead of their visit and, once that budget had been exhausted, cease to gamble any further. It would appear that these casinos are more interested in appearing to be responsible, which helps improve their reputation for social responsibility, than in actually effecting improvements in deterring problem gamblers.

In fact, many casino executives will claim that they support responsible gambling from a business perspective: As long as patrons can control their gambling, they are likely to remain customers for a much longer period of time (Pitcher, 1999). However, Williams and Wood (2004) find that Canada's casinos likely make 23% of their revenue from problem gamblers, and they report that the figures for Australia, New Zealand, and the United States range from 15% to 33%. Given these figures, it seems unlikely that casinos would so willingly forfeit such a substantial chunk of their profits. Indeed, it seems that while talking the talk of responsible gambling, casinos are not walking the walk – the ATM scenario given above, for instance, serves as a prime example.

In fact, the use of CSR as a strategic tool – the business case for CSR, which promotes the overall economic success of the corporation (or other casino operator) – does not support most of the efforts to address responsible gambling, such as ATM removal, that would have a real impact on problem gamblers. Under this approach, CSR actions are only supported if they will eventually return some financial benefit, especially if significant costs are incurred by engaging in CSR.

The advantage of casinos' engagement in responsible gambling primarily falls into two categories: overall reputation and government relations. On a gut level, it seems as though no amount of responsible gambling efforts will adequately create a public perception of gaming as an industry with a good reputation, even if attitudes toward gambling have moderated significantly in the past few decades (Hing, 2002). Additionally, it seems that public perception of the casino industry or individual casino operators is unlikely to affect patrons' decision to go to casinos in any kind of significant way.

Presenting an image of support for responsible gambling can, however, benefit casinos in terms of government relations. In fact, it is the very notion that casinos will take responsibility for the negative costs of gambling that has allowed the industry to expand into new jurisdictions. An overall image of social responsibility, in addition to the promise of economic development, can help casinos gain legalization in new jurisdictions and argue for lower taxes and removal of other regulatory barriers in existing jurisdictions. In this way also, casinos' efforts to promote responsible gambling are highly functional as they allow the casinos to continue operating.

Notes

1 MGM Resorts, Caesars Entertainment, and Las Vegas Sands dedicate sections of their corporate websites to featuring information about their environmental policies. Wynn Las Vegas features this information on its dedicated website that addresses the meeting and convention industry, which is significant considering that green practices have become a strong selection factor in determining meeting and convention sites (Draper, Dawson, & Casey, 2011) and attendees rate green meetings highly, as long as they are not required to pay extra for them (Rittichainuwat & Mair, 2012).

2 Interview participants were given pseudonyms in order to protect confidentiality. A list of participants' job positions and their pseudonyms can be found in the Appendix.

7 Trouble points

Implications of strategic CSR

This chapter establishes discussion points that arise when considering the case of corporate social responsibility in the casino industry. Although these points primarily arise from the case study explored here in-depth in chapter 6 (Las Vegas, Nevada), they will also reference the three gambling locations explored in chapter 4 – Australia, Canada, and Macau. As has been demonstrated in previous chapters, the widely varied range of characteristics of the casino industry – such as whether casinos are operated by governments or corporations, and whether their profits go toward public or private benefit – directly influences the issues about CSR raised by its use in the casino industry.

The points made in this chapter will serve as touchstones for this book's conclusion, which considers how the implementation of conventional CSR in the gaming industry might have unintended effects on the industry itself, society, and the professionals who work to enact CSR programs and communicate them to important stakeholders via public relations. This chapter looks first at some practical and ethical concerns about the use of strategic CSR by casino corporations. It then turns to the particular challenges of communicating CSR and the importance of this element of the CSR process. The chapter then looks at specific issues regarding corporations' efforts to support their local communities, often by engaging with nonprofit organizations. Finally, the chapter draws some conclusions from the Las Vegas case study that can be applied more broadly to discussions about CSR and the role that business should play in society.

Unintended consequences of a functional approach to CSR

There is considerable reason for concern that a business case for CSR in the casino industry may result in a standard for CSR actions that allows the corporation to fall short of its moral obligations. In other words, the amount of CSR effort required to achieve the necessary benefits of CSR (such that its costs are justified and the actions have a positive impact on the corporation's financial bottom line) might be considerably lower than the efforts required to fulfill the corporation's moral obligations, especially given that the industry's product may have negative social externalities.

As discussed previously, the distinction between a company's efforts to fulfill its functional obligations – those actions it must take in order to be successful – and its need to fulfill moral obligations to various stakeholders carries particular significance in the casino industry. In the case of the former, a casino company may engage in CSR to improve its reputation, to encourage purchase decisions by customers, or to improve employee morale. However, a casino corporation's moral obligations to those stakeholders that are less powerful and/or dependent on the corporation take on a different nature entirely and might include the corporation's obligation to protect the environment, to support its local community, and to interact with employees in ways that ultimately may not positively affect the company's financial profitability, but will benefit the employee's wellbeing.

An element of CSR unique to the casino industry, the issue of promotion of responsible gambling, falls into an ambiguous middle ground between moral and functional CSR. Certainly there is a strong moral element to a corporation's obligation to address gambling problems that may have been directly or indirectly caused by the operation of its casinos; this is even more true in the case of governments that operate gambling enterprises for the purpose of generating public revenue. However, casino corporations' engagement in responsible gambling efforts as a part of their overall CSR program serves a significant functional goal as well: It protects their reputation as responsible members of a community and it can benefit the corporation, or at least enable its operations to remain legal, by reflecting well on the corporation when it comes to government regulation.

Participation in CSR can help a casino corporation appear more responsible to government stakeholders and often results in more lenient regulation of the company and/or its industry. This raises a particular concern in the state of Nevada, which is heavily dependent on the gaming industry: Does the state give tax breaks (as a result of casino corporations' CSR actions and ensuing positive effects on their reputation) to the gaming corporations at the expense of its citizens? With the very legitimate concern that governments might become reliant on tax revenue from gambling, it bears considering that they might therefore be willing to overlook corporate behavior that is not adequately socially responsible, or even downright harmful to the people they are supposed to protect, in order to ensure the continuation of this revenue stream.

Additionally, if a company views CSR strategically and engages in CSR behavior based on a traditional cost–benefit framework, certain consequences may ensue:

1   In order to obtain the greatest financial benefit in terms of CSR, the corporation might prefer certain socially responsible actions that it feels will generate the greatest return on investment. For instance, the corporation may prioritize its efforts for environmental sustainability because "green" efforts may result in customer purchase decisions, although further research is needed to know whether this is true in the hotel and/or casino industry. A strategic approach or business case perspective may then lead corporations to spend less time and effort on other aspects of CSR such as labor relations.

2   Additionally, if CSR is ultimately intended to benefit the financial bottom line, corporations might direct their philanthropic efforts to support more mainstream nonprofits and issues. This may cause them to exclude groups whose causes may be equally important but not as palatable to the potential consumer, such as organizations that prevent animal cruelty or child abuse. Such a preference creates a process for determining which nonprofits a corporation will support that lacks procedural justice; this may lead to nonprofits perceiving that they are being treated unfairly. By choosing to engage with stakeholders such as nonprofit managers and community leaders through CSR, corporations set a high standard for ethical communication and fairness that they are compelled to uphold to ensure that their efforts do not backfire. Decisions about supporting certain philanthropic or community causes based on the business case for CSR, not a sense of fairness or justice in directing funding where it is most needed, can also lead nonprofits to misuse their resources by approaching corporations for funding when they are unlikely to receive it based on the nature of their mission.

3   In an economic crisis where resources contract, corporations might de-prioritize CSR efforts because they perceive these efforts as not essential to ensuring the financial survival of the corporation. In a business case approach to CSR, corporations only engage in these efforts such that they benefit the corporation's bottom line, and in an economic downturn, CSR may be reduced or eliminated entirely because these efforts do not generate as great a return on investment as other expenditures. However, it is during times of economic crisis that certain CSR efforts, such as local community support, are most badly needed.

The considerable conflicts generated by the business case for CSR in the casino industry will be explored further in the next chapter.

Communicating CSR: challenges and ethical concerns

The efforts of casino corporations to communicate their CSR efforts – and the fact that many of them, ultimately, decide not to communicate about these efforts because they fear negative repercussions – raises several issues about these corporations' use of CSR and their decisions about communicating these efforts.

A natural connection exists between the discussion of strategic CSR and the news media. After all, strategic CSR efforts often intend to improve a corporation's image, and the news media play an important role in bestowing positive reputation via third-party endorsement. A closer look at the Las Vegas case reveals that this is a rather complicated issue. When news media show no interest in covering casino corporations' CSR events, the corporations are less likely to engage in CSR because the expected reputational benefit will not be as significant. However, reporters often do not want to cover CSR because they see it as "free advertising" for the corporation, and here the two sides are at a bit of an impasse.

Nonprofit managers in Las Vegas suggested that local news media must also play a key watchdog role to ensure that corporations are engaging in CSR: Without outside pressure, casino corporations might not engage in CSR, or might not engage in enough CSR to address negative externalities created by their operations. However, current pressures in the news industry suggest that exposés about casino CSR are likely to be low on the priority list for Las Vegas news media, especially when advertising and sponsorship revenues from those corporations may be threatened by any criticism levied against them.

The notion of CSR as a functional tool to drive corporations' financial success also ignores the fact that corporations may have a moral obligation to communicate their CSR actions externally even if doing so does not ultimately promote the corporation's financial interests. This suggests that public relations practitioners might need to consider communicating to stakeholders such as area nonprofits, local media, and the local community, even though it might not prove to be financially beneficial. The decision of whether to include these stakeholders based on a moral obligation certainly addresses an issue at the heart of corporate social responsibility: whether socially responsible actions should be undertaken for functional purposes, such as advancing reputation or promoting purchase decisions, or whether they must be done altruistically or to satisfy the corporation's obligation to society.

Without communication about CSR with important stakeholders, corporations also may not know whether they share a common definition of appropriate gaming CSR with those stakeholders. If corporations set a certain bar for adequate CSR efforts, and stakeholders set the bar at a higher level, the corporation will not know if it is disappointing the stakeholders, and the stakeholders might become dissatisfied because the corporation has not met their expectations. If corporations believe their CSR efforts are adequate (even though other stakeholders may not), they might not engage in CSR at a level that is high enough to fulfill even their functional obligations, because improved reputation and stakeholder relations are intended outcomes of CSR expenditures.

Casino corporations may be hesitant to communicate or publicize their CSR efforts, fearing that doing so might have negative effects on reputation and thus diminish the expected returns on CSR efforts. This may have implications for several stakeholders, including:

1   the local community, especially when the corporation belongs to an industry leader. If citizens are not aware of the corporation's socially responsible efforts, they may be less likely to engage in the community themselves. A similar effect might be seen in businesses outside of the dominant industry.
2   employees of the corporation. If the corporation does not publicize its efforts, employees will not experience the expected benefit from CSR for that particular public (generally thought to be improved morale and job satisfaction), although the corporation may still benefit from the actions, either financially or through an improved reputation.

3   local nonprofits. The development directors of nonprofit organizations, who often use news reports and other public communication about corporate giving to aggregate information about corporations' involvement with other nonprofits, are at a disadvantage to assess the corporations' giving priorities and the likelihood that the corporation will get involved with the nonprofit.

As long as CSR is justified with a business case, public relations is required to communicate about these efforts only because CSR's benefits require knowledge of the actions among stakeholders such as employees, local communities, media, etc. In order to ensure an ethical implementation of CSR, though, it is important to make sure the causal arrow points in the correct direction: Public relations should be used to communicate about CSR, but CSR decisions should not be made on the basis of PR considerations.

In fact, the act of engaging in CSR might itself be seen as an act of public relations: Ideally, it facilitates engagement with stakeholders in a two-way dialogue that creates mutual benefit. The notion of CSR as dialogue and the possibilities for this concept to be used to prosocial ends are explored in chapter 8.

Casino CSR and community/nonprofit support

Corporations often work with community nonprofits as a part of their strategic CSR efforts. When casino corporations engage in this kind of CSR with local nonprofits, nonprofits may suffer some consequences that may work against their efforts to fulfill their mission.

1   Nonprofits may spend a lot of time trying to woo corporations' support, either by responding to calls for proposals or through more traditional fundraising and prospect management. Nonprofits may also be required to report in some formal way how they have spent donations from corporations, so that the corporations can prove their donations have been used well (for their own reporting purposes) and so the corporations can measure more closely their return on investment (benefits vs. costs). The time spent fundraising and reporting necessarily takes away from the time a nonprofit can spend fulfilling its mission of feeding the hungry, improving the educational system, etc.
2   Because the pool of corporate dollars is limited, nonprofits may find themselves competing for corporate donations, when collaboration would likely be more efficient and effective. Again, this may result in nonprofits' efforts and resources being diverted from their primary missions.

As has been discussed previously, corporations often do not communicate their CSR efforts to certain stakeholders because a business case approach suggests that it is not financially prudent to do so. When this happens, nonprofits are not publicly identified as being worthy recipients of these corporation's philanthropic efforts, rendering them unable to use this reputational capital to procure support from other corporate donors. Due to the fact that they have more power than the nonprofits, casino corporations have a moral obligation to help these nonprofits by communicating their CSR efforts to external stakeholders so that the nonprofits can gain the advantage – a sort of "third-party approval" – that is communicated by the casino corporations' financial support.

When casino corporations engage with local nonprofits as a part of their CSR efforts, considerable concerns about power imbalances can arise. An inherent power dynamic in the relationship between corporations and nonprofits makes these relationships unstable in the long run and may lead to nonprofit managers compromising in order to meet the demands of the corporation. Additionally, nonprofits often provide services to employees of gaming corporations regardless of whether the corporations provide financial assistance to the nonprofit; in some ways, this amounts to an exploitative relationship.

And finally, although this concern may seem somewhat trivial and nominal compared to other more practical ones, a corporation's strategic use of CSR implies that nonprofits should speak in the same terms, forcing the nonprofit into a functional orientation even if its primary motivation is moral. This may require nonprofits to go outside their mission-specific abilities and consider how they can best "sell" the benefits of donation to corporations. Ultimately, this traces back to the difference between moral and functional CSR: Should a corporation engage in CSR because such efforts can prove useful to the corporation's bottom line, or because it has a moral obligation to help where and when it can?

Learning from Las Vegas

The case of Las Vegas shows that CSR is not only industry-specific, but also location-specific. This suggests that discussions about CSR need to happen more frequently on a micro level where specific elements of both the industry and location can be considered and the corporation's complete realm of obligations (both moral and functional) to stakeholders can be identified and assessed.

Las Vegas provides an example of a location with a dominant industry. This type of location has special considerations when it comes to the use of CSR by that industry and the impacts it can have on the community. As mentioned previously, dominant industries need to "lead by example" when it comes to CSR, or other industries likely will not follow suit. This involves not only participating in CSR actions, but also publicizing them – "walking the walk" doesn't really have much of an impact if people don't know what the corporation is doing, so in this case "talking the talk" is just as important. (This is an interesting reversal of one of the enduring complaints/criticisms about CSR, which is that corporations are reaping false praise by promoting and receiving credit for actions that they do not actually engage in.)

Any discussion about the casino industry or any other "vice" industry must consider the possibility that these industries may be fundamentally incapable of true social responsibility due to the potentially damaging and addictive nature of their product. As Palazzo and Richter (2005) explain, it seems difficult to describe what an ethical use of CSR by the tobacco industry would look like. However, it is more feasible to consider that corporations in this industry might employ CSR to benefit their bottom line, such as the support of community causes and the employment of responsible labor relations policies, in an amoral use of strategic CSR.

All corporations in vice industries also share a unique characteristic that affects their participation in CSR: Their product may be harmful to the user and, in the case of gambling problems and secondhand smoke, negative externalities may even be felt by non-users. Additionally, it is the continued consumption of the product that drives financial profitability of the corporations that provide it. It remains very possible that the mere existence of casino corporations is by nature fundamentally irresponsible due to these negative externalities.

If the responsibility of casino corporations is questionable, then the operation of government-run gambling for generating public revenue, such as is the case in Canada and Australia, is even more morally dubious. If the government exists to maintain a society that is orderly and safe for the people who live within it, the operation of gambling enterprises may by nature breach that obligation regardless of the intended purpose of the revenue derived from them. In addition, the use of a purported public benefit as a rationale for legalized gambling may in turn be gaining residents' support by convincing them that the gambling enterprise is intended for their own benefit.

CSR in the casino industry is primarily understood and expressed as support for responsible gambling programs and treatment of problem gamblers. However, current discourse about and definition of problem gambling locates the "problem" with the individuals, not with the system that enables them to gamble. Therefore, by funding programs that promote responsible gambling and treat those who have developed addictions, casino corporations (and governments) reinforce the cultural notion that the fault of "problem" gambling lies with the individual, thereby essentially exonerating themselves from responsibility.

Wider implications of the business case for CSR

It is difficult to deny that many of today's corporations are making considerable (and visible) strides toward improving their impact on society. Many of the sustainability practices initiated by Caesars Entertainment, for instance, have considerably reduced the multinational casino operator's environmental impact. However, they have also resulted in considerable financial savings for the casino corporation, and Caesars has been able to sell its environmental CSR efforts to investors largely on the basis of these savings.

If a corporation thinks of CSR in the business case, it will primarily focus on CSR actions that have a positive financial impact for the corporation. This could include, for instance, encouraging purchase decisions by promoting its socially responsible actions and using the corporation's involvement in CSR as a unique selling proposition. This can be especially successful in industries where other companies in the industry do not traditionally engage in CSR; it can also be helpful in industries where companies' actions may generate some sort of negative externalities.

If CSR were intended to serve as a business strategy and ultimately promote purchase decisions, then the primary stakeholders to whom the corporation would communicate would be potential customers, and possibly journalists for a mediated message (third-party endorsement) and a wider reach. Other stakeholders would not be central to the strategic communication and communication to these stakeholders would be de-prioritized. When CSR is approached using a cost–benefit analysis – where costs should be minimized so that return on investment can be maximized – these stakeholders would likely not be communicated to at all; this seems to be the case in Las Vegas, where local community members receive very little communication about the casino corporations' CSR efforts.

But a corporation's failure to communicate its CSR message to all stakeholders might have negative externalities, such as a local community that is less involved in volunteerism and civic engagement and businesses that will not feel pressured to engage in CSR by the presence of an active leading industry or a proactive local media. Thus, the case study of Las Vegas shows that a corporation needs to communicate its CSR actions not just to its consumers, who may make purchase decisions, but also to a wider range of stakeholders in order to fill the moral obligations that extend beyond its functional ones.

8   Conclusions and future directions

The noteworthy financial success of casino gaming in places like Las Vegas and Macau has fueled growth in this industry in locations all over the world. But one has to look no farther than Atlantic City, New Jersey to know that casinos are not a cure-all for ailing cities. The former seaside resort town enjoyed a few decades of success after legalizing casino gambling in the late 1970s, but ultimately, casinos failed to provide the financial redemption to Atlantic City that they had bestowed on other places around the world.

There are certainly discussions to be had about the Atlantic City casino industry and why it failed. More important to this research, however, is the discussion about how the casino industry failed Atlantic City, and the effects that casino gambling has had upon this city. Even in Atlantic City's heyday, when money was flowing into its casinos, Atlantic City simply was not seen as a nice place to live (Simon, 2004). The success of the industry did not translate to the health of the community.

It is this kind of inconsistency that the idea of corporate social responsibility is intended to address: A situation where a corporation or an entire industry benefits at the expense of a local community (or the environment, or its employees) is not only unfair, it is untenable. When the voters of New Jersey approved legal gambling in Atlantic City in 1976, the state established laws requiring casino corporations to give a pittance from their profits (less than 2%, with easily executed loopholes to avoid paying) toward community development (Schwartz, 2003; Simon, 2004). Other than this small legal obligation, though, casinos were not expected to contribute toward the city – their presence and projected economic benefits (e.g. tax revenue, jobs) were considered to be contribution enough.

Because Atlantic City perceived legalized gambling as a last-gasp option to save the failing city, the state was more than happy to give free reign to corporations willing to open these casinos. The legal requirements for community involvement, therefore, were set very low.

> Casinos, lawmakers promised, would act as a "unique tool of urban renewal."
> But the phrase, important as it was, dangled like a catfish on a line – it was
> hard to grasp, and even harder to know exactly what it meant. Did it mean

that casinos – private corporations – would become urban planners? What sort of city would they build? What role would the state play? For whom would they build the city?

(Simon, 2004, pp. 180–181)

The implication in the state's approach – that what was good for the casino corporations would de facto be good for New Jersey – seems almost laughable in hindsight. Casinos came into Atlantic City as a purported savior for the ailing beach town, but the corporations that opened them came for economic reasons. The interests of Atlantic City were not their priority – the interests of their shareholders ruled supreme.

In the late 1970s and early 1980s, casinos rolled into Atlantic City much like the literal bulldozers that tore down decades of the beach town's fabled history. Driven by economic motivation, real estate developers assembled parcels of land in order to sell them to incoming casino corporations. Landlords inflated rents and in some cases even illegally cut off utilities in order to force out tenants so they could cash in on the land grab (Simon, 2004). Even the community, it seems, was overtaken by the primacy of economic profit that was modeled by the casino corporations.

Atlantic City's casinos made decisions based on promoting their own economic success, not the community's. Parking decks and walkways were built with the intention to shuttle visitors directly from their cars into the casino without interacting with the city; this is designed to assuage visitors' fears about Atlantic City's notorious crime problems. In order to preserve precious parking space for paying customers, casinos built remote parking lots for employees on the outskirts of the city (Simon, 2004). This system, which benefits the casinos, deprives local businesses of the patronage of casino employees by reducing their foot traffic.

No one would argue that casino corporations should be responsible for community design and redevelopment; in fact, as Simon (2004) argues, the example of Atlantic City shows that they are particularly ill-suited for that charge. However, the fact that casino corporations (much like all corporations) will naturally prioritize their own economic and operational considerations only serves to reinforce the importance of expecting these corporations to also consider their social responsibilities and factor them into decisions that may affect the community.

This final chapter draws conclusions based on the book's consideration of corporate social responsibility in the casino industry. The first section separates the theoretical and practical concerns about CSR in this industry and others: While an academic and theoretical examination of CSR draws certain conclusions, it is important to acknowledge that there are real-life forces that affect the implementation of CSR by casino corporations. The second section in this chapter looks at the impact of casino corporations, both direct and indirect, and the ways that CSR can help mitigate those negative externalities that are generated by casinos. Finally, a third section makes concrete recommendations for change, based on the research presented here, that are directed at two primary audiences – the corporations that operate (and often profit considerably) from casinos and the public relations practitioners who play a vital role in communicating with stakeholders as a part of the CSR process.

Theoretical considerations and practical concerns

The issue of motivation is central to many theoretical discussions about CSR, whether it is addressed implicitly (e.g. Basu & Palazzo, 2008; Lantos, 2001; Moir, 2001; Pedersen & Neergaard, 2009; Porter & Kramer, 2002) or explicitly (see Brønn & Vidaver-Cohen, 2009; Graafland & Mazereeuw-Van der Duijn Schouten, 2012; Graafland & van de Ven, 2006). Does it matter *why* corporations engage in CSR, or does it merely matter that they *do*?

The points raised by this book aim to frame the discussion somewhat differently; answering the question of motivation lies beyond the scope of this book, nor is it its intention. However, the book suggests that what may be most important is not trying to answer the question, but merely asking it and discussing it from the perspective of the corporation and its stakeholders. Doing so can help a corporation and its stakeholders align their beliefs about CSR in order to identify where discrepancies may exist, then allow them to negotiate through further discussion how they might address those areas where the two may not align. This two-way communication would have the added benefit of strengthening the relationship between the organization and its stakeholders through dialogue.

As argued in chapter 7, casino corporations have a moral obligation to communicate about their CSR actions to a wider range of stakeholders, even if those communications might not support (and may even actively work against) the strategic motivation for engaging in CSR, which is to improve the corporation's bottom line financially. However, this sort of communication requires the commitment of resources by the corporation, and it seems unlikely that corporations would engage in this sort of behavior in practice. The popularity of the business case for CSR also makes it less likely that such a cost expenditure would be supported if it did not ultimately result in financial gain. This sort of communication would probably have to be mandated by legal regulation in order for corporations to allocate the appropriate resources. Given the immense power differential between casino corporations and most, if not all, stakeholders, it seems unlikely that even strong pressure from one or more stakeholders would be sufficient to mandate this sort of communication.

On a conceptual level, a business case approach to corporate social responsibility clearly has some flaws. As detailed in chapter 7, several inconsistencies can be found between the execution of CSR efforts designed to support an organization's bottom line and the fundamental idea that businesses should interact with and support society in an appropriate manner. However, the use of CSR that is justified on a purely moral basis does not satisfy the demands of shareholders that the corporation be a responsible steward of their money. Thus, from a practical perspective, a functional approach to CSR is likely to be more successful in establishing a corporation's support for CSR and integrating these actions into the corporation's core operations, which will then perpetuate the continued inclusion of CSR in the corporation's efforts.

In this way, the corporation finds itself paradoxically unable to take a moral approach to CSR even if it wishes to avoid some of the contradictions and negative externalities inherent in the functional approach. Further complicating this choice is the fact that CSR decisions are technically made not by amoral "corporations" but by people within those corporations, often several of them, who have their own beliefs about the appropriate relationship between business and society. This can lead to even more contradictions as one person's perspective might differ from another's in key ways.

Impact of casino corporations' CSR and some wider thoughts for other industries

A search of academic journals and trade publications in fields like business, management, and communication will yield hundreds of articles on the ways that CSR can be deployed to a business's strategic advantage. Very little of the research on corporate social responsibility, however, has considered the direct and indirect impacts of a business's strategic approach to CSR. As CSR increasingly becomes a part of the ongoing interaction between business and society, it is important to take a consequential look at what effects these actions might be having on a variety of stakeholders.

Chapter 7 identified various impacts that casino corporations' functional approach toward CSR might have, including prioritization of environmental efforts that save cost and encourage purchase decisions; limited support for workers' rights to a healthy and fair work environment; reduced support for nonprofits in times of economic crisis, when that support might be needed most; and other impacts on the nonprofits in a casino's local community that might negatively affect the nonprofits' ability to fulfill their mission-based goals. Additionally, when stakeholders are negatively impacted by a corporation's CSR efforts, they may find it hard to challenge the corporation's actions taken under the auspices of CSR for a number of reasons.

Clearly, CSR is not intended to support certain stakeholders at the expense of others, and the idea that stakeholders should suffer negative impacts in the name of CSR in order to benefit the corporation would not fit into most conceptions of the word "responsible." These situations may arise because a lack of forethought or an overly narrow scope for considering CSR's potential consequences leaves the corporation without any knowledge that negative externalities may exist; alternatively, a corporation (or some actor within the corporation) may have made a conscious choice to deem these consequences acceptable given the benefits that are to accrue to the corporation, its shareholders, and/or other stakeholders.

As discussed in chapter 7, some of CSR's effects may be less direct and more generally felt by society rather than particular stakeholders. For instance, an increasing trend toward a business case approach to CSR implies that corporate decisions should be made solely to benefit the financial bottom line and ultimately the corporation's shareholders. This concept of shareholder primacy places emphasis on financial success over all else and leads to the kind of decisions that can make functional CSR so problematic.

Considering CSR in the casino industry is especially important because of the negative externalities that the industry can generate. However, the corporation's moral obligation to engage in CSR comes not from the type of industry or the product it creates but from the dynamic between business and society and the relative wealth and power of corporations relative to many other stakeholders. Thus, a great deal of the concerns raised in this book can be applied more broadly to other industries, especially those in which corporations are especially large and powerful or dominate a local community.

The case of the casino industry, and in particular the case study of Las Vegas examined in chapter 6, suggests that corporations must take a more holistic approach to CSR that also examines potential consequences of its CSR actions for stakeholders, especially if they might be negative. Often this may entail actually speaking with members of the stakeholder group, where possible, as they may be able to give unique insight that the corporation might not have. A big-picture approach to a corporation's CSR efforts, which includes the possible negative externalities generated by these efforts or the particular stakeholder groups that may be disadvantaged by them, speaks to the suggestions by nonprofit managers in Las Vegas that the corporations' CSR programs should be more holistic and proactive if they are to best serve the Las Vegas community.

Another interesting point raised in interviews with managers of Las Vegas nonprofits is that casino corporations' CSR actions might have an impact on the level of CSR efforts by other corporations, both inside and outside of an industry. As discussed in chapter 3, under a business case approach to CSR the corpora- tion will not participate in CSR unless it feels that there is a significant economic advantage to be gained from its efforts. Engagement in CSR as a unique selling proposition (USP) – an attempt to differentiate the corporation from others in the industry for the purpose of influencing purchase decisions – will only exist if other corporations in the industry are not engaging in CSR. Conversely, the existence of significant CSR efforts on the part of other corporations in the industry may force a particular corporation to engage in CSR lest the corporation appear irresponsible by comparison. In vice industries such as casino gaming, this is especially signifi- cant as corporations strive to establish an appearance that the corporation is taking steps to address negative externalities it may be creating.

While a duty-based approach to decision making, which looks at an actor's obligations to stakeholders and the ways that various actions may uphold those duties, is an important element of considering topics like CSR, a consequential approach that looks at outcomes and impacts must be included as well in order to ensure a well-reasoned ethical decision (Bivins, 2009). While discussions of CSR in the academic and popular literature have amply examined the strategic advan- tage of engaging in CSR and the moral obligations that can be fulfilled with these efforts, so far very few scholars have considered the ramifications of corporations' socially responsible actions, especially those that might be counter-intuitive to the notion of CSR. In order for corporate social responsibility to be enacted as a genuine attempt to improve society, and not merely as window-dressing to improve the corporation's reputation, this big-picture approach remains crucial to ensuring that CSR is enacted ethically and responsibly.

What next? CSR in the casino industry

It seems clear that casino corporations, in no small part due to the negative externalities their operations cause in their communities, should bear some responsibility to the society that allows them to operate. However, as this book shows, the current efforts by casino corporations to engage in strategic CSR – in hopes of ultimately benefiting their financial bottom line and reinforcing their primary allegiance to shareholders – may ultimately be causing as much harm as they are doing good.

If casino corporations are going to continue engaging with various stakeholders as a part of their CSR efforts, this research suggests several steps that should be taken in order to make these actions most productive for all involved.

1   Casino corporations should take a macro-level approach to CSR, considering all stakeholders, not just those who might directly impact the corporation's bottom line.
2   Planning and research should be involved in the coordination of casino corporations' CSR to ensure that these efforts do not prioritize certain stakeholders at the expense of creating negative externalities for others. In order to do this effectively, these corporations should engage all stakeholders in dialogue about the casino's CSR and how it affects the stakeholder in positive and negative ways.
3   In order to ensure that their efforts will achieve the maximum benefit for stakeholders, casino CSR efforts should be communicated to all stakeholders, regardless of their ability to affect the casino's bottom line. This will prevent negative externalities as discussed in chapters 6 and 7 and may even have the effect of multiplying the positive benefits to society of the corporation's efforts.
4   Casinos should offer support to nonprofits in the community based on the nonprofits' need and/or the casinos' ability to provide specialized expertise (e.g. casino executives as board members) rather than because the nonprofits' mission fits into the casino corporations' prescribed giving priorities.
5   Casinos' efforts to ameliorate their environmental impacts, especially in natural resource-strapped locations like Las Vegas and Macau, should prioritize actions that have the greatest ability to positively impact the natural environment. This may require that the corporations commission research from independent experts so that their decisions are guided by evidence, not by the potential influence on corporate profits.
6   In addition to being granted rights to form unions and other benefits given to most service employees, workers in casinos should not be forced to subject

themselves to the negative health impacts of casinos, such as secondhand smoke, as conditions of their continued employment. Casinos should make decisions on labor relations topics based on what is best for the workers, not the corporations' financial success.

7   Although casino corporations' efforts to prevent problem gambling should be continued, they should endeavor to deviate from traditional medical approaches, which locate the "problem" in the individual, and instead accept that some of the fault lies with the system that makes gambling opportunities easy to access.

The casino industry has seen many attempts by well-meaning corporations to engage in socially responsible actions. Sometimes these efforts achieve their intended goal of benefiting a particular stakeholder group or society in general; other times, these actions have unintended consequences. However, the most ethical way for casino corporations to engage in CSR is to dialogue with key stakeholders to ensure that the corporations' actions are actually achieving their intended goals (Hing & McKellar, 2004). For this reason, the involvement of public relations professionals in casino CSR plays a vital role in ensuring that these actions reach their maximum benefit.

What's next? Implications for public relations professionals

In 1994, L'Etang theorized the potential ethical conflicts between the use of CSR by corporations and the responsibility, often given to public relations professionals, of communicating these actions to stakeholder publics. Her concerns centered around whether PR was being used to communicate CSR to stakeholders, as an ethical approach would suggest, or whether corporations were in fact engaging in actions that appeared socially responsible solely for the function of improving relationships with certain key stakeholders.

Too often, CSR actions are employed as a corporation struggles to regain its footing after a crucial ethical misstep, such as Nike's employment of child-labor in the sweatshops that produced its product (Hamil, 1999; Schoenberger-Orgad & McKie, 2005). Sims and Brinkman (2003) noted that even the Enron corporation deployed a robust slate of CSR actions before its eventual collapse due to massive ethical breaches. In reporting on the use of strategic CSR by multinational oil companies in Africa, Frynas (2005, pp. 585–586) gives perhaps the most chilling possibility, that these corporation's attempts at "window-dressing" CSR might actually impede the progress of development in these countries:

> If PR priorities take precedence over development priorities, this is likely to affect the planning and the implementation of CSR initiatives. PR needs may, for instance, prioritize media-friendly projects such as donating medical equipment or helping to construct a new hospital, rather than slow local capacity-building or the training of village nurses . . . There is a real danger that PR needs may constrain developmental efforts.

The use of CSR as a public relations tactic also presents "a danger that companies will misuse the new paradigm to win over citizens with highly publicized social initiatives only to divert their attention from unjust corporate practices, such as underpaying workers or exposing them to unsafe conditions" (Smith, 1994, p. 112).

As Lantos (2001) argues, strategic CSR is not necessarily wrong just because it can be useful in helping an organization achieve its financial objectives by improving relationships with key stakeholders. However, the strategic use of PR solely for public relations purposes runs the risk that CSR becomes what Frankental (2001, p. 22) calls "an adjunct of PR" and not something that is "embedded across the organisation horizontally and vertically." In vice industries such as gambling, the danger of CSR that is merely "window dressing" seems amplified because of the negative externalities generated by corporations in these industries (Cai, Jo, & Pan, 2012, p. 467; see also Palazzo & Richter, 2005).

Because forces from within the casino corporation will likely advocate for actions that promote financial success even at the risk of negative consequences, the onus may fall on the public relations professional – or other professionals tasked with conducting CSR programs – to ensure that the actions being chosen are truly intended to benefit society and are not merely "self-serving philanthropic initiatives that lend themselves to photo opportunities without effecting real change" (Hamil, 1999, p. 105). While public relations practitioners are accustomed to calls that they bear the ethical responsibility for an organization's actions (Bowen, 2008), in practice this may put a good deal of pressure on public relations practitioners to make a stand against traditional concepts of shareholder primacy. This also suggests that public relations practitioners may want to consider further education in the theory of corporate social responsibility so that they can better appreciate the "big picture" approach necessary to ensure that CSR actions are being undertaken responsibly.

Public relations practitioners often become engaged in a corporation's social responsibility efforts as part of an effort to align the corporation's efforts with stakeholders' expectations by opening lines of dialogue about CSR with these stakeholders. This co-orientation makes for improved execution of CSR actions (Pava & Krausz, 1997), but ultimately may be merely an element of the strategic deployment of CSR that aims to improve relationships with key stakeholders. Echoing Grunig and Hunt's (1984) concept of two-way symmetrical public relations, these efforts at CSR dialogue must genuinely attempt to achieve mutual benefit for both the corporation and its stakeholders.

Beyond merely communicating a corporation's efforts to key stakeholders, public relations practitioners can play an important role in ensuring that CSR serves a broader purpose of contributing to society in an appropriate way. Miles, Munilla, & Darroch (2006) suggest that public relations practitioners play a vital role in conducting "strategic conversations" with stakeholders that can ensure the corporation is taking a broad approach to CSR.

> In fact, without engaging stakeholders in strategic conversations, top management runs the risk of intellectual isolation from its stakeholders and its

own BSEs [boundary-spanning employees, i.e. employees who interact with other stakeholders], creating a "bunker mentality" that offers a very management-centric, limited perspective of the firm, its capabilities, and potential futures.

(Miles, Munilla, & Darroch, 2006, p. 198)

Conversations with stakeholders can broaden the corporation's view of CSR beyond the traditional business justification and can bring in new ideas for how the corporation's efforts can best serve all stakeholders, not just those with a financial interest (i.e. shareholders).

Public relations practitioners can also play a vital role in establishing the way that both corporations and their stakeholders define CSR and the corporation's responsibility to society. In fact, Guthey and Morsing (2014) suggest that the wide variety of definitions of CSR is actually an opportunity rather than a disadvantage. By engaging in dialogue with stakeholders about the corporation's responsibility and the appropriateness of certain CSR actions, public relations professionals can facilitate "a forum for sensemaking, diversity of opinion, and debate over the social norms and expectations attached to corporate activity" (Guthey & Morsing, 2014, p. 556). In fact, it may be these discussions themselves that provide the greatest benefit of CSR, as they allow us to continue debating and defining the appropriate role of corporations in our society and the ways that they must act in order for our system to achieve long-term sustainability.

In this way, CSR is not a solution to society's problems, nor is it a penance for sins a corporation may have committed against society or certain stakeholder groups within it. Instead, CSR is an important (two-way) discussion we need to have about the role that corporations play in our society. Because so many elements of CSR are culturally constructed and situationally based in an industry or location (Schultz, Castelló, & Morsing, 2013), these are conversations that need to happen constantly as cultural mores and contextual factors change – the economic situation in Las Vegas, Nevada provides a prime example of how this is important.

As the boundary-spanners between the corporation and key stakeholders, public relations practitioners are uniquely positioned to facilitate these conversations. Further, in order to ensure that CSR benefits not only the corporation but also society as a whole, professionals must not merely serve a functional role in ensuring that CSR will best fit the corporation's strategic business goals. Rather, they must ensure that the dialogue takes an approach focused on macro-level aspects of CSR and considers the various impacts the corporation's actions may have in this regard and the corporation's duties to avoid creating negative impact on stakeholders with its actions.

Challenging corporate social responsibility: final thoughts

That CSR is so hotly debated as a topic indicates the important position it inhabits in the discussion about today's society and its priorities.

> The discussion [about the role of business in society] is rooted in the deep concern existing in postmodern societies that economic reasoning dominates human and social issues. While observing the increase of corporate power, postmodern societies have witnessed heated discussions on the purpose and scope of corporations, touching the very basic foundations of their economic systems.
>
> (Richter, 2010, p. 629)

The business case for CSR holds that a perceived "convergence of financial and social interests" (Paine, 2000, p. 319) has facilitated the growth in CSR, as corporations can now justify involvement in social or ethical issues with an economic rationale. However, as Newell (2008) points out, the mere fact that corporations feel the need to invoke a financial "excuse" for participation in social issues belies a more concerning situation, especially given that corporations are increasingly invoking rights of personhood (Winkler, 2014) – which should, in theory, come with the accompanying moral obligations assigned to all individuals.

As Paine (2000, p. 327) argues, the business case for CSR follows as one instance in an insidious trend of prioritizing financial gain in decision making, as "implicit in the appeal to economics as a justification for ethics is acceptance of economics as the more authoritative rationale. *Rather than being a domain of rationality capable of challenging economics, ethics is conceived only as a tool of economics*" (emphasis added). In a society where economics are the driving motivation for corporate actions – and indeed, the behavior of most actors in society – traditional noneconomic values such as human rights, fairness, and beneficence no longer hold any sway. Even the most coldly rational thinker should certainly realize the potential evolution toward trouble when financial success holds more value than human dignity.

The example of CSR in the casino industry shows us that the successful execution of corporate social responsibility is far more complex than the enactment of programs that advance the corporation's reputation and/or address the negative externalities it may cause. In the case of Las Vegas, for instance, casino corporations' efforts to enact CSR programs have resulted in a number of negative (presumably unintended) consequences for a variety of stakeholders. Government attempts to enact legalized gambling for public benefit in countries like Canada and Australia have addressed the negative externalities of gambling as best they can, but it remains unclear whether any degree of CSR can suffice to balance out casinos' often negative social impact on communities.

Indeed, it may even be that efforts by casino corporations to engage in CSR may be a form of "window dressing" that masks the true effect that casinos are having on our society. If this is the case, these CSR efforts paradoxically may even be doing more harm than good. This raises serious questions for professionals everywhere and should prompt an examination of not only the motivations for but also the effects of a corporation's social responsibility program, ensuring that CSR is being enacted for the benefit of society and stakeholders and not merely for the bottom line of the corporation.

Appendix

List of participant pseudonyms referenced in the book

Table A.1

Pseudonym	Job Title	Type of Nonprofit	Years at Current Position	Years of Nonprofit Experience
Francine Donovan	Public Relations	Children/Family	4	4
Beverly Hanson	Director of Development	Children/Family	1.5	1.5
Eleanor Golden	Executive Director	Parenting	12	12
Natasha Delatour	Executive Director	Childhood disease	3.5	4.5
Kent Charleston	Executive Director, local chapter	Health advocacy	4.5	8
Maria Islington	Co-founder/ Executive Director	Literacy	9	9
Tina Goldstein	Development Manager	Hospice	0.5	7
Thomas Denton	Executive Director	Disability/job placement	14	–
Marion Islip	State Director	Education	6.5	27
Karen Carpenter	Executive Director, local chapter	Education	–	–
Katherine Matthews	Executive Director	Youth/medical	3	23
Victor Newsome	Interim Executive Director	Homelessness/ youth	1.5	1.5
Noreen king	Director of Development	Disability	6.5	–
Kevin Roberts	Development Assistant	Disability	0.5	0.5
Mary Dunston	Executive Director	HIV/AIDS, LGBT	5	5

References

A stress test for good intentions. (2009, May 16). *Economist, 391*, 69–70.

Abbugao, M. (2010, August 29). Singapore's bet on casino resorts paying off big. *Agence France-Presse*. Retrieved from http://www.eturbonews.com/18166/singapores-bet-casino-resorts-paying-big

Aguilera, R. V., Rupp, D. E., Williams, C. A., & Ganapathi, J. (2007). Putting the S back in corporate social responsibility: A multilevel theory of social change in organizations. *Academy of Management Review, 32*(3), 836–863.

Alexander, C. (2002). Rise to power: The recent history of the Culinary Union in Las Vegas. In Rothman, H. K., M. Davis (Eds.), *The grit beneath the glitter: Tales from the real Las Vegas* (pp. 145–175). Berkeley, CA: University of California Press.

American Association of Fund-Raising Counsel. (2009). *Giving USA 2009: The annual report on philanthropy for the year 2008*. New York: American Association of Fund-Raising Counsel.

Andersen, K. (1994). Las Vegas, USA. *Time, 143*, 36–43.

Ap, J. (1992). Residents' perceptions on tourism impacts. *Annals of Tourism Research, 19*(4), 665–690.

Associated Press. (1993, January 16). Sam Boyd, 82, a roulette dealer who became a builder of casinos. Lexis-Nexis Academic: http://www.lexisnexis.com/

Associated Press. (2011, December 3). Is Nevada's economy recovering? Some say yes, some say no. *USA Today*. Retrieved from http://www.usatoday.com/news/nation/story/2011-12-03/nevada-las-vegas-economy/51623464/1

Aupperle, K. E., Carroll, A. B., & Hatfield, J. D. (1985). An empirical examination of the relationship between corporate social responsibility and profitability. *Academy of Management Journal, 28*(2), 446–463.

Axelrod, R. (1980). Effective choice in the prisoner's dilemma. *Journal of Conflict Resolution, 24*(1), 3–25.

Azzone, G., & Noci, G. (1998). Seeing ecology and "green" innovations as a source of change. *Journal of Organizational Change Management, 11*(2), 94–111.

Back, K.-J., & Lee, C.-K. (2012). Residents' perceptions of casino development in Korea: the Kangwon Land casino case. *UNLV Gaming Research & Review Journal, 9*(2), 45–53.

Balsas, C. J. L. (2013). Gaming anyone? A comparative study of recent urban development trends in Las Vegas and Macau. *Cities, 31*, 298–307.

Barr, M. S. (2005). Credit where it counts: The Community Reinvestment Act and its critics. *New York University Law Review, 80*, 101–133.

Basu, K., & Palazzo, G. (2008). Corporate social responsibility: A process model of sensemaking. *Academy of Management Review, 33*(1), 122–136.

Belanger, Y. D., & Williams, R. J. (2011). Neoliberalism as colonial embrace: Evaluating Alberta's regulation of First Nations gaming, 1993–2010. *Business and Politics, 13*(4), 1–34.

Belanger, Y. D., & Williams, R. J. (2012). The First Nations' contribution to Alberta's charitable gaming model: Assessing the impacts. *Canadian Public Policy, 38*(4), 551–572.

Beliveau, B., Cottrill, M., & O'Neill, H. M. (1994). Predicting corporate social responsiveness: A model drawn from three perspectives. *Journal of Business Ethics, 13*, 731–738.

Bellringer, M. E., Perese, L. M., Abbott, M. W., & Williams, M. M. (2006). Gambling among Pacific mothers living in New Zealand. *International Gambling Studies, 6*(2), 217–235.

Bernhard, B. J., Green, M. S., & Lucas, A. F. (2008). From maverick to mafia to MBA: Gaming industry leadership in Las Vegas from 1931 through 2007. *Cornell Hospitality Quarterly, 49*(2), 177–190.

Bhattacharya, C. B., & Sen, S. (2004). Doing better at doing good: When, why, and how consumers respond to corporate social initiatives. *California Management Review, 47*(1), 9–24.

Binkley, C. (2008). *Winner takes all.* New York: Hyperion.

Birth, G., Illia, L., Lurati, F., & Zamparini, A. (2008). Communicating CSR: practices among Switzerland's top 300 companies. *Corporate Communications: An International Journal, 13*(2), 182–196.

Bivins, T. (2009). *Mixed media* (2nd ed.). New York: Routledge.

Black, R., & Ramsay, H. (2003). The ethics of gambling: guidelines for players and commercial providers. *International Gambling Studies, 3*(2), 199–215.

Blanco, B., Guillamón-Saorín, E., & Guiral, A. (2013). Do non-socially responsible companies achieve legitimacy through socially responsible actions? The mediating effect of innovation. *Journal of Business Ethics, 117*(1), 67–83.

Blaszczynski, A., Ladouceur, R., Nower, L., & Shaffer, H. (2008). Informed choice and gambling: Principles for consumer protection. *Journal of Gambling Business and Economics, 2*(1), 103–118.

Blevins, A., & Jensen, K. (1998). Gambling as a community development quick fix. *The Annals of the American Academy of Political and Social Science, 556*(1), 109–123.

Bloom, P. N., Hoeffler, S., Keller, K. L., & Meza, C. E. B. (2006). How social-cause marketing affects consumer perceptions. *MIT Sloan Management Review, 47*(2), 49–55.

Blowfield, M., & Frynas, J. G. (2005). Setting new agendas: critical perspectives on corporate social responsibility in the developing world. *International Affairs, 81*(3), 499–513.

Blumenthal, D., & Bergstrom, A. J. (2003). Brand councils that care: Towards the convergence of branding and corporate social responsibility. *The Journal of Brand Management, 10*(4–5), 327–341.

Boatright, J. R. (1996). Business ethics and the theory of the firm. *American Business Law Journal, 34*(2), 217–238.

Bondy, K., Matten, D., & Moon, J. (2004). The adoption of voluntary codes of conduct in MNCs: A three-country comparative study. *Business and Society Review, 109*(4), 449–477.

Borch, A. (2012). Gambling in the news and the revelation of market power: the case of Norway. *International Gambling Studies, 12*(1), 55–67.

Boris, E. T., & Steuerle, C. E. (2006). Scope and dimentions of the nonprofit sector. In R. Steinberg & W. W. Powell (Eds.), *The nonprofit sector: A research handbook* (2nd ed.) (pp. 66–88). New Haven, CT: Yale University Press.

Bowen, H. R. (1953). *Social responsibilities of the businessman*. New York: Harper and Row.

Bowen, S. A. (2008). A state of neglect: Public relations as "corporate conscience" or ethics counsel. *Journal of Public Relations Research, 20*(3), 271–296.

Braunlich, C. G. (1996). Lessons from the Atlantic City casino experience. *Journal of Travel Research, 34*(3), 46–56.

Breen, H., Buultzens, J., & Hing, N. (2012). The responsible gambling code in Queensland, Australia: Implementation and venue assessment. *UNLV Gaming Research & Review Journal, 9*(1), 43–60.

Brønn, P. S., & Vidaver-Cohen, D. (2009). Corporate motives for social initiative: Legitimacy, sustainability, or the bottom line? *Journal of Business Ethics, 87*(S1), 91–109.

Buchanan, J., Elliott, G., & Johnson, L. (2009). The marketing of legal but potentially harmful products and corporate social responsibility: The gaming industry view. *International Journal of Interdisciplinary Social Sciences, 4*(2), 81–97.

Buchanan, J., & Johnson, L. W. (2007). Corporate social responsibility and the gaming industry: A contradiction in terms? Presented at the Australia and New Zealand Marketing Academy, Dunedin, New Zealand.

Burke, L., & Logsdon, J. M. (1996). How corporate social responsibility pays off. *Long Range Planning, 29*(4), 495–502.

Burnham, J. C. (1993). *Bad habits: Drinking, smoking, taking drugs, gambling, sexual misbehavior, and swearing in American history*. New York: NYU Press.

Bybee, S. (1999). History, development, and legislation of Las Vegas casino gaming. In C. H. C. Hsu (Ed.), *Legalized casino gaming in the United States: The economic and social impact* (pp. 3–24). Binghamton, NY: Haworth Hospitality Press.

Caesars, Circus Circus and Hilton in Casino Deal. (1993, December 4). *The New York Times*. Retrieved from http://www.nytimes.com/

Caesars Entertainment. (2014). *Vibrant communities: Our holistic approach to sustainability*. Retrieved from http://www.caesars.com/images/corporate/community/CE-CSR-OneSheet%20Facts-FINAL-02.pdf

Cai, Y., Jo, H., & Pan, C. (2012). Doing well while doing bad? CSR in controversial industry sectors. *Journal of Business Ethics, 108*(4), 467–480.

Campbell, C. S. (1994). *Gambling in Canada: The bottom line*. Criminology Research Centre, School of Criminology, Simon Fraser University.

Campbell, C. S., & Smith, G. J. (1998). Canadian gambling: Trends and public policy issues. *The Annals of the American Academy of Political and Social Science, 556*(1), 22–35.

Campbell, C. S., & Smith, G. J. (2003). Gambling in Canada – From vice to disease to responsibility: A negotiated history. *Canadian Bulletin of Medical History/Bulletin Canadien D'histoire de La Médecine, 20*(1), 121–149.

Campbell, J. L. (2007). Why would corporations behave in socially responsible ways? An institutional theory of corporate social responsibility. *Academy of Management Review, 32*(3), 946–967.

Caneday, L., & Zeiger, J. (1991). The social, economic, and environmental costs of tourism to a gaming community as perceived by its residents. *Journal of Travel Research, 30*(2), 45–49.

Capriotti, P., & Moreno, Á. (2007). Corporate citizenship and public relations: The importance and interactivity of social responsibility issues on corporate websites. *Public Relations Review, 33*(1), 84–91. doi:10.1016/j.pubrev.2006.11.012

Carroll, A. B. (1991). The pyramid of corporate social responsibility: toward the moral management of organizational stakeholders. *Business Horizons, 34*(4), 39–48.

Carroll, A. B. (1999). Corporate social responsibility evolution of a definitional construct. *Business & Society, 38*(3), 268–295.

Carroll, C. E. (2011). Media relations and corporate social responsibility. In O. Ihlen, J. Bartlett, & S. May (Eds.), *Handbook of Communication and Corporate Social Responsibility* (Chichester: Wiley-Blackwell), 423–444.

Cheney, G., Roper, J., & May, S. (2007). Overview. In S. May, G. Cheney, & J. Roper (Eds.), *The debate over corporate social responsibility* (pp. 3–12). New York: Oxford University Press.

Chhabra, D., & Gursoy, D. (2007). Perceived impacts of gambling: Integration of two theories. *UNLV Gaming Research & Review Journal, 11*(1), 27–40.

Christensen, L. T., Morsing, M., & Thyssen, O. (2013). CSR as aspirational talk. *Organization, 20*(3), 372–393.

Christie, L. (2008, February 5). Las Vegas tops foreclosure list. *CNNMoney.* Retrieved from http://money.cnn.com/2008/02/05/real_estate/zip_code_foreclosures/

City of Las Vegas. (2009). *History.* Retrieved from http://www.lasvegasnevada.gov/FactsStatistics/history.htm

Clark, C. E. (2000). Differences between public relations and corporate social responsibility: An analysis. *Public Relations Review, 26*(3), 363–380.

Clarkson, M. E. (1995). A stakeholder framework for analyzing and evaluating corporate social performance. *Academy of Management Review, 20*(1), 92–117.

Clayton, C. H. (2013). Macau's "sort-of sovereignty." *The Newsletter,* (64), 26–27.

Coolican, J. P. (2012, February 20). Was life really better when the Mob ruled Las Vegas? *Las Vegas Sun.* Retrieved from http://www.lasvegassun.com/

Cotti, C. (2008). The effect of casinos on local labor markets: A county level analysis. *Journal of Gambling Business and Economics, 2*(2), 17–41.

Cragg, W. (2002). Business ethics and stakeholder theory. *Business Ethics Quarterly, 12*(2), 113–142.

Crawford, R. L., & Gram, H. A. (1978). Social responsibility as interorganizational transaction. *Academy of Management Review, 3*(4), 880–888.

Culinary Union Local 226. (2014). *History.* Retrieved from http://www.culinaryunion226.org/union/history

Dahlsrud, A. (2008). How corporate social responsibility is defined: an analysis of 37 definitions. *Corporate Social Responsibility and Environmental Management, 15*(1), 1–13.

Davis, K. (1960). Can business afford to ignore social responsibilities? *California Management Review, 2*(3), 70–76.

De Colle, S., & York, J. G. (2009). Why wine is not glue? The unresolved problem of negative screening in socially responsible investing. *Journal of Business Ethics, 85*(S1), 83–95.

Den Hond, F., & De Bakker, F. G. (2007). Ideologically motivated activism: How activist groups influence corporate social change activities. *Academy of Management Review, 32*(3), 901–924.

Dentchev, N. A. (2004). Corporate social performance as a business strategy. *Journal of Business Ethics, 55*(4), 395–410.

Despite health risks, casino dealers still exposed to cigarette smoke. (2010, February 14). *Las Vegas Sun.* Retrieved from http://www.lasvegassun.com/

Dhaliwal, D. S., Li, O. Z., Tsang, A., & Yang, Y. G. (2011). Voluntary nonfinancial disclosure and the cost of equity capital: The initiation of corporate social responsibility reporting. *The Accounting Review, 86*(1), 59–100.

Dief, M. E., & Font, X. (2010). The determinants of hotels' marketing managers' green marketing behaviour. *Journal of Sustainable Tourism, 18*(2), 157–174.

Dimanche, F., & Speyrer, J. F. (1996). Report on a comprehensive five-year gambling impact research plan in New Orleans. *Journal of Travel Research, 34*(3), 97–100.

Dioko, L. A. N., & So, S.-I. (2012). Branding destinations versus branding hotels in a gaming destination—Examining the nature and significance of co-branding effects in the case study of Macao. *International Journal of Hospitality Management, 31*(2), 554–563.

Doane, D. (2005). The myth of CSR. *Stanford Social Innovation Review, 3*(3), 22–29.

Dombrink, J. (1996). Gambling and the legislation of vice: Social movements, public health and public policy in the United States. In *Gambling cultures: Studies in history and interpretation* (pp. 43–64). London: Routledge.

Donaldson, T. (1982). *Corporations and morality*. Englewood Cliffs, NJ: Prentice-Hall.

Donaldson, T., & Preston, L. E. (1995). The stakeholder theory of the corporation: Concepts, evidence, and implications. *Academy of Management Review, 20*(1), 65–91.

Doran, B., & Young, M. (2010). "Mobile mindsets": EGM venue usage, gambling participation, and problem gambling among three itinerant groups on the Sunshine Coast of Australia. *International Gambling Studies, 10*(3), 269–288.

Doughney, J. (2007). Ethical blindness, EGMs and public policy: A tentative essay comparing the EGM and tobacco industries. *International Journal of Mental Health and Addiction, 5*(4), 311–319.

Draper, J., Dawson, M., & Casey, E. (2011). An exploratory study of the importance of sustainable practices in the meeting and convention site selection process. *Journal of Convention & Event Tourism, 12*(3), 153–178.

Dreier, H. (2013, July 6). Macau, Chinese gambling boomtown, remakes gambling world, Las Vegas. *Huffington Post*. Retrieved from http://www.huffingtonpost.com/

Du, S., Bhattacharya, C. B., & Sen, S. (2007). Reaping relational rewards from corporate social responsibility: The role of competitive positioning. *International Journal of Research in Marketing, 24*(3), 224–241.

Du, S., Bhattacharya, C. B., & Sen, S. (2010). Maximizing business returns to corporate social responsibility (CSR): The role of CSR communication. *International Journal of Management Reviews, 12*(1), 8–19.

Du, S., & Vieira, E. T. (2012). Striving for legitimacy through corporate social responsibility: Insights from oil companies. *Journal of Business Ethics, 110*(4), 413–427.

Du Cros, H. (2009). Emerging issues for cultural tourism in Macau. *Journal of Current Chinese Affairs, 38*(1), 73–99.

Durham, S., & Hashimoto, K. (2010). *The history of gambling in America*. Upper Saddle River, NJ: Pearson Education.

Eadington, W. R. (1975). Economic implications of legalizing casino gambling. *Journal of Behavioral Economics, 4*(1), 55–77.

Eadington, W. R. (1996). The legalization of casinos: Policy objectives, regulatory alternatives, and cost/benefit considerations. *Journal of Travel Research, 34*(3), 3–8.

Eadington, W. R. (2003). Values and choices: The struggle to find balance with permitted gambling in modern society. In *Gambling: Who wins? who loses?* (pp. 31–48). Amherst, NY: Prometheus Books.

Eadington, W. (2005). Ethical and policy considerations in the spread of commercial gambling. In *Gambling cultures: Studies in history and interpretation* (pp. 222–239). New York: Routledge.

Eadington, W. R. (2012). Analyzing the trends in gaming-based tourism for the state of Nevada: Implications for public policy and economic development. *UNLV Gaming Research & Review Journal, 15*(1), 37–50.

Eadington, W. R., & Siu, R. C. S. (2007). Between law and custom – examining the interaction between legislative change and the evolution of Macao's casino industry. *International Gambling Studies, 7*(1), 1–28.

Easterling, D. S. (2004). The residents' perspective in tourism research: A review and synthesis. *Journal of Travel & Tourism Marketing, 17*(4), 45-62.

Edwards, L. (2006). Rethinking power in public relations. *Public Relations Review, 32*(3), 229–231.

Ellen, P. S., Webb, D. J., & Mohr, L. A. (2006). Building corporate associations: Consumer attributions for corporate socially responsible programs. *Journal of the Academy of Marketing Science, 34*(2), 147–157.

Elving, W. J. L. (2013). Scepticism and corporate social responsibility communications: the influence of fit and reputation. *Journal of Marketing Communications, 19*(4), 277–292.

Esrock, S. L., & Leichty, G. B. (1998). Social responsibility and corporate web pages: self-presentation or agenda-setting? *Public Relations Review, 24*(3), 305–319.

Evan, W. M., & Freeman, R. E. (1988). A stakeholder theory of the modern corporation: Kantian capitalism. In T. Beauchamp & N. Bowie (Eds.), *Ethical theory and business* (pp. 75-93). Englewood Cliffs, NJ: Prentice-Hall.

Evans, W. N., & Topoleski, J. H. (2002). *The social and economic impact of Native American casinos*. National Bureau of Economic Research.

Fanstein, S. F., & Judd, D. R. (1999). Global forces, local strategies, and urban tourism. In D. R. Judd & S. F. Fanstein (Eds.), *The tourist city* (pp. 1–17). New Haven, CT: Yale University Press.

Ferrari, M., & Ives, S. (2005). *Las Vegas: An unconventional history*. Boston, MA: Bulfinch Books.

Firat, A. F. (2001). The meanings and messages of Las Vegas: The present of our future. *M@n@gement, 4*(3), 101–120.

Fletcher, M. (2001, October 26). Luck of Las Vegas runs out for 15,000. *London Times*.

Fong, D. K. C., Fong, H. N., & Li, S. Z. (2011). The social cost of gambling in Macao: before and after the liberalisation of the gaming industry. *International Gambling Studies, 11*(1), 43–56.

Forehand, M. R., & Grier, S. (2003). When is honesty the best policy? The effect of stated company intent on consumer skepticism. *Journal of Consumer Psychology, 13*(3), 349–356.

Forrest, D. (2013). An economic and social review of gambling in Great Britain. *Journal of Gambling Business and Economics, 7*(3), 1–33.

Frankental, P. (2001). Corporate social responsibility–a PR invention? *Corporate Communications: An International Journal, 6*(1), 18–23.

Frederick, W. C. (1986). Toward CSR: Why ethical analysis is indispensable and unavoidable in corporate affairs. *California Management Review, 28*(2), 126–141.

Frederick, W. C. (1994). From CSR1 to CSR2: The maturing of business-and-society thought. *Business & Society, 33*(2), 150–164.

Freeman, R. E. (1984). *Strategic management: A stakeholder approach*. Boston: Pitman.

Friedman, M. (1962). *Capitalism and freedom*. Chicago, IL: University of Chicago Press.

Friedman, M. (1970, September 13). The social responsibility of business is to increase its profits. *New York Times Magazine*, 122–126.

Friedman, J., Hakim, S., & Weinblatt, J. (1989). Casino gambling as a "growth pole" strategy and its effect on crime. *Journal of Regional Science, 29*(4), 615–623.

Fry, L. W., Keim, G. D., & Meiners, R. E. (1982). Corporate contributions: altruistic or for-profit? *Academy of Management Journal, 25*(1), 94–106.

Frynas, J. G. (2005). The false developmental promise of corporate social responsibility: evidence from multinational oil companies. *International Affairs, 81*(3), 581–598.

Gardberg, N. A., & Fombrun, C. J. (2006). Corporate citizenship: Creating intangible assets across institutional environments. *Academy of Management Review, 31*(2), 329–346.

Garrett, T. A., & Nichols, M. W. (2008). Do casinos export bankruptcy? *Journal of Socio-Economics, 37*(4), 1481–1494.

Garriga, E., & Melé, D. (2004). Corporate social responsibility theories: Mapping the territory. *Journal of Business Ethics, 53*(1–2), 51–71.

Geran, T. (2006). *Beyond the glimmering lights: The pride and perseverance of African Americans in Las Vegas.* Las Vegas, NE: Stephens Press.

German, J. (2009, August 22). Station Casinos founder left his mark as philanthropist. *Las Vegas Sun.* Retrieved from http://www.lasvegassun.com/

Gioia, D. A. (1999). Practicability, paradigms, and problems in stakeholder theorizing. *Academy of Management Review, 24*(2), 228–232.

Godfrey, P. C., Merrill, C. B., & Hansen, J. M. (2009). The relationship between corporate social responsibility and shareholder value: An empirical test of the risk management hypothesis. *Strategic Management Journal, 30*(4), 425–445.

Godinho, J. (2013). A history of games of chance in Macau: Part 2 – The foundation of the Macau gaming industry. *Gaming Law Review and Economics, 17*(2), 107–116.

González, M. D. L. C., & Martinez, C. V. (2004). Fostering corporate social responsibility through public initiative: From the EU to the Spanish case. *Journal of Business Ethics, 55*(3), 275–293.

Gorman, T. (2001, August 30). Charities find themselves on the losing end in Las Vegas. *Los Angeles Times.* Retrieved from http://www.latimes.com/

Gose, B. (2005). Putting down stakes near the Strip. *Chronicle of Philanthropy, 17*(6), 10–14.

Gottdiener, M., Collins, C. C., & Dickens, D. R. (1999). *Las Vegas: The social production of an all-American city.* Malden, MA: Blackwell.

Graafland, J. J., Eijffinger, S. C., & Smid, H. (2004). Benchmarking of corporate social responsibility: Methodological problems and robustness. *Journal of Business Ethics, 53*(1–2), 137–152.

Graafland, J., & Mazereeuw-Van der Duijn Schouten, C. (2012). Motives for corporate social responsibility. *De Economist, 160*(4), 377–396.

Graafland, J., & van de Ven, B. (2006). Strategic and moral motivation for corporate social responsibility. *Journal of Corporate Citizenship, 2006*(22), 111–123.

Grant, D. (1994). *On a roll: A history of gambling and lotteries in New Zealand.* Wellington, NZ: Victoria University Press.

Green, S. (2009, July 28). Station Casinos files for Chapter 11. *Las Vegas Sun.* Retrieved from http://www.lasvegassun.com/

Green, S. (2012a, March 19). Moody's analysts: "The Las Vegas recovery is under way." *VEGAS INC.* Retrieved from http://www.vegasinc.com/

Green, S. (2012b, April 3). New reports confirm Las Vegas lagging in economic *Las Vegas Sun.* Retrieved from http://www.lasvegassun.com/

Green, S. (2012c, May 22). Report: Nevada won't see full jobs recovery until after 2017. *Las Vegas Sun News.* Retrieved from http://www.lasvegassun.com/

Greenhouse, S. (2004, June 3). ORGANIZED; Local 226, "the Culinary," makes Las Vegas the land of the living wage. *New York Times*. Retrieved from http://www.nytimes.com/

Greening, D. W., & Turban, D. B. (2000). Corporate social performance as a competitive advantage in attracting a quality workforce. *Business & Society, 39*(3), 254–280.

Griffin, J. J., & Mahon, J. F. (1997). The corporate social performance and corporate financial performance debate twenty-five years of incomparable research. *Business & Society, 36*(1), 5–31.

Grinols, E. L., & Mustard, D. B. (2001). Management and information issues for industries with externalities: The case of casino gambling. *Managerial and Decision Economics, 22*(1–3), 143–162.

Griswold, M. T., & Nichols, M. W. (2006). Social capital and casino gambling in U.S. communities. *Social Indicators Research, 77*(3), 369–394.

Groza, M. D., Pronschinske, M. R., & Walker, M. (2011). Perceived organizational motives and consumer responses to proactive and reactive CSR. *Journal of Business Ethics, 102*(4), 639–652.

Grunig, J. E., & Hunt, T. (1984). *Managing public relations*. New York: Holt, Rinehart and Winston.

Gu, X., Li, G., & Tam, P. S. (2013). Casino tourism, social cost and tax effects. *International Gambling Studies, 13*(2), 221–239.

Gu, X., & Tam, P. S. (2011). Casino taxation in Macao: An economic perspective. *Journal of Gambling Studies, 27*(4), 587–605.

Gu, Z. (2004). Macau gaming: Copying the Las Vegas style or creating a Macau model? *Asia Pacific Journal of Tourism Research, 9*(1), 89–96.

Gu, Z. (2012). Performance gaps between US and European casinos: a comparative study. *UNLV Gaming Research & Review Journal, 6*(2), 53–62.

Guthey, E., & Morsing, M. (2014). CSR and the mediated emergence of strategic ambiguity. *Journal of Business Ethics, 120*(4), 555–569.

Haigh, M., & Jones, M. T. (2006). The drivers of corporate social responsibility: a critical review. In *Proceedings of the 2006 Global Business and Economics Research conference* (pp. 1–8). Istanbul, Turkey: GBER.

Hall, P. D. (1987). A historical overview of the private nonprofit sector. *The nonprofit sector: A research handbook, 12*, 341–361.

Hall, S. (1997). *Representation: Cultural representations and signifying practices* (Vol. 2). Thousand Oaks, CA: Sage.

Ham, S., Brown, D. O., & Jang, S. (2004). Proponents or opponents of casino gaming: A qualitative choice model approach. *Journal of Hospitality & Tourism Research, 28*(4), 391–407.

Hamer, T. P. (2002). Casino mergers and economic concentration issues. The acquisition of Caesars by Park Place Entertainment in Atlantic City. *International Gambling Studies, 2*(1), 27–50.

Hamil, S. (1999). Corporate community involvement: A case for regulatory reform. *Business Ethics: A European Review, 8*(1), 14–25.

Hampson, R. (2014, July 6). Once fabled Atlantic City hits free fall. *USA Today*. Retrieved from http://www.usatoday.com/

Han, H., Hsu, L.-T. J., Lee, J.-S., & Sheu, C. (2011). Are lodging customers ready to go green? An examination of attitudes, demographics, and eco-friendly intentions. *International Journal of Hospitality Management, 30*(2), 345–355.

Han, L. C. (2011, September). Corporate social responsibility and gambling industry: An exploratory study. Presented at the Corporate Responsibility Research Conference, Leeds, UK.

Hannigan, J. (2007). Casino cities. *Geography Compass, 1*(4), 959–975.

Hao, Z. (2011). *Macau: History and society.* Hong Kong: Hong Kong University Press.

Harding, L. (2009, June 29). Game over for Russia's punters as gambling ban closes casinos. *The Guardian.* Retrieved from http://www.theguardian.com/world/2009/jun/29/russia-bans-gambling-casino-putin

Harrill, R., Uysal, M., Cardon, P. W., Vong, F., & Dioko, L. D. (2011). Resident attitudes towards gaming and tourism development in Macao: Growth machine theory as a context for identifying supporters and opponents. *International Journal of Tourism Research, 13*(1), 41–53.

Harris, R. (2005). When giving means taking: Public relations, sponsorship, and morally marginal donors. *Public Relations Review, 31*(4), 486–491.

Heath, R., & Ni, L. (2008). *The challenge of corporate social responsibility.* Gainesville, FL: The Institute for Public Relations. Retrieved from http://www.instituteforpr.org/corporate-social-responsibility/

Heath, R. L., & Ryan, M. (1989). Public relations' role in defining corporate social responsibility. *Journal of Mass Media Ethics, 4*(1), 21–38.

Henriksson, L. E. (2001). Gambling in Canada: some insights for cost–benefit analysis. *Managerial and Decision Economics, 22*(1–3), 113–123.

Hess, D., Rogovsky, N., & Dunfee, T. W. (2002). The next wave of corporate community involvement: Corporate social initiatives. *California Management Review, 44*(2), 110–125.

Hing, L. S. (2005). Casino politics, organized crime and the post-colonial state in Macau. *Journal of Contemporary China, 14*(43), 207–224.

Hing, N. (2002). The emergence of problem gambling as a corporate social issue in Australia. *International Gambling Studies, 2*(1), 101–122.

Hing, N. (2012a). Club gaming in New South Wales, Australia: The transition to industry maturity. *UNLV Gaming Research & Review Journal, 3*(1), 13–32.

Hing, N. (2012b). Competing forces in sustainable gambling: Towards a balanced approach. *UNLV Gaming Research & Review Journal, 4*(1), 43–61.

Hing, N., & McKellar, J. (2004). Challenges in responsible provision of gambling: Questions of efficacy, effectiveness and efficiency. *UNLV Gaming Research & Review Journal, 8*(1), 43–58.

Hing, N., & McMillan, J. (2002). A conceptual framework of the corporate management of social impacts: The case of problem gambling. *Business and Society Review, 107*(4), 457–488.

Historical Las Vegas Visitor Statistics (1970–2011). (2012, February). Las Vegas Convention and Visitors Authority (LVCVA). Retrieved from http://www.lvcva.com/includes/content/images/media/docs/Historical-1970-to-2011.pdf

Historical Las Vegas Visitor Statistics (1970–2012). (2013, February). Las Vegas Convention and Visitors Authority (LVCVA). Retrieved from http://www.lvcva.com/includes/content/images/media/docs/Historical-1970-to-2012.pdf

Hoeffler, S., & Keller, K. L. (2002). Building brand equity through corporate societal marketing. *Journal of Public Policy & Marketing, 21*(1), 78–89.

Holme, R., & Watts, P. (2000). *Corporate social responsibility: Making good business sense.* Conches-Geneva, Switzerland: World Business Council for Sustainable Development.

Hoye, R. (2005). A sure bet: Privatisation of the Victorian TAB. *International Gambling Studies, 5*(1), 85–94.

Hsu, C. H. C. (1998). Impacts of riverboat gaming on community quality. *Journal of Hospitality & Tourism Research, 22*(4), 323–337.

Hsu, C. H. C. (2000). Residents' support for legalized gaming and perceived impacts of riverboat casinos: Changes in five years. *Journal of Travel Research, 38*(4), 390–395.

Husted, B. W., & de Jesus Salazar, J. (2006). Taking Friedman seriously: Maximizing profits and social performance. *Journal of Management Studies, 43*(1), 75–91.

In U.S. building industry, is it too easy to be green? (2013, June 13). *USA TODAY*. Retrieved from http://www.usatoday.com/

Ives, S. (Director). (2005). *Las Vegas: An unconventional history* [motion picture]. United States: PBS Paramount.

Jamali, D., & Mirshak, R. (2007). Corporate social responsibility (CSR): Theory and practice in a developing country context. *Journal of Business Ethics, 72*(3), 243–262.

Jo, H., & Na, H. (2012). Does CSR reduce firm risk? Evidence from controversial industry Sectors. *Journal of Business Ethics, 110*(4), 441–456.

Jones, B., Bowd, R., & Tench, R. (2009). Corporate irresponsibility and corporate social responsibility: competing realities. *Social Responsibility Journal, 5*(3), 300–310.

Jones, M. T. (1999). The institutional determinants of social responsibility. *Journal of Business Ethics, 20*(2), 163–179.

Judd, D. R. (1999). Constructing the tourist bubble. In D. R. Judd & S. S. Fanstein (Eds.), *The tourist city* (pp. 35–53). New Haven, CT: Yale University Press.

Kagan, R. A., Gunningham, N., & Thornton, D. (2003). Explaining corporate environmental performance: how does regulation matter? *Law & Society Review, 37*(1), 51–90.

Kang, S. K., Lee, C.-K., Yoon, Y., & Long, P. T. (2008). Resident perception of the impact of limited-stakes community-based casino gaming in mature gaming communities. *Tourism Management, 29*(4), 681–694.

Kang, Y.-S., Long, P. T., & Perdue, R. R. (1996). Resident attitudes toward legal gambling. *Annals of Tourism Research, 23*(1), 71–85.

Kearney, M. S. (2005). *The economic winners and losers of legalized gambling*. National Bureau of Economic Research. Retrieved from http://www.nber.org/papers/w11234

Keim, G. D. (1978). Corporate social responsibility: An assessment of the enlightened self-interest model. *Academy of Management Review, 3*(1), 32–39.

Kennelly, R. (2013, May 21). Nevada's economic recovery: Gaming and tourism. UNLV Center for Business & Economic Research. Retrieved from http://cber.unlv.edu/commentary/CBER-21May2013.pdf

Kilcullen, M., & Kooistra, J. O. (1999). At least do no harm: Sources on the changing role of business ethics and corporate social responsibility. *Reference Services Review, 27*(2), 158–178.

Kim, H. S. (2007). A multilevel study of antecedents and a mediator of employee–organization relationships. *Journal of Public Relations Research, 19*(2), 167–197.

Kimery, K. M., & Rinehart, S. M. (1998). Markets and constituencies: an alternative view of the marketing concept. *Journal of Business Research, 43*(3), 117–124.

Kingma, S. (2004). Gambling and the risk society: The liberalisation and legitimation crisis of gambling in the Netherlands. *International Gambling Studies, 4*(1), 47–67.

Knox, S., & Maslan, S. (2004). Corporate social responsibility: Moving beyond investment towards measuring outcomes. *European Management Journal, 22*(5), 508–516.

Komenda, E. (2013, July 15). The Culinary Union: A history of striking. *VEGAS INC*. Retrieved from http://www.vegasinc.com/business/gaming/2013/jul/15/culinary-union-history-striking/

Korn, D. A. (2000). Expansion of gambling in Canada: Implications for health and social policy. *Canadian Medical Association Journal, 163*(1), 61–64.

Kraft, J. P. (2010). *Vegas at odds: Labor conflict in a leisure economy, 1960–1985*. Baltimore, MD: JHU Press.

Krause, N., Scherzer, T., & Rugulies, R. (2005). Physical workload, work intensification, and prevalence of pain in low wage workers: Results from a participatory research project with hotel room cleaners in Las Vegas. *American Journal of Industrial Medicine, 48*(5), 326–337.

Laczniak, E., & Murphy, P. (2008). Distributive justice: Pressing questions, emerging directions, and the promise of Rawlsian analysis. *Journal of Macromarketing, 28*(1), 5–11.

Land, B., & Land, M. (1999). *A short history of Las Vegas*. Reno, NV: University of Nevada Press.

Langlois, C. C., & Schlegelmilch, B. B. (1990). Do corporate codes of ethics reflect national character? Evidence from Europe and the United States. *Journal of International Business Studies, 21*, 519–539.

Lantos, G. P. (2001). The boundaries of strategic corporate social responsibility. *Journal of Consumer Marketing, 18*(7), 595–632.

Las Vegas CVA (Convention and Visitors Authority). (2009). *Statistics and facts*. Retrieved from http://www.lvcva.com/stats-and-facts/

Las Vegas Sands. (2014). *More than just an idea … it's our way of doing business*. Retrieved from http://www.sands.com/sands-eco-360/our-vision.html

Leap, T., & Loughry, M. L. (2004). The stakeholder-friendly firm. *Business Horizons, 47*(2), 27–32.

Lee, C.-K., & Back, K.-J. (2003). Pre- and post-casino impact of residents' perception. *Annals of Tourism Research, 30*(4), 868–885. doi:10.1016/S0160-7383(03)00060-4

Lee, C.-K., & Back, K.-J. (2009). An overview of residents' perceptions toward gaming development in local community: Theory and practice. *Worldwide Hospitality and Tourism Themes, 1*(4), 300–319.

Lee, C.-K., Kang, S. K., Long, P., & Reisinger, Y. (2010). Residents' perceptions of casino impacts: A comparative study. *Tourism Management, 31*(2), 189–201.

Lee, C.-K., Song, H.-J., Lee, H.-M., Lee, S., & Bernhard, B. J. (2013). The impact of CSR on casino employees' organizational trust, job satisfaction, and customer orientation: An empirical examination of responsible gambling strategies. *International Journal of Hospitality Management, 33*, 406–415.

Lee, S., & Park, S.-Y. (2009). Do socially responsible activities help hotels and casinos achieve their financial goals? *International Journal of Hospitality Management, 28*(1), 105–112.

Lenkowsky, L. (2002). Foundations and corporate philanthropy. In L. Salamon (Ed.), *The state of nonprofit America* (pp. 355–386). Washington, DC: Brookings Institution Press.

L'Etang, J. (1994). Public relations and corporate social responsibility: Some issues arising. *Journal of Business Ethics, 13*(2), 111–123.

Levy, R. (1999). Corporate philanthropy comes of age: Its size, its import, its future. In C. T. Clotfelter & T. Ehrlich (Eds.), *Philanthropy and the nonprofit sector in a changing America* (pp. 99–121). Bloomington, IN: Indiana University Press.

Levy, S. E., & Park, S.-Y. (2011). An analysis of CSR activities in the lodging industry. *Journal of Hospitality and Tourism Management, 18*(1), 147–154.

Lewin, A. Y., Sakano, T., Stephens, C. U., & Victor, B. (1995). Corporate citizenship in Japan: Survey results from Japanese firms. *Journal of Business Ethics, 14*(2), 83–101.

Lewis, S. (2001). Measuring corporate reputation. *Corporate Communications: An International Journal, 6*(1), 31–35.

Li, J. S., & Chen, G. Q. (2014). Water footprint assessment for service sector: A case study of gaming industry in water scarce Macao. *Ecological Indicators.*

Lichtenstein, D. R., Drumwright, M. E., & Braig, B. M. (2004). The effect of corporate social responsibility on customer donations to corporate-supported nonprofits. *Journal of Marketing, 68*(4), 16–32.

Lindgreen, A., Swaen, V., & Johnston, W. J. (2009). Corporate social responsibility: An empirical investigation of US organizations. *Journal of Business Ethics, 85*(2), 303–323.

Lindorff, M., Prior Jonson, E., & McGuire, L. (2012). Strategic corporate social responsibility in controversial industry sectors: The social value of harm minimisation. *Journal of Business Ethics, 110*(4), 457–467.

Littlejohn, D. (1999). Introduction: The ultimate company town. In D. Littlejohn (Ed.), *The real Las Vegas: Life beyond the Strip* (pp. 1–40). New York: Oxford University Press.

Livingstone, C. (2001). The social economy of poker machine gambling in Victoria. *International Gambling Studies, 1*(1), 46–65.

Livingstone, C., & Woolley, R. (2007). Risky business: A few provocations on the regulation of electronic gaming machines. *International Gambling Studies, 7*(3), 361–376.

Llewellyn, J. (2007). Government, business, and the self in the United States. In *The debate over corporate social responsibility* (pp. 177–189). New York: Oxford University Press.

Loi, K. I., & Kim, W. G. (2010). Macao's casino industry: Reinventing Las Vegas in Asia. *Cornell Hospitality Quarterly, 51*(2), 268–283.

Luke, T. W. (2010). Gaming space: Casinopolitan globalism from Las Vegas to Macau. *Globalizations, 7*(3), 395–405.

MacDonald, M., McMullan, J. L., & Perrier, D. C. (2004). Gambling households in Canada. *Journal of Gambling Studies, 20*(3), 187–236.

Macleod, S. (2001). Why worry about CSR? *Strategic Communication Management, 5*(5), 8–9.

Madhusudhan, R. G. (1996). Betting on casino revenues: Lessons from state experiences. *National Tax Journal, 49*(3), 401–412.

Madichie, N. O. (2007). Gaming UK: How prepared is Manchester (UK) for Vegas-style supercasinos? *Problems and Perspectives in Management, 5*, 153–165.

Maignan, I., Ferrell, O., & Ferrell, L. (2005). A stakeholder model for implementing social responsibility in marketing. *European Journal of Marketing, 39*(9/10), 956–977.

Maignan, I., Ferrell, O. C., & Hult, G. T. M. (1999). Corporate citizenship: cultural antecedents and business benefits. *Journal of the Academy of Marketing Science, 27*(4), 455–469.

Margolis, J. D., & Walsh, J. P. (2003). Misery loves companies: Rethinking social initiatives by business. *Administrative Science Quarterly, 48*(2), 268–305

Marshall, D. (2005). The gambling environment and gambler behaviour: Evidence from Richmond-Tweed, Australia. *International Gambling Studies, 5*(1), 63–83.

Martin, R. L. (2002). The virtue matrix: Calculating the return on corporate responsibility. *Harvard Business Review, 80*(3), 68–75.

Matten, D., & Moon, J. (2008). "Implicit" and "explicit" CSR: A conceptual framework for a comparative understanding of corporate social responsibility. *Academy of Management Review, 33*(2), 404–424.

McAllister, I. (2014). Public opinion towards gambling and gambling regulation in Australia. *International Gambling Studies, 14*(1), 146–160.

McCartney, G. J. (2005). Casinos as a tourism redevelopment strategy – The case of Macao. *Journal of Macau Gaming Research Association, 2*, 40–54.

McCracken, G. (1988). *The long interview.* Thousand Oaks, CA: Sage.

McKechnie, D. S., Grant, J., Sadeghi, H., Khan, L., & Taymaskhanov, Z. (2009). Casinos and Gambling in Dubai: finding common ground between polarized stakeholders. Presented at the 3rd International Conference on Destination Branding and Marketing, Macau, China, December 2–4.

McMahon, L., & Lloyd, G. (2006). "Rien ne va Plus." Casino developments and land use planning? *Planning Practice and Research, 21*(2), 257–266.

McMillan, J. (1996). From glamour to grind: The globalization of casinos. In *Gambling cultures: Studies in history and interpretation* (pp. 263–287). London: Routledge.

McMillan, J. J. (2007). Why corporate social responsibility: Why now? In *The debate over corporate social responsibility* (pp. 15–29). New York: Oxford University Press.

McWilliams, A., & Siegel, D. (2001). Corporate social responsibility: A theory of the firm perspective. *Academy of Management Review, 26*(1), 117–127.

Mellen, S. R., & Okada, S. S. (2005). Forecasting market-wide gaming revenue (win) for the Macau Special Administrative Region. *HVS International, San Francisco, CA*. Retrieved from http://pt.hvs.com/Content/1830.pdf

Menon, S., & Kahn, B. E. (2003). Corporate sponsorships of philanthropic activities: When do they impact perception of sponsor brand? *Journal of Consumer Psychology, 13*(3), 316–327.

Meyerson, H. (2004). Las Vegas as a workers' paradise. *The American Prospect, 13*, 168–169.

Meznar, M. B., & Nigh, D. (1995). Buffer or bridge? Environmental and organizational determinants of public affairs activities in American firms. *Academy of Management Journal, 38*(4), 975–996.

MGM Resorts International. (2014). *Environmental sustainability: A greener business is a better business*. Retrieved from http://www.mgmresorts.com/csr/environmental/

Midttun, A., Gautesen, K., & Gjølberg, M. (2006). The political economy of CSR in Western Europe. *Corporate Governance, 6*(4), 369–385.

Mikle, J., & Diamond, M. L. (2014, July 20). Jersey shore braces for casino closings. *USA Today*. Retrieved from http://www.usatoday.com/

Miles, M. P., & Covin, J. G. (2000). Environmental marketing: A source of reputational, competitive, and financial advantage. *Journal of Business Ethics, 23*(3), 299–311.

Miles, M. P., Munilla, L. S., & Darroch, J. (2006). The role of strategic conversations with stakeholders in the formation of corporate social responsibility strategy. *Journal of Business Ethics, 69*(2), 195–205.

Miller, V. (2005). Philanthropy takes off in Las Vegas. *Las Vegas Business Press*. Retrieved from http://www.lvbusinesspress.com/

Millions of people worldwide to switch off lights for eighth Earth Hour. (2014, March 29). *ABC News Australia*. Retrieved from http://www.abc.net.au/news/2014-03-29/earth-hour-support-increasing-in-australia-world/5353966

Mishra, K. E. (2006). Help or hype: Symbolic or behavioral communication during Hurricane Katrina. *Public Relations Review, 32*(4), 358–366.

Mitchell, R. K., Agle, B. R., & Wood, D. J. (1997). Toward a theory of stakeholder identification and salience: Defining the principle of who and what really counts. *Academy of Management Review, 22*(4), 853–886.

Moir, L. (2001). What do we mean by corporate social responsibility? *Corporate Governance, 1*(2), 16–22.

Moreno, A., & Capriotti, P. (2009). Communicating CSR, citizenship and sustainability on the web. *Journal of Communication Management, 13*(2), 157–175.

Morsing, M. (2006). Corporate social responsibility as strategic auto-communication: on the role of external stakeholders for member identification. *Business Ethics: A European Review, 15*(2), 171–182.

Morsing, M., & Schultz, M. (2006). Corporate social responsibility communication: stakeholder information, response and involvement strategies. *Business Ethics: A European Review, 15*(4), 323–338.

Motion, J., & Leitch, S. (1996). A discursive perspective from New Zealand: Another world view. *Public Relations Review, 22*(3), 297–309.

Munilla, L. S., & Miles, M. P. (2005). The corporate social responsibility continuum as a component of stakeholder theory. *Business and Society Review, 110*(4), 371–387.

Murphy, P. E., Öberseder, M., & Laczniak, G. R. (2013). Corporate societal responsibility in marketing: Normatively broadening the concept. *Academy of Marketing Science Review, 3*(2), 86–102.

Murray, K. B., & Montanari, J. B. (1986). Strategic management of the socially responsible firm: Integrating management and marketing theory. *Academy of Management Review, 11*(4), 815–827.

Nader, R. (1965). *Unsafe at any speed*. New York: Grossman.

Nagourney, A. (2013, July 31). Crowds return to Las Vegas, but gamble less. *New York Times*. Retrieved from http://www.nytimes.com/

National Museum of Organized Crime and Law Enforcement. (2013). *The game continues*. Exhibit. National Museum of Organized Crime and Law Enforcement, Las Vegas, NV.

NEA wire service. (1931, March 4). Jobless form big problem in Boulder Dam's expected "boom town" as boom fails. *Spokane Daily Chronicle*, p. B1.

Newell, P. (2008). CSR and the limits of capital. *Development and Change, 39*(6), 1063–1078.

Nickerson, N. P. (1995). Tourism and gambling content analysis. *Annals of Tourism Research, 22*(1), 53–66.

Nisbet, S. (2005). Alternative gaming machine payment methods in Australia: Current knowledge and future implications. *International Gambling Studies, 5*(2), 229–252.

Oh, H. (1999). Social impacts of casino gaming: The case of Las Vegas. In C. H. C. Hsu (Ed.), *Legalized casino gaming in the United States: The economic and social impact* (pp. 177–200). Binghamton, NY: Haworth Hospitality Press.

Paine, L. S. (1996). Moral thinking in management: An essential capability. *Business Ethics Quarterly*, 477–492.

Paine, L. S. (2000). Does ethics pay? *Business Ethics Quarterly, 10*(1), 319–330.

Palazzo, G., & Richter, U. (2005). CSR business as usual? The case of the tobacco industry. *Journal of Business Ethics, 61*(4), 387–401.

Papiez, M. R., Potosnak, M. J., Goliff, W. S., Guenther, A. B., Matsunaga, S. N., & Stockwell, W. R. (2009). The impacts of reactive terpene emissions from plants on air quality in Las Vegas, Nevada. *Atmospheric Environment, 43*(27), 4109–4123.

Parker, R. E. (1999). Las Vegas: Casino gambling and local culture. In D. R. Judd & S. S. Fanstein (Eds.), *The tourist city* (pp. 107–123). New Haven, CT: Yale University Press.

Parker, R. E. (2002). The social costs of rapid urbanization in southern Nevada. In H. K. Rothman & M. Davis (Eds.), *The grit beneath the glitter: Tales from the real Las Vegas* (pp. 126–144). Berkeley, CA: University of California Press.

Patrick, T. I. (2000). No dice: violations of the criminal code's gaming exceptions by provincial governments. *Criminal Law Quarterly, 44*, 108–126.

Pava, M. L., & Krausz, J. (1997). Criteria for evaluating the legitimacy of corporate social responsibility. *Journal of Business Ethics, 16*(3), 337–347.

Pearce, J. A. (1982). The company mission as a strategic tool. *Sloan Management Review, 23*(3), 15–24.

Pearce, J. A., & Doh, J. P. (2005). The high impact of collaborative social initiatives. *MIT Sloan Management Review, 46*(3), 30–38.

Pedersen, E. R. (2006). Making corporate social responsibility (CSR) operable: How companies translate stakeholder dialogue into practice. *Business and Society Review, 111*(2), 137–163.

Pedersen, E. R., & Neergaard, P. (2009). What matters to managers? The whats, whys, and hows of corporate social responsibility in a multinational corporation. *Management Decision, 47*(8), 1261–1280.

Perdue, R. R., Long, P. T., & Kang, Y. S. (1999). Boomtown tourism and resident quality of life: The marketing of gaming to host community residents. *Journal of Business Research, 44*(3), 165–177.

Pickernell, D., Brown, K. A., Keast, R. L., & Yousefpour, N. (2009). The public management issues of access to electronic gaming machines (EGMs): a case study of policy in Victoria, its effects and requirements for evaluation. Presented at the 13th International Research Society for Public Management Conference, Fredericksberg, Denmark, April 6–8. Retrieved from http://epubs.scu.edu.au/bus_pubs/802/

Pickernell, D., Keast, R., Brown, K., Yousefpour, N., & Miller, C. (2013). Gambling revenues as a public administration issue: Electronic gaming machines in Victoria. *Journal of Gambling Studies, 29*(4), 689–701.

Pickernell, D. G., Keast, R. L., & Brown, K. A. (2010). Social clubs and social capital: The effect of electronic gaming machines in disadvantaged regions on the creation or destruction of community resilience. Presented at the 14th Annual Conference of the International Research Society for Public Management, Bern, Switzerland, April 7–9. Retrieved from http://epubs.scu.edu.au/bus_pubs/793/

Pirsch, J., Gupta, S., & Grau, S. L. (2007). A framework for understanding corporate social responsibility programs as a continuum: An exploratory study. *Journal of Business Ethics, 70*(2), 125–140.

Pitcher, A. (1999). Responsible promotion of gaming and dealing with problem gamblers. *Journal of Gambling Studies, 15*(2), 149–159.

Pizam, A., & Pokela, J. (1985). The perceived impacts of casino gambling on a community. *Annals of Tourism Research, 12*, 147–165.

Porter, M., & Kramer, M. R. (2002). The competitive advantage of corporate philanthropy. *Harvard Business Review, 80*(12), 56–68.

Porter, M. E., Kramer, M. R., & Zadek, S. (2006). *Redefining corporate social responsibility*. Harvard Business School Publishing. Retrieved from http://storage.globalcitizen.net/data/topic/knowledge/uploads/20110330143737705.pdf

Porteous, J. D. (1970). The nature of the company town. *Transactions of the Institute of British Geographers*, (51), 127–141.

Posner, B., & Kiron, D. (2013). How Caesars Entertainment is betting on sustainability. *MIT Sloan Management Review, 54*(4), 63–71.

Putnam, R. D. (2000). *Bowling alone: The collapse and revival of American community*. New York: Simon and Schuster.

Qaiser, K., Ahmad, S., Johnson, W., & Batista, J. R. (2013). Evaluating water conservation and reuse policies using a dynamic water balance model. *Environmental Management, 51*(2), 449–458.

Quelch, J. A., & Jocz, K. E. (2009). Can corporate social responsibility survive recession? *Leader to Leader, 53*, 37–43.

Rampell, C. (2009, March 11). "Great Recession": A brief etymology. *New York Times*. Retrieved from http://economix.blogs.nytimes.com/2009/03/11/great-recession-a-brief-etymology/

Ramstack, T. (2001, December 11). Gloom amidst glitter; Decline in gambling costs jobs. *Washington Times*, p. C8.

Ramus, C. A., & Monteil, I. (2005). When are corporate environmental policies a form of greenwashing? *Business & Society, 44*(4), 377–414.

Rapoza, K. (2013, August 1). Macau Is "Vegas on steroids." *Forbes*. Retrieved from http://www.forbes.com/

Rawlins, B. (2006). *Prioritizing stakeholders for public relations*. Gainesville, FL: The Institute for Public Relations. Retrieved from http://www.instituteforpr.org/wp-content/uploads/2006_Stakeholders_1.pdf

Raylu, N., & Oei, T. P. (2004). Role of culture in gambling and problem gambling. *Clinical Psychology Review, 23*(8), 1087–1114.

Reith, G. (2003). *Gambling: Who wins? Who loses?* Amherst, NY: Prometheus Books.

Richter, U. H. (2010). Liberal thought in reasoning on CSR. *Journal of Business Ethics, 97*(4), 625–649.

Riley, C. (2014, January 6). Macau's gambling industry is now 7 times bigger than Vegas. *CNNMoney*. Retrieved from http://money.cnn.com/2014/01/06/news/macau-casino-gambling/index.html

Rim, H., & Song, D. (2013). The ability of corporate blog communication to enhance CSR effectiveness: The e. *International Journal of Strategic Communication, 7*(3), 165–185.

Rittichainuwat, B., & Mair, J. (2012). An exploratory study of attendee perceptions of green meetings. *Journal of Convention & Event Tourism, 13*(3), 147–158.

Robison, J. (2009, July 17). Las Vegas unemployment soars to 12.3 percent. *Las Vegas Review-Journal*. Retrieved from http://www.lvrj.com/

Robison, J. (2010a, January 22). Nevada's jobless rate hits 13 percent; state to lose more jobs. *Las Vegas Review-Journal*. Retrieved from http://www.reviewjournal.com/

Robison, J. (2010b, May 21). Las Vegas jobless rate jumps to 14 percent. *Las Vegas Review-Journal*. Retrieved from http://www.reviewjournal.com/

Roehl, W. S. (1999). Quality of life issues in a casino destination. *Journal of Business Research, 44*(3), 223–229.

Rose, I. N. (2013). A tale of two cities, Macau and Las Vegas. *Gaming Law Review and Economics, 17*(6), 393–403.

Rothman, H. (2002). *Neon metropolis: How Las Vegas started the twenty-first century*. New York: Routledge.

Rothman, H. (2003). Cultural tourism and the future: What the new Las Vegas tells us about ourselves. In H. K. Rothman (Ed.), *The culture of tourism, the tourism of culture: Selling the past to the present in the American Southwest* (pp. 229–244). Albuquerque, NM: University of New Mexico Press.

Rothman, H., & Davis, M. (2002). Introduction: The many faces of Las Vegas. In *Las Vegas: The grit beneath the glitter* (pp. 1–16). Berkeley, CA: University of California Press.

Rowley, T., & Berman, S. (2000). A brand new brand of corporate social performance. *Business & Society, 39*(4), 397–418.

Rowley, T. I., & Moldoveanu, M. (2003). When will stakeholder groups act? An interest- and identity-based model of stakeholder group mobilization. *Academy of Management Review, 28*(2), 204–219.

Ryan, M., & Martinson, D. L. (1983). The PR officer as corporate conscience. *Public Relations Quarterly, 28*(2), 20–23.

Saiia, D. H., Carroll, A. B., & Buchholtz, A. K. (2003). Philanthropy as strategy: When corporate charity "begins at home." *Business & Society, 42*(2), 169–201.

Salamon, L. M. (2002). The resilient sector: The state of nonprofit America. In L. M. Salamon (Ed.), *The state of nonprofit America* (pp. 3–61). Washington, DC: Brookings Institution Press.

Scalet, S., & Kelly, T. F. (2010). CSR rating agencies: What is their global impact? *Journal of Business Ethics, 94*(1), 69–88.

Schoenberger-Orgad, M., & McKie, D. (2005). Sustaining edges: CSR, postmodern play, and SMEs. *Public Relations Review, 31*(4), 578–583.

Schultz, F., Castelló, I., & Morsing, M. (2013). The construction of corporate social responsibility in network societies: A communication view. *Journal of Business Ethics, 115*(4), 681–692.

Schwartz, D. G. (2003). *Suburban Xanadu*. New York: Routledge.

Schwartz, D. G. (2012, February 23). Mob neighbors. *Vegas Seven*. Retrieved from http://vegasseven.com/

Schwartz, D. G. (2013a). *Roll the bones: The history of gambling* (2nd ed.). Las Vegas, NE: Winchester Books.

Schwartz, D. G. (2013b). *Grandissimo: The first emperor of Las Vegas: How Jay Sarno won a casino empire, lost it, and inspired modern Las Vegas*. Las Vegas, NE: Winchester Books.

Scull, S., & Woolcock, G. (2005). Problem gambling in Non-English speaking background communities in Queensland, Australia: A qualitative exploration. *International Gambling Studies, 5*(1), 29–44.

Sen, S., Bhattacharya, C. B., & Korschun, D. (2006). The role of corporate social responsibility in strengthening multiple stakeholder relationships: A field experiment. *Journal of the Academy of Marketing Science, 34*(2), 158–166.

Shannon, M., & Mitchell, C. J. A. (2012). Deconstructing place identity? Impacts of a "racino" on Elora, Ontario, Canada. *Journal of Rural Studies, 28*(1), 38–48.

Shapiro, A. (2010). Hold'em or fold'em: Gambling laws in Asia. *Penn State Journal of Law and International Affairs, 29*, 385–412.

Sharfman, M. (1996). The construct validity of the Kinder, Lydenberg & Domini social performance ratings data. *Journal of Business Ethics, 15*(3), 287–296.

Sheng, L., & Tsui, Y. (2009a). A general equilibrium approach to tourism and welfare: The case of Macao. *Habitat International, 33*(4), 419–424.

Sheng, L., & Tsui, Y. (2009b). Casino boom and local politics: The city of Macao. *Cities, 26*(2), 67–73.

Shocker, A. D., & Sethi, S. P. (1973). An approach to incorporating societal preferences in developing corporate action strategies. *California Management Review, 15*(4), 97–105.

Shrestha, E., Ahmad, S., Johnson, W., & Batista, J. R. (2011). The carbon footprint associated with water management policy options in the Las Vegas Valley, Nevada. *Journal of the Nevada Water Resources Association, 6*(1), 2–9.

Simon, B. (2004). *Boardwalk of dreams: Atlantic City and the fate of urban America*. New York: Oxford University Press.

Simpson, T. (2012). Tourist Utopias: Las Vegas, Dubai, Macau. Asia Research Institute. Retrieved from http://repository.umac.mo/dspace/bitstream/10692/1258/2/wps12_177.pdf

Simpson, W. G., & Kohers, T. (2002). The link between corporate social and financial performance: evidence from the banking industry. *Journal of Business Ethics, 35*(2), 97–109.

Sims, R. R., & Brinkmann, J. (2003). Enron ethics (or: culture matters more than codes). *Journal of Business Ethics*, *45*(3), 243–256.

Siu, R. C. (2006). Evolution of Macao's casino industry from monopoly to oligopoly: Social and economic reconsideration. *Journal of Economic Issues*, *40*(4), 967–990.

Siu, R. C. S. (2007). Is casino gaming a productive sector? A conceptual and cross-jurisdiction analysis. *Journal of Gambling Business and Economics*, *1*(2), 129–146.

Skapinker, M. (2004, July 21). Why corporate laggards should not win ethics awards. *Financial Times*. Retrieved from http://www.ft.com/

Skolnik, S. (2011). *High stakes*. Boston, MA: Beacon Press.

Skopchevskiy, K. (2008, June 15). *Russia reshapes its gaming industry*. CIS Legal Newswire. Retrieved from http://www.chadbourne.com/files/Publication/45879028-eb56-4997-9db9-b1a1289d56f7/Presentation/PublicationAttachment/ca1a8540-da13-4b89-a02a-b30167eda535/CIS%20Newswire-061508.pdf

Smith, C. (1994). The new corporate philanthropy. *Harvard Business Review*, *72*(3), 105–116.

Smith, G. J., & Campbell, C. S. (2007). Tensions and contentions: An examination of electronic gaming issues in Canada. *American Behavioral Scientist*, *51*(1), 86–101.

Smith, G. J., Schopflocher, D. P., el-Guebaly, N., Casey, D. M., Hodgins, D. C., Williams, R. J., & Wood, R. (2011). Community attitudes toward legalised gambling in Alberta. *International Gambling Studies*, *11*(1), 57–79.

Smith, J. L. (1999, May 2). The double life of Moe Dalitz. *Las Vegas Review-Journal*. Retrieved from http://www.lexisnexis.com/

Smith, J. (2000). Gambling taxation: Public equity in the gambling business. *Australian Economic Review*, *33*(2), 120–144.

Smith, N. C. (2003). Corporate social responsibility: Whether or how? *California Management Review*, *45*(4), 52–76.

Smith, S., & Kumar, A. (2013). Impact of corporate social responsibility on employee organizational commitment within the gaming industry. *Advances in Hospitality and Leisure*, *9*, 49–67.

Snider, J., Hill, R. P., & Martin, D. (2003). Corporate social responsibility in the 21st century: A view from the world's most successful firms. *Journal of Business Ethics*, *48*(2), 175–187.

Song, H. J., Lee, H.-M., Lee, C.-K., & Song, S.-J. (2014). The role of CSR and responsible gambling in casino employees' organizational commitment, job satisfaction, and customer orientation. *Asia Pacific Journal of Tourism Research*, 1–17. DOI: 10.1080/10941665.2013.877049

Stake, R. E. (2005). Qualitative case studies. In N. K. Denizen & Y. S. Lincoln (Eds.), *The Sage handbook of qualitative research* (3rd ed.) (pp. 443–466). Thousand Oaks, CA. Sage.

Stansfield, C. (2006). The rejuvenation of Atlantic City: The resort cycle recycles. In R.W. Butler (Ed.), *The tourism area life cycle: Applications and modifications* (pp. 287–305). Clevedon, UK: Channelview Publications.

Starck, K., & Kruckeberg, D. (2004). Ethical obligations of public relations in an era of globalisation. *Journal of Communication Management*, *8*(1), 29–40.

Stokowski, P. A. (1993). Undesirable lag effects in tourist destination development: A Colorado case study. *Journal of Travel Research*, *32*(2), 35–41.

Stokowski, P. A., & Park, M. (2012). Resident quality-of-life in gaming communities. In M. Uysal, R. Perdue, & M. J. Sirgy (Eds.), *Handbook of tourism and quality-of-life research* (pp. 653–666). New York: Springer.

Stone, A. (2009, December 3). Las Vegas' big gamble opens. *ABC News*. Retrieved from http://abcnews.go.com/Travel/BusinessTraveler/city-center-opens-las-vegas-massive-gamble-mgm/story?id=9231196

Storer, J., Abbott, M., & Stubbs, J. (2009). Access or adaptation? A meta-analysis of surveys of problem gambling prevalence in Australia and New Zealand with respect to concentration of electronic gaming machines. *International Gambling Studies, 9*(3), 225–244.

Strauss, J. (2010). *Obligation as a relationship antecedent: A qualitative study of the Las Vegas community*. Unpublished doctoral dissertation. University of Oregon, Eugene, OR.

Strauss, J. R. (2015). Gambling on community development: Building commerce and community in downtown Las Vegas. *Community Development* (forthcoming).

Strauss, J. R. and Maxian, W. (2014). *What happens in Vegas . . . never stays in Vegas: How smartphones, the 24-hour news cycle, and social media have subverted one of the iconic advertising campaigns of the 21st century*. Unpublished manuscript.

Stroup, M. A., Neubert, R. L., & Anderson Jr, J. W. (1987). Doing good, doing better: Two views of social responsibility. *Business Horizons, 30*(2), 22–25.

Suchman, M. C. (1995). Managing legitimacy: Strategic and institutional approaches. *Academy of Management Review, 20*(3), 571–610.

Sun, Y., Tong, S. T. Y., Fang, M., & Yang, Y. J. (2013). Exploring the effects of population growth on future land use change in the Las Vegas Wash watershed: An integrated approach of geospatial modeling and analytics. *Environment, Development and Sustainability, 15*(6), 1495–1515.

Swanson, D. L. (1995). Addressing a theoretical problem by reorienting the corporate social performance model. *Academy of Management Review, 20*(1), 43–64.

Swarbrooke, J. (1999). *Sustainable tourism management*. Wallingford, UK: CABI.

Sweeney, L., & Coughlan, J. (2008). Do different industries report corporate social responsibility differently? An investigation through the lens of stakeholder theory. *Journal of Marketing Communications, 14*(2), 113–124.

Tam, F., Tsai, H., & Chen McCain, S.-L. (2013). Tourists' and residents' perceptions toward casino gaming development in Hong Kong. *Asia Pacific Journal of Tourism Research, 18*(4), 385–407.

Taylor, J. (2014, March 27). Clark County population tops 2 million, new census report estimates. *Las Vegas Sun*. Retrieved from http://www.lasvegassun.com/

Tench, R., Bowd, R., & Jones, B. (2007). Perceptions and perspectives: corporate social responsibility and the media. *Journal of Communication Management, 11*(4), 348–370.

Thompson, W. N. (1999). Casinos in Las Vegas: Where impacts are not the issue. In C. H. C. Hsu (Ed.), *Legalized casino gaming in the United States: The economic and social impact* (pp. 93–112). Binghamton, NY: Haworth Hospitality Press.

Thompson, W. N. (2001). *Gambling in America: An encyclopedia of history, issues, and society*. Santa Barbara, CA: ABC-CLIO.

Thompson, W. N. (2012). Two countries, one system: Las Vegas and Macau – sharing the future. *Gaming Law Review and Economics, 16*(3), 81–90.

Thompson, W. N., Lutrin, C., & Friedberg, A. (2012). Political culture and gambling policy: A cross-national study. *UNLV Gaming Research & Review Journal, 8*(1), 1–12.

Thompson, W. N., Schwer, R. K., Hoyt, R., & Brosnan, D. (1993). Not in my backyard: Las Vegas residents protest casinos. *Journal of Gambling Studies, 9*(1), 47-62.

Turner, N. E., Wiebe, J., Falkowski-Ham, A., Kelly, J., & Skinner, W. (2005). Public awareness of responsible gambling and gambling behaviours in Ontario. *International Gambling Studies, 5*(1), 95–112.

Urevich, R. (2008, August 18). When the living's not easy, the giving's not so easy either. *Las Vegas Sun*. Retrieved from http://www.lasvegassun.com/

Valenzuela, F.-R., & Fisher, J. (2012). Poker machine wars: Social responsibility and marketing. *World Journal of Social Sciences, 2*(3), 69–77.

van Marrewijk, M. (2003). Concepts and definitions of CSR and corporate sustainability: Between agency and communion. *Journal of Business Ethics, 44*(2/3), 95–105.

Varadarajan, P. R., & Menon, A. (1988). Cause-related marketing: A coalignment of marketing strategy and corporate philanthropy. *Journal of Marketing, 52(3*), 58–74.

Vasiliev, P. V., & Bernhard, B. (2012). Prohibitions and policy in the global gaming industry: A Genealogy and media content analysis of gaming restrictions in contemporary Russia. *UNLV Gaming Research & Review Journal, 15*(1), 71–86.

Velotta, R. N. (2012, July 10). International tourists in Las Vegas outspend domestic travelers, analyst says. *VEGAS INC*. Retrieved from http://www.vegasinc.com/

Venkatesan, A. K., Ahmad, S., Johnson, W., & Batista, J. R. (2011). Systems dynamic model to forecast salinity load to the Colorado River due to urbanization within the Las Vegas Valley. *Science of the Total Environment, 409*(13), 2616–2625.

Verona, R. (2012). An overview of Italian gaming: The state of the industry. *UNLV Gaming Research & Review Journal, 14*(1), 55–70.

Vogel, D. J. (2005). Is there a market for virtue? The business case for corporate social responsibility. *California Management Review, 47*(4), 19–45.

Vogel, D. (2006). *The market for virtue: The potential and limits of corporate social responsibility*. Washington, DC: Brookings Institution Press.

von Herrmann, D. (Ed.). (2006). *Resorting to casinos: The Mississippi gambling industry*. Jackson, MS: University Press of Mississippi.

Vong, F. (2010). Perception of Macao teachers and students regarding gaming operators' social responsibility. *UNLV Gaming Research & Review Journal, 14*(1), 1–13.

Vong, F., & Wong, I. A. (2013). Corporate and social performance links in the gaming industry. *Journal of Business Research, 66*(9), 1674–1681.

Waddock, S. A., & Graves, S. B. (1997). The corporate social performance–financial performance link. *Strategic Management Journal, 18*(4), 303–319.

Waddock, S., & Smith, N. (2000). Relationships: The real challenge of corporate global citizenship. *Business and Society Review, 105*(1), 47–62.

Wagner, T., Lutz, R. J., & Weitz, B. A. (2009). Corporate hypocrisy: Overcoming the threat of inconsistent corporate social responsibility perceptions. *Journal of Marketing, 73*(6), 77–91.

Walker, D. M. (2009). The economic effects of casino gambling: A perspective from the US. In *Macao Polytechnic Institute Global Gaming Management Seminar Series*. Retrieved from http://walkerd.people.cofc.edu/pubs/Walker_Macao_ss.pdf

Walker, D. M., & Jackson, J. D. (1998). New goods and economic growth: Evidence from legalized gambling. *Review of Regional Studies, 28*(2), 47–70.

Wan, Y. K. P. (2010). Exploratory assessment of the Macao casino dealers' job perceptions. *International Journal of Hospitality Management, 29*(1), 62–71.

Wan, Y. K. P. (2012). The social, economic and environmental impacts of casino gaming in Macao: The community leader perspective. *Journal of Sustainable Tourism, 20*(5), 737–755.

Wan, Y. K. P., & Li, X. (2013). Sustainability of tourism development in Macao, China: Sustainability of tourism development in Macao. *International Journal of Tourism Research, 15*(1), 52–65.

Wan, Y. K. P., Li, X. C., & Kong, W. H. (2011). Social impacts of casino gaming in Macao: A qualitative analysis. *Tourism, 59*(1), 63–82.

Wan, Y. K. P., & Pinheiro, F. V. (2014). Macau's tourism planning approach and its shortcomings: A case study. *International Journal of Hospitality & Tourism Administration, 15*(1), 78–102.

Wanderley, L. S. O., Lucian, R., Farache, F., & de Sousa Filho, J. M. (2008). CSR information disclosure on the web: A context-based approach analysing the influence of country of origin and industry sector. *Journal of Business Ethics, 82*(2), 369–378.

Wang, L., & Juslin, H. (2009). The impact of Chinese culture on corporate social responsibility: The harmony approach. *Journal of Business Ethics, 88*(S3), 433–451.

Weaver, G. R., Trevino, L. K., & Cochran, P. L. (1999). Integrated and decoupled corporate social performance: Management commitments, external pressures, and corporate ethics practices. *Academy of Management Journal, 42*(5), 539–552.

Webb, D. J., & Mohr, L. A. (1998). A typology of consumer responses to cause-related marketing: From skeptics to socially concerned. *Journal of Public Policy & Marketing, 17*(2), 226–238.

Weiss, R. S. (1994). *Learning from strangers: The art and method of qualitative interview studies.* New York: The Free Press.

Welch, J., & Welch, S. (2009, July 1). Giving in an unforgiving time. *Business Week, 4133,* 80.

Wells, J. (September 1, 2009a). Is Vegas housing a safe bet now? *CNBC.* Retrieved from http://www.cnbc.com/

Wells, J. (September 1, 2009b). MGM mirage's CEO "playing offense." *CNBC.* Retrieved from http://www.cnbc.com/

Wenz, M. (2014). Casinos, gambling, and economic development: An introduction to the special issue: Casinos, gambling, and economic development. *Growth and Change, 45*(1), 1–4.

Wheeler, D., Colbert, B., & Freeman, R. E. (2003). Focusing on value: Reconciling corporate social responsibility, sustainability and a stakeholder approach in a network world. *Journal of General Management, 28*(3), 1–28.

Wheeler, D., Fabig, H., & Boele, R. (2002). Paradoxes and dilemmas for stakeholder responsive firms in the extractive sector: Lessons from the case of Shell and the Ogoni. *Journal of Business Ethics, 39*(3), 297–318.

Whitehair, J. (2009, July 24). Flashback Friday: Braving the economic crisis of 1955. *Las Vegas Blog.* Retrieved from http://blog.vegas.com/more-las-vegas-news/flashback-friday-braving-the-economic-crisis-of-1955/

Williams, C. C. (2008). Toward a taxonomy of corporate reporting strategies. *Journal of Business Communication, 45*(3), 232–264.

Williams, R. J., & Wood, R. T. (2004). The proportion of gaming revenue derived from problem gamblers: Examining the issues in a Canadian context. *Analyses of Social Issues and Public Policy, 4*(1), 33–45.

Winkler, A. (2014, March 17). Yes, corporations are people. *Slate.* Retrieved from http://www.slate.com/

Wong, I. A. (2012). Research note: Forecasting Macau's gaming revenue and its seasonality. *UNLV Gaming Research & Review Journal, 15*(1), 87–93.

Wood, D. J. (1991). Corporate social performance revisited. *Academy of Management Review, 16*(4), 691–718.

WWF. (2014). Earth Hour 2014 summary July 2014. Retrieved from http://www.earth-hour.org

Yani-de-Soriano, M., Javed, U., & Yousafzai, S. (2012). Can an industry be socially responsible if its products harm consumers? The case of online gambling. *Journal of Business Ethics, 110*(4), 481–497.

Yin, R. K. (1998). The abridged version of case study research: Design and method. In L. Bickman & D. L. Rog (Eds.), *Handbook of applied social research methods* (pp. 229–259). Thousand Oaks, CA: Sage.

Yoo, J. J.-E., Zhou, (Joe) Yong, Lu, T. (Ying), & Kim, T. (Terry). (2014). The moderating effects of resident characteristics on perceived gaming impacts and gaming industry support: The case of Macao. *Journal of Travel & Tourism Marketing, 31*(2), 229–250.

Yoon, Y., Gürhan-Canli, Z., & Schwarz, N. (2006). The effect of corporate social responsibility (CSR) activities on companies with bad reputations. *Journal of Consumer Psychology, 16*(4), 377–390.

Young, M., Barnes, T., Stevens, M., Paterson, M., & Morris, M. (2007). The changing landscape of indigenous gambling in Northern Australia: Current knowledge and future directions. *International Gambling Studies, 7*(3), 327–343.

Yu, X. (2008). Growth and degradation in the Orient's "Las Vegas": Issues of environment in Macau. *International Journal of Environmental Studies, 65*(5), 667–683.

Zadek, S. (2004). The path to corporate responsibility. *Harvard Business Review, 82*(12), 125–132.

Zeng, Z., Forrest, D., & McHale, I. G. (2013). Happiness and job satisfaction in a casino-dominated economy. *Journal of Gambling Studies, 29*(3), 471–490.

Zhang, J., & Swanson, D. (2006). Analysis of news media's representation of corporate social responsibility (CSR). *Public Relations Quarterly, 51*(2), 13–17.

Zheng, V., & Hung, E. P. W. (2012). Evaluating the economic impact of casino liberalization in Macao. *Journal of Gambling Studies, 28*(3), 541–559.

Index

activism 34, 37
addiction *see* problem gambling
Alberta 77, 79
altruism 22–4
American Gaming Association 1, 58, 113
annual reports 45
Atlantic City 53, 123–4; gambling's fall
  from grace 82–3
ATMs 113
Australia 4, 121, 132; spread and
  containment of gambling 80–2
auto industry 90
Axelrod, R. 69

benefits of CSR 13, 24–6
Bivins, T. 14
Boatright, J.R. 21–2
boomtowns 62
Boulder City 6, 86
Boyd, Sam 94
Boyd Gaming 4, 90, 94
brand identity 25
Buchanan, J. 68
Burnham, J.C. 52
business case for CSR 7, 18–28, 64, 114,
  127, 132; evolution of 20–1; flaws
  125–6; implications of 115–22, 126; oil
  companies 47; *see also* strategic CSR
business-society relationship 12, 28–31, 48

Caesars Entertainment 4, 90, 121
Caesars Palace 89
Caesars Windsor Hotel and Casino 78
Campbell, C.S. 78, 79
Canada 51, 114, 121, 132; government-run
  gaming 75–9

capitalism 98–9
Carnegie, Andrew 10, 17, 32
Carroll, A.B. 32
casino industry 5–6, 49–69; characteristics
  of casino communities and their residents
  54–5; contraction 57–8; corporate
  influence 52–4; cost-benefit framework
  for evaluating casino proposals 56–7;
  CSR in 60–9; expansion 1, 56–7; future
  for CSR in 128–32; history and current
  regulation 50–2; impact of CSR in
  126–8; public relations in 58–60; size
  1; and tourism 56, 57, 61–3, 69; unique
  characteristics 61
Castelló, I. 48
cause-related marketing (CRM) 25, 46
charitable donations 65
China 4, 5, 71–2, 73; *see also* Macau
Circus Circus 89
CityCenter 91, 99
Clayton, C.H. 72
Cleveland crime syndicate 3
codes of ethics 29
Colorado 59, 61–2
communication of CSR 35–48, 125,
  128; challenges and ethical concerns
  117–19; cost of 40, 109; employees
  37–8, 118; failure to communicate
  and negative externalities 122; keys to
  successful 41–2; Las Vegas 109–13;
  local community 38–9, 118; public
  relations 45–7, 119, 129–31; reasons for
  and against 39–41; stakeholder dialogue
  47–8, 119, 127, 128, 129, 130–1; via
  news media 37, 42–4, 117–18; via the
  Web 44–5; vice industries 65

community, local *see* local community
Community Benefit Statement (CBS) 80
community development, contributions to
   123
community groups 57
Community Reinvestment Act 1977 20
company towns 101
competitors 37
consequential approach 127–8
construction projects 90, 91–2
consumer protection 81–2
consumer skepticism 27, 40, 46
consumer sovereignty 81
consumption 61, 98
contraction 57–8
convention trade 90–1
corporate social investment (CSI) funds 15
corporate social performance (CSP) 39–40,
   48
corporate social responsibility (CSR) 1–2,
   9–48; benefits of 13, 24–6; business
   case for *see* business case for CSR;
   casino industry 60–9; communicating
   see communication of CSR; cost-benefit
   proposition 24–6; cultural influences
   16–18, 73; definitions and terminology
   11–15; in an economic crisis 22–3,
   117; functional *see* functional CSR;
   future for in the casino industry
   128–32; history 10–11; impact of
   casino corporations' CSR 126–8; Las
   Vegas 101–14; measurement of 27–8;
   moral *see* moral CSR; motivations
   for 14, 125; nonprofits and their role
   31–5; perception of 29; and responsible
   gambling 65–8, 113–14, 116, 121;
   social construction 15–16; societal
   implications 28–31; strategic *see*
   strategic CSR; theoretical considerations
   and practical concerns 125–6; in vice
   industries 63–5, 120–1
corporations 4–5, 10; role and degree of
   influence on the casino industry 52–4
corporatization of Las Vegas 3–4, 88–90
cost-benefit analysis 62, 122; CSR as a
   cost-benefit proposition 24–6; evaluation
   of casino proposals 56–7; unintended
   consequences of strategic CSR 116–17
cost of CSR communication 40, 109

Cragg, W. 22
crown corporations 78
Crown Resorts 4–5
Culinary Union 90, 106
cultural heritage 72
cultural icon 85, 98–100
cultural influences on CSR 16–18, 73
customers 37

Dalitz, Moe 3, 87
Darroch, J. 130–1
Davis, M. 99
De Colle, S. 15
De Jesus Salazar, J. 23
Desert Inn 87, 88
Detroit 90
developing countries 17, 39
dialogue with stakeholders 47–8, 119, 127,
   128, 129, 130–1
distributors 37
dominant industries 1, 2, 120
Du, S. 47
'Dutch disease' 74

Earth Hour 104
economic crisis 22–3, 117; Great
   Recession 33, 90–2, 100, 106
economic impacts of casinos 55
economic reasoning 31
electronic gaming machines (EGMs) 68,
   76, 79; Australia 80–2
Elliott, G. 68
Elving, W.J.L. 40
employees 128–9; communication of CSR
   37–8, 118; Las Vegas 90, 106–8, 111;
   Macau 74; remote parking lots for 124
enlightened self-interest 29, 30, 69
Enron 129
environmental CSR 25; Las Vegas 104–6,
   110–11
environmental impacts 55, 74, 128
environmental sustainability 75, 110–11,
   121
Europe 50, 51
European Union (EU) 18
executives 23–4
expansion of casino industry 1, 56–7
expectations: consumer 40; stakeholder
   15–16, 118

fantan 70
Fertitta, Frank, Jr 94
financial crisis 22–3, 117; Great Recession
    33, 90–2, 100, 106
First Nation tribes 56–7, 77
fit 26–7, 40
Ford Motors 90
Forrest, D. 108
Friedman, M. 18–19, 20, 21
Frontier hotel-casino 106
Fry, L.W. 25
Frynas, J.G. 38, 129
functional CSR 14, 63, 125–6; Las Vegas
    109, 110–12; possible impacts of
    115–22, 126

gambling/gaming stocks 89
gambling zones 58
General Motors 90
Ghana 17
gigantism 99
globalization 17
Goodman, Oscar 91
government: casino industries with strong
    ties to 55; regulation *see* regulation;
    relations and support for responsible
    gambling 114; revenues from gambling
    2, 51–2, 76–7, 79, 80, 121
government-run gambling 121; Australia
    80–2; Canada 75–9
Great Recession 33, 90–2, 100, 106
Greenpeace 44
Grunig, J.E. 48
Guardian Angel Cathedral 3
Gunningham, N. 44
Guthey, E. 131

Haigh, M. 31, 35
Harrah's Entertainment 94
Hilton, Barron 89
Hilton, Conrad 89
Hing, N. 69, 82
Ho, Pansy 83
Ho, Stanley 4–5, 60, 71
Hoffa, Jimmy 89
holistic approach to CSR 127
Holme, R. 39
Hoover Dam workers 6, 86
hotel chains 89

hotel room statistics 92
housekeepers 107
housing market 92
Hsieh, Tony 92
Hsu, C.H.C. 60
Hughes, Howard 3, 88
human resources *see* employees
Hunt, T. 48
Husted, B.W. 23

index of social responsibility (KLD index)
    14–15, 28
industry competitors 37
institutional CSR 46
Internal Revenue Service 32
Internet 44–5
intrinsic case study approach 85
investment, CSR as 25–6

Japan 18
job creation 56; Las Vegas 90, 95–6, 108;
    Macau 74
Johnson, L. 68
Jones, M.T. 31, 35
journalists 43–4; *see also* news media
Juslin, H. 73

Kagan, R.A. 44
Kang, Y.S. 57
Kearney, M.S. 56–7
Kefauver, Estes 87–8
Kimery, K.M. 36–7
Kinder, Lydenburg and Domini (KLD)
    index 14–15, 28
Krause, N. 107

labor *see* employees
labor unions 89, 90, 106
Las Vegas 1, 2, 6, 50, 70, 85–100, 122,
    132; communication of CSR 109–13;
    CSR in 101–14; as cultural icon 85,
    98–100; employees 90, 106–8, 111;
    environmental issues 104–6, 110–11;
    history 3–4, 86–93; influence on Macau
    72–3; local community 94–6, 102–4,
    110; location-specificity of CSR 120–1;
    moral vs functional CSR 109, 110–12;
    negative externalities 96–8, 113–14;
    nonprofits 86, 93–4, 102–4; organized

crime 3, 4, 53, 86–8; social impact of gaming 96–8, 113–14; tourism 91, 92–3, 96–8
Las Vegas Sands 4, 4–5, 52, 90, 94, 104–5
Las Vegas Strip 6, 52, 86, 95
Leap, T. 47–8
legalization of gambling 6–7, 50–1, 59; Canada 76; Macau 70–1; Nevada 3, 50, 86; New Jersey 82–3, 123–4
legitimacy 41, 42
L'Etang, J. 30, 46, 129
liberalization 71–2
'license to operate' view 13
Lloyd, G. 52
local community 53; characteristics of casino communities and their residents 54–5; communication of CSR 38–9, 118; CSR and tourism 61–3; implications of the business case for CSR 119–20; Las Vegas 94–6, 102–4, 110
location-specificity of CSR 120–1
Long, P.T. 57
Los Angeles Times 94
Loughry, M.L. 47–8

Macau (also Macao) 1, 4–5, 17–18, 50, 51, 108; class divisions 55; corporations 4–5, 52; evolution of the casino industry 70–5; philanthropy 60
major investors 37
managers 23–4
Margolis, J.D. 12–13, 28
Martin, R.L. 21
McCracken, G. 102
McHale, I.G. 108
McMahon, L. 52
measurement of CSR 27–8
media *see* news media
mega-resort hotels 99
MGM Grand 99
MGM Mirage 90, 94
MGM Resorts 4, 52, 83, 91, 104–5
migration 91
Miles, M.P. 130–1
misallocation 19
misappropriation 19
Mississippi 52
Mohr, L.A. 23

Monaco 50
Monteil, I. 105
moral CSR 14, 63, 116, 125–6; Las Vegas 109, 110–12
Morsing, M. 48, 131
motivations for CSR 14, 125
Munilla, L.S. 130–1

Nader, Ralph 10
National Center for Responsible Gaming (NCRG) 67
National Council on Responsible Gaming 113
National Museum of Organized Crime and Law Enforcement 87
Native American tribes 56–7, 77
negative externalities 27, 47, 55, 127, 132; failure to communicate CSR and 122; implications of strategic CSR 115–22; Las Vegas 96–8, 113–14; Macau 74–5; social exchange theory 56; vice industries 64
Nevada 3, 50, 53, 86, 95, 107
Nevada Gaming Commission 3, 89
New Jersey 82–3, 123
news media 16, 34; communication of CSR 37, 42–4, 117–18
Nike 129
nonprofit organizations (nonprofits) 128; communication of CSR and becoming a 'target' for 112; fighting back against pressure from 44; implications of the business case for CSR 117, 119, 119–20; Las Vegas 86, 93–4, 102–4; and their role in CSR 31–5

Obama, Barack 90–1
oil companies 47
online gambling 58
Ontario 78
organized crime 59; Las Vegas 3, 4, 53, 86–8; Macau 71

Paine, L.S. 30, 132
Palazzo, G. 42, 64, 67, 120
papacio 70
peer encouragement 34–5
perception of CSR 29
Perdue, R.R. 57

philanthropy 12, 26–7, 32–3, 60, 65, 87
Pitcher, A. 53
population growth 95–6, 96, 105
Porteous, J.D. 101
Portugal 70–1, 72
postmodern city 98
power imbalances 35, 120
prisoner's dilemma 68, 69
private enterprise 78
privatization 55, 81
problem gambling 66–7, 121, 129;
   Australia 81–2; Canada 77, 78;
   gambling addiction programs 52, 121;
   Las Vegas 113–14; Macau 75
procedural justice 34
product sales 24–5
profits 53–4; distribution of 55
promotional CSR 46
proposal evaluation 56–7
public relations: casino industry 58–60;
   communication of CSR 45–7, 119,
   129–31
purchase decisions 121–2, 127
Putin, Vladimir 58

Ramus, C.A. 105
regulation 18, 20, 50–2, 68; Canada
   75–6; Las Vegas 89; Macau 71–2;
   participation in CSR and 116
reputation 114, 117
responsible gambling (RG) 65–8, 113–14,
   116, 121
revenues, government 2, 51–2, 76–7, 79,
   80, 121
Richter, U. 42, 64, 67, 120, 132
Rinehart, S.M. 36–7
riverboat casinos 60
Riviera hotel-casino 3
Rockefeller, John 10, 17
Rothman, H. 99
Rugulies, R. 107
Russia 57–8

Salamon, L.M. 31–2
Scherzer, T. 107
Schultz, F. 48
Schwartz, D.G. 95
segmentation of publics 59
self-interest 29–30, 69

self-promotion 112
service jobs 90
shareholder primacy 19, 21–2, 36, 126–7
Siegel, Benjamin 'Bugsy' 3, 86
Simon, B. 123–4
Singapore 50
SJM 4
Skolnik, S. 67
Smith, C. 130
Smith, G.J. 60, 78, 79
smoking 107
social capital 54
social clubs 80–1
social construction of CSR 15–16
social contract 13
social exchange theory 56
social impact 28, 55; Las Vegas 96–8,
   113–14
social profits 23, 48
society, role of business in 12, 28–31, 48
South Dakota 61–2
Stake, R.E. 85
stakeholder dialogue 47–8, 119, 127, 128,
   129, 130–1
stakeholder expectations 15–16, 118
stakeholder theory 36–7
Stansfield, C. 83
Station Casinos 4, 90, 94
STDM 4, 5, 71
stigma 89
Stokowski, P.A. 53, 59
strategic conversations 130–1
strategic CSR 7, 23–8, 64, 114, 130;
   implications of 115–22, 126;
   measurement of initiatives 27–8; and the
   notion of fit 26–7; *see also* business case
   for CSR
Summa Corporation 3
sustainable tourism 62–3

Tai Xing company 71
Taiwan 17
Tattersall, George 60
taxes 51–2, 69, 78
Teamsters' Union 89
Thompson, W.N. 97
Thornton, D. 44
tobacco industry 42, 64, 67, 120–1
Totaliser Agency Board 81

tourism: casino gaming and 56, 57, 61–3, 69; Las Vegas 91, 92–3, 96–8; Macau 73–4
transparency 47
two-way symmetrical/asymmetrical communication 48, 54–5

unemployment 91–2, 93
unintended consequences 115–17
unique selling proposition (USP) 121, 127
United States (US) 17, 51, 69; Community Reinvestment Act 1977 20; Las Vegas *see* Las Vegas; size of casino industry 1; *see also under individual cities and states*

vendors 37
vice industries 63–5, 120–1
Victoria, Australia 81
video lottery terminals (VLTs) 76–7, 79
Vieira, E.T. 47
voluntary disclosure 45

Walsh, J.P. 12–13, 28
Wan, Y.K.P. 62, 108
Wang, L. 73
water use 74, 84, 105
Watts, P. 39
Web, the 44–5
Webb, D.J. 23
Weiss, R.S. 102
welfare capitalism 10, 17
Williams, R.J. 114
window-dressing 104, 129, 130, 132; hypothesis 65
Winkler, Garth 94
Wood, D.J. 1–2, 11–12
Wood, R.T. 114
Wynn Resorts 4–5, 52, 90, 94

York, J.G. 15

Zappos 92
Zeng, Z. 108

For Product Safety Concerns and Information please contact our EU
representative GPSR@taylorandfrancis.com
Taylor & Francis Verlag GmbH, Kaufingerstraße 24, 80331 München, Germany